The Allure of Decadent Thinking

The Allure of Decadent Thinking

Religious Studies and the Challenge of Postmodernism

CARL OLSON

OXFORD
UNIVERSITY PRESS

OXFORD
UNIVERSITY PRESS

Oxford University Press is a department of the
University of Oxford. It furthers the University's objective
of excellence in research, scholarship, and education
by publishing worldwide.

Oxford   New York
Auckland   Cape Town   Dar es Salaam   Hong Kong   Karachi
Kuala Lumpur   Madrid   Melbourne   Mexico City   Nairobi
New Delhi   Shanghai   Taipei   Toronto

With offices in
Argentina   Austria   Brazil   Chile   Czech Republic   France   Greece
Guatemala   Hungary   Italy   Japan   Poland   Portugal   Singapore
South Korea   Switzerland   Thailand   Turkey   Ukraine   Vietnam

Oxford is a registered trade mark of Oxford University Press
in the UK and certain other countries.

Published in the United States of America by
Oxford University Press
198 Madison Avenue, New York, NY 10016

© Oxford University Press 2013

Library of Congress Cataloging-in-Publication Data
Olson, Carl.
The allure of decadent thinking : religious studies and the challenge of postmodernism / Carl Olson.
p. cm.
Includes bibliographical references (p.) and index.
ISBN 978-0-19-995983-9 (hardcover : alk. paper)
1. Religion—Methodology.   2. Religion—Study and
teaching.   3. Postmodernism.   I. Title.
BL41.O47   2013
200.72—dc23   2012030466

1 3 5 7 9 8 6 4 2

Printed in the United States of America
on acid-free paper

To Lloyd Michaels and Lefty,
companions on the Holzwege *of dialogical life*

Contents

Acknowledgments	ix
Preface	xi
1. Introduction	3
2. Eroticism, Violence, and Sacrifice	17
3. Excess, Time, and the Pure Gift	36
4. Genealogy, Power, and Discourse	59
5. Hermeneutics, Comparison, Context, and Difference	80
6. The Problematic Nature of Representational Thinking	108
7. Responding to the Postmodern Challenge	128
Notes	153
Bibliography	181
Index	201

Acknowledgments

ALTHOUGH THE INDIVIDUAL chapters have been rethought and rewritten, parts of them have been previously published. The second, third, and fourth chapters were published in the journal *Method and Theory in the Study of Religion* respectively as the following essays: "Eroticism, Violence, and Sacrifice: A Postmodern Theory of Ritual and Religion," 6/3 (1994): 231–250; "Excess, Time, and the Pure Gift: Postmodern Transformations of Marcel Mauss' Theory," 14/3–4 (2002): 350–374; "Politics, Power, Discourse and Representation: A Critical Look at Said and Some of His Children," 17/4 (2005): 317–336. Aspects of chapter 5 concerning the work of Mircea Eliade were published as "Eliade, the Comparative Method, Historical Context, and Difference," in *Changing Religious Worlds: The Meaning and End of Mircea Eliade*, edited by Bryan Rennie (Albany: State University of New York Press, 2001), pp. 59–76.

I want to acknowledge the financial support by the Faculty Review Committee of Allegheny College, and I want to thank Dean Linda DeMerritt and President James Mullen, both providing leadership with a smile, for approving my sabbatical leave of absence in order to complete this book at Clare Hall, University of Cambridge. My colleagues Glenn, Eric the Younger, Eric the Elder, Bill, and Rabbi Ron are simply the best. Peggy, a traveling phenomenon, provided a comfortable diversion from my labors with friendly conversation and a quiet environment in which to work.

Preface

SOME YEARS AGO at the book display at an annual convention of the American Academy of Religion, I encountered a former professor and racket-ball partner from my seminary and graduate school days whose field of study was the Hebrew Bible. He proudly showed me with a certain amount of delight and even giddiness a festschrift that a group of his former students and colleagues put together and published in his honor, and I was delighted to see an old friend so happy. After discussing some of the contents and contributors to this festschrift, he began to lament his younger colleagues who were using methods of deconstruction and gene- alogy, whereas he believed that he was the only scholar left in his department placing the texts within their cultural and historical time and place in order to discern their meaning. Because it seemed to be a natural follow-up to some of my previous work, when I began to think about this book I was reminded of this enjoyable chance encounter, during the good old days when the AAR and Society of Biblical Literature held their con- ventions jointly, a situation that is now corrected with a revision back to the older format of the convention. My former professor felt out of style with respect to new approaches in his field, which also held consequences for other fields of religious studies. Thus I decided to think about the impact of postmodern thinking on the field of religious studies in how it has contested methods and categories used by scholars.

Religious studies is an artificially constructed field for the study of reli- gious narratives, thoughts, actions, and phenomena by scholars. This relatively infant field of scholarship, in comparison to a field such as phi- losophy with its roots in ancient Greek culture, is still experiencing growing pains and experimenting with various types of methodological approaches to the study of religion, which is itself a human construct with limited cross-cultural application. Without a generally agreed-upon method for the study of its subject, religious studies is characterized at present by the use of many methods, which tend to be adopted and used based on the latest trends in the field. A current trend in religious studies is the adoption of postmodern thought to discuss religion, which is a dangerous development because the very radical skepticism of such thinking undermines, subverts, and distorts the study of religion, and it is difficult to hermeneutically grasp aspects of religion, a confusing topic in itself, by uncritically adopting any of the various postmodern positions.

Since religious studies is a product of the European Enlightenment with its values and representational mode of thinking, it is threatened, or at the very least challenged, by postmodern thought that calls into question many of its values, basic presuppositions, and convictions. In order to streamline this book and make it a bit more focused, anthropologist and feminist adoptions of postmodern perspectives will not be considered in any depth. After an introductory chapter, each of the remaining chapters of the book is devoted to examining various postmodern positions related to the study of religion and examines their allure for scholars of religious studies.

Chapter 2 critically discusses the theory of religion developed by Georges Bataille with respect to the themes of eroticism, violence, and sacrifice because the interconnections and workings of these aspects help to explain the nature of religion that he identifies with the sacred. The key to understanding Bataille's theory of religion is to focus on his concept of eroticism, a lifelong obsession of his. According to Bataille, a common feature of eroticism, sacrifice, and religion is violence, representing a danger that might overflow at anytime. If eroticism opens the way to death, sacrifice affects death, creating an intimate connection between eroticism and sacrifice. Because Bataille does not use ample examples from various religious traditions to support his theory, this chapter tests his ideas by applying them to the Sun Dance of the Native American Sioux. Bataille's notion of the gift and Jacques Derrida's inquiry into the possibility of a pure gift are covered within the context of Marcel Mauss's classic theory reviewed in chapter 3. The chapter places these three theories of the gift within the context of theoretical work on the Hindu notion of the gift in order to test their reflections about the nature of the gift within the context of a particular tradition. The fourth chapter considers the method of genealogy, concept of power, and theory of discourse of Michel Foucault as they are used by Edward W. Said and his notion of Orientalism, a style of scholarship that also affects cross-cultural studies. Using Mircea Eliade, Wendy Doniger, and Jonathan Z. Smith as examples of scholars from the area of the history of religions, the fifth chapter compares these figures with selected postmodern thinkers on the topics of hermeneutics, comparison, and difference. Because many scholars of religion use the representational mode of thinking as they attempt to make sense of religious phenomena, the sixth chapter explores the rationale for the subversion of this type of thinking by looking at the theory and method of Eliade as representative of a type of scholarship within religious studies. This chapter examines the theme of representational thinking that many postmodern thinkers perceive as a form of intellectual bondage to the past with the intention of breaking free of the constraints of the Enlightenment. Thus, this chapter examines the problematic nature of representational thinking in history, ontology, epistemology, and representational thinking itself. Finally, this critical study of the postmodern challenge in the final chapter considers ways in which scholars in religious studies might critically respond to this test.

The Allure of Decadent Thinking

I

Introduction

IN ONE QUARTER of the field, religious studies is considered an artificially constructed discipline for the study of religious narratives, thoughts, actions, and phenomena by scholars. This relatively infant field of scholarship, in comparison to a field such as philosophy with its roots in ancient Greek culture, is still experiencing growing pains and experimenting with various types of methodological approaches to the study of religion, a term that is also itself a human construct with limited cross-cultural application. In fact, the term *religion* is considered problematic by some scholars who advocate doing away with it.[1] There are also others who think that the term *religion* possesses some utility, even though it has drawbacks when used in a cross-cultural context.[2] It is possible to see its cross-cultural limitations by comparing the Latin terms for religion and those in ancient China and India.

We can identify three Latin terms for religion: *religare*, meaning to bind together; *religio*, referring to obligation, reverence, or fear of God or other divine beings; and *religere*, implying to reread, to ponder upon, to gather together, or to repeatedly pass over. Although the precise etymology is uncertain, both *religare* and *religere* suggest social aspects of *religio*. In the early fifth century, Saint Augustine, a bishop in North Africa and influential intellectual and shaper of the early church, confirms that *religio* includes human social bonds and relationships. If the term is used to refer to worship of God, this is bound to cause confusion for Augustine. This brief examination of the etymology of the term suggests its uncertainty and ambiguity, a situation that leads to attempts to construct a viable definition of the term by scholars over the centuries.

During the nineteenth century, scholars doing comparative work in religion were influenced by Darwin's theory of evolution, which motivated them to seek the origins of religion in order to determine its nature. Herbert Spencer (1820–1903) attempted, for instance, to trace the origins of religion from ancestor worship and to argue that remnants of such practice can still be discerned in such Christian notions as the Holy Ghost and funeral customs. Because of his conviction that the evolutionary process consisted of a course of increasing differentiation that culminated in ultimate integration, Spencer's use of the comparative method was an attempt to construct a rational a priori argument for the evolutionary development of particular and similar notions into different conceptions.[3]

In addition to Spencer, other theorists made contributions to the discussion about the nature of religion. Eward B. Tylor (1832–1917) identified animism with the basis of religion in archaic cultures, whereas Lucien Lévy-Bruhl (1857–1939) focused on an archaic form of "prelogical reasoning," which he characterized as mystical, prelogical, and pervaded by a sense of affectional participation because some people thought of themselves as animals without thinking metaphorically or symbolically about this kind of identity. Sir James G. Frazer (1854–1941), a pioneer of the field of comparative religion and acknowledged founding father of anthropology, argued that religion was a form of propitiation and conciliation of assumed superior powers to human beings that was to be distinguished from magic, a necessarily false discipline and basic mistaken application of the association of ideas and an erroneous system of natural law and science. These types of theories about the nature and origin of religion are called "dreamtime" by Tomoko Masuzawa.[4] The twentieth century manifested further attempts to define religion in terms of psychological experience, a feeling of absolute dependence, a subjective experience of the numinous that is an irreducible or sui generis phenomenon, distinctions between the sacred and profane, identification with power, a psychological projection of infantile forms of dependency onto external reality that suggests mental illness by Sigmund Freud (1856–1939), or a tracing of its origins to a collective unconscious and its archetypes by Carl Jung (1875–1961). More recently, findings in the field of cognitive science are being applied to religion to isolate its origins within the human brain and its shaping by the process of evolution.[5] There are thus scholars who perceive an opportunity to integrate science with the humanistic field of religious studies.[6]

In spite of these definitions of and approaches to religion, if we attempt to apply the term *religion* to a cross-cultural context, we discover that is not possible to find equivalent terms in ancient China, although the term *zongjiao*, which refers to ancestral teaching or pious doctrine, comes closest to the Latin terms. The term *zongjiao* can be traced to Buddhist origins, while its contemporary usage includes such things as dogmas, rituals, institutions, and superstitions. If we separate the terms, *zong* is related to the worship of ancestors and concern with family lineage, denoting an ancestral temple, a clan or families with common ancestors, and chief spirits identified with ancestors worshipped in a temple. The importance of family lineage is even more evident with the term *jiao*, which means family or home; it can also mean a teaching transmitted from the past, as is evident by the Chinese threefold character for the term consisting of signs for instruction, a son or junior person, and a hand holding a stick. This ancient character suggests authority that comes from a teacher instructing a child to adhere to good behavior by following examples from the past embodied in the wisdom of the ancient sages, whereas the modern character of *jiao* includes two parts: *xiao* (filial piety) and *wen* (culture). As a combined term *zongjiao* stresses communication between humans and spirits and correspondence and mutuality.[7] The etymology of the Chinese term implies that religion looks backward toward the past, is founded on order and harmony, and represents a search for conformity and enhancement by complex rituals.

If classical China does not have a precise equivalent for religion, the same is true of ancient and classical Indian culture, even though a Western observer could recognize behavior and practices that appear to be connected to religion. As is similar in the case of China, it is difficult to really separate religion from Indian culture. The closest approximation of the term *religion* in India is the notion of *dharma*, an elusive term to precisely define. The origin of *dharma* can be traced to a Sanskrit root *dhar* (meaning to hold or uphold, to maintain, to support, to be firm, or to be durable). In classical Indian texts, dharma can be viewed from two perspectives: physical and individual moral worlds. Both perspectives refer to a revealed and eternal dharma. When the term *dharma* is applied to the universe it signifies the cosmic laws that govern and maintain it, which are laws guarded by the gods. In addition to the physical realm, dharma also includes the moral world of humans, representing a set of personal and social obligations and duties that depend on a person's station in life and social standing. These obligations associated with personal and moral dharma basically govern how a person should act, embodying social custom. In short, dharma includes a harmony of cosmic laws, social customs, legal requirements, and religious rules.[8] It is thus preferable to conceive of religion in India and China as a way of life that is intertwined within their cultures. These remarks suggest the limited application of the Western notion of religion within a cross-cultural context.

The serious scholarly study of religion began to take shape in the nineteenth century in Europe before it spread to Canada and America. Without a generally agreed upon method for the overall study of its subject, religious studies is characterized at present by the use of many methods, such as comparative, historical, theological, philosophical, phenomenological, psychological, sociological, anthropological, economical, feminist, hermeneutical, cognitive science, and postmodern. Unlike other approaches to the study of religion, the last mentioned approach represents a genuine challenge to the shaky foundations of this new discipline because it represents a reaction to and challenge of the pillars of Enlightenment philosophy of which religious studies is a direct outgrowth. It is the overall purpose of this book to examine the allure and challenge of postmodernism to the new and continually developing field of religious studies and to attempt to discern if it undermines or enhances the development of methodological approaches to the study of religion.

Enlightenment, Romanticism, and Postmodernism

Because of the cacophony of voices among postmodern thinkers, it is difficult to derive an all-encompassing definition of it. Jeremy Carrette thinks that *postmodernism* is a misleading term, which tends to obfuscate matters rather than clarify them, arguing that it is best to separate postmodernism from post-structuralism. His major reason for doing this is that "the specificity of post-structuralism will allow us to appreciate the historical context of French thought in the 1960s and move the discussion away from simple charges of relativism and anti-modernism."[9] He goes on to write that post-structuralism represents a critique of the Enlightenment by including a critical assessment of the problem of representation in its theory of knowledge. Since postmodernism does the same thing, I have opted to adopt the term *postmodernism* in order to avoid splitting terminological hairs and adding to further obfuscation within a context in which no terms can be applied universally.

With this type of clarification made, it is useful to attempt to discern what postmodernism is reacting against in order to get a better sense of its position. Postmodernism is a reaction to both the Enlightenment program and the development of certain trends in modernism. The significance of liberty to human welfare, human equality, tolerance for the actions, cultures, and beliefs of others, recognition of the value of common sense, and the importance of reason are just some of the aspects that evolved from Enlightenment thought, along with an ardent belief in the natural goodness and perfectibility of human nature and a conviction about a natural law that prescribes the pursuit of pleasure, profit, and property.

With reason as one's guideline and convictions about its powers to solve every genuine question, there was a belief that it could know all questions and find answers to them that would be compatible with other answers. This confidence in reason made thinkers optimistic about their ability to know, rendering mind the only source of truth, which resulted in the rejection of faith as a source of truth. Although the age of the Enlightenment insisted on the predominance of rational a priori concepts, Louis Dupré refines his characterization of the intellectual period in the following way: "The Enlightenment was not so much an age of reason as an age of self-consciousness."[10] This type of trend motivated thinkers of the period to have contempt for tradition and authority, which were often identified with the Roman Catholic Church and kingship as a mode of governance.

In contrast to the prior historical period, the Enlightenment ushered into existence secularization of knowledge and thought. This development was grounded in the conviction that rational reflection was liberating and that there was virtually nothing that the human mind could not under-stand because reason was autonomous and life was rationally ordered. Consequently, the rational individual was privileged over the social body. This tendency made it difficult to preserve genuine otherness. Dupré critically assets, "A self reduced to a meaning-giving function—a mere subject—loses its personal identity and, as a result, is no longer able to recognize the identity of the other."[11] A corollary of this situation is a lack of self-understanding.

The Enlightenment also gave birth to democracy, the growth of the nation-state, capitalism, and the establishment of science as the standard for all dependable truth and knowledge. These various values and convic-tions were derived from a representational mode of thinking, a way of thinking that produced an image for any thought by a person, with the human mind functioning as a mirror in a metaphorical way. During this age, the revolution of science undermined any stable concept of time. The significance of this subversive development for a human understanding of time meant that one did not have to repeat the past because "time was pregnant with novelty and directed toward the future rather than repeating the past."[12] There was a generally held conviction that an individual could now alter the course of history because he or she represented a source of meaning and value.

Scholars of the Enlightenment have argued about its scope, with Peter Gay insisting on a single Enlightenment that he defines as a kind of "modern paganism"[13] and that approach being countered by more recent studies stressing its national contexts and claims that there were plural Enlightenments.[14] In contrast to these positions, Dan Edelstein argues that the genealogy of the Enlightenment narrative is primarily a product of France. Edelstein elucidates his position when he asserts, "The Enlightenment was never just the sum of its parts: instead of an aggregate of ideas, actions, and events, it provided a matrix in which ideas, actions, and events acquired new meanings."[15] Moreover, it marked "a change in the way people thought about the way people thought."[16] The change of thinking took place within the context of a quarrel over the merits of the ancients and the moderns. This quarrel did not directly cause the Enlightenment, but it functioned as a catalyst for its narrative. Edelstein defines the French narrative this way: "the present age (*siècle*) was 'enlightened' (*éclairé*) because the 'philosophical spirit' of the Scientific Revolution had spread to the educated classes, institutions of learning, and even parts of the government."[17] Thereby, this development contributed to a new self-awareness of the educated elite. In fact, the expression *l'esprit philosophique* in French was used to characterize the period, whereas it was called *Aufklärung* in Germany. The French expression suggested a mind purified by philosophy, although it had a wide application and was interpreted differently by thinkers.

A major product of the Enlightenment in France was the publication of the *Encyclopédie,* which functioned to both justify and serve as an exemplary work of the Enlightenment. Edelstein summarizes the importance of this text in the following way: "To become 'enlightened' was to think and act in accordance with a new set of norms, but these norms were only rarely self-imposed."[18] The implication of this observation means that a person must think and act according to a new set of norms that included embracing progress, rediscovering the past, and undergoing social transformation.

Romanticism represents a reaction to the Enlightenment; it was an intellectually disparate movement rooted in Pietism, a historical consequence of Lutheranism characterized by Bible study and respect for a sincere personal relationship with God. The romantics believed in fighting for their beliefs, martyrdom for the truth, the importance of individuals over collective bodies, nobility of failure, purity of soul, a drive forward, and dedication to a personal ideal. Within the context of these convictions, a person is always active and perpetually creating.[19]

If the Enlightenment represented applying a scientific and rational approach to the study of religion, romantics countered its spirit by stressing the aesthetic and emotional quality of religion, and opposing the rationalistic view of religion by making aesthetics primary, rendering religion an individual experience and beyond rational criticism by interiorizing it within the heart or soul. If religion represented a naturally inherent human potential as some romantics thought, religion was something sui generis, making it irreducible to other phenomena and impossible to explain as a form of intuition, which stands in sharp contrast to the Enlightenment discourse concerned with the problem of reconciling reason and religion.[20] This type of scenario influences Hans Kippenberg to locate the origins of religious studies as an academic discipline in the romantic period, but he traces the sociology of religion back to the Enlightenment.[21] Besides its relativizing and individualizing conception of religion, romanticism tended to also stress its pluralizing, social, and communicative aspects. Therefore, there is no one religion that embodies absolute truth.

Postmodernists criticized the enduring values and optimistic convictions of Enlightenment thinking for the static world envisioned by its philosophers, which is a debatable position if one considers the concepts of time and history in such thinkers as Kant and Hegel. Instead of what they conceived to be the static world of the Enlightenment, postmodernists stressed becoming, contingency, relativity, chance, and difference. Methods of inquiry or modes of classification that were grounded on similarity needed to be rejected, as did imitation of models or conformity to paradigms because there were no metaphysical essences or ontological foundations for such things. Within a world of continual flux, some postmodern thinkers stressed the absence of any universal or timeless truths, which made it impossible to have complete knowledge of anything. Thus, everything is relative and indeterminate, which necessarily means that one's knowledge is always incomplete, fragmented, and conditioned by historical and cultural forces, and no philosophical position or theory possesses any foundation. If reason affirms that something is valid, it is best to become suspicious of such claims from a postmodern perspective. Moreover, the individual person, society, culture, or history lacks a center because everything is decentered and fragmented. Some postmodern thinkers even refer to the demise of a stable enduring self as a result of this process of temporal flux.

Besides these features, postmodernism is also characterized by discontinuity, rupture, irregularity, plurality, and an emphasis on difference and a rejection of sameness. The possibility of a utopia on earth or in a transcendent sphere is impossible because there is no transhistorical value or metaphysical entity, a conviction based on the acceptance of the death of God. The postmodern iconoclastic spirit also embraces a revolutionary ethos that is democratic in the sense that anyone with the ability to write can become a revolutionary, although writing condemns one to a wandering, erring, experimental, and socially marginal lifestyle.

The postmodernist wanders as an erring and marginal being on the surfaces of life because human existence is devoid of ontological depth or a foundation. Wanting to think "difference," a positive and disruptive mode of cognition, Gilles Deleuze and Félix Guatttari affirm surfaces or planes as constitutions of a fluctuating series that forms them. These surfaces or planes are not derivative or secondary because they are a series of waves that lack depth as concepts.[22] A plane is abstract, an indivisible milieu, and a horizon of events that is populated by philosophically linked concepts. This position stresses immanence without any foundation beneath it and represents a rejection of all forms of transcendence.

This affirmation of surfaces without ontological depth is associated with simulacrum, which is difference itself for Deleuze in that it possesses no identity and appears by disguising itself as demonic images lacking any resemblance that function by themselves.[23] Being constructed on a difference, the simulacrum, a Dionysian machine, internalizes a dissimilarity that is a positive power that "denies *the original and the copy, the model and the reproduction.*"[24] The simulacrum, a simulated phantasm itself, stands in opposition to any Kantian perspective because it is nonconceptual and nonrepresentational.

This notion is also used by Jean Baudrillard, a postmodern cultural critic, to indicate an era in which simulation dominates and all references are liquidated. For Baudrillard, simulation cannot be represented, and possesses no relationship to meaning or the real. Both the real and illusion are rendered simultaneously impossible because the latter is no longer possible without the former.[25] Simulation manifests a hyperreality, a phantom of simulation that is more real than the real within a context in which the real never did truly exist.[26] Within the simulacrum, difference reigns supreme without linear time and is dominated by a cyclical reversal realm that implies the loss of history, metaphysics, economic exchange, wealth, and power.

This peripatetic, tentative, and subsidiary lifestyle is decadent or destined to end in decadence. The pornographic life and work of Georges Bataille, discussed in chapters 2 and 3, represent an excellent example of the importance of decadence, as do Michel Foucault's sexual proclivities, through which he reads and writes about the history of sexuality.[27] As with the honesty of Bataille, the decadent nature of postmodern thought, which resists modernity and comes after it, is made apparent by Fredric Jameson.[28] Jameson's remark reminds one of Nietzsche's observations about the necessity of decadence as absolutely necessary to every age, but there are also some significant implications for decadence, namely skepticism and nihilism, forming its logical outcome and not its cause.[29] Besides its intended shock effect, the openly acknowledged decadent nature of postmodernism can be grasped as symptomatic of a disintegration of the social fabric, the transitory nature of life, an uncertain nature of thinking, and a wavering assurance about the Enlightenment in general and its belief in the power of reason and progress.

Postmodern thought is experimentally playful, as is evident in the philosophy of Jean-François Lyotard with his notion of rewriting, which represents a new beginning that is exempt from any prejudice. A second sense of rewriting reflects Freud's notion of *Durcharbeitung* (working through), which suggests operating with a hidden thought obscured by past prejudice and future possibilities. Another experiment involves problematizing time, where the roots of logocentrism (a metaphysics of presence), authority, the scientific worldview, hierarchy, and universal narratives can be found. Instead of past or future moments of time, postmodern thinkers tend to stress the present in order to indifferently focus on the free play of different discourses.

The precise roots of postmodernism are difficult to discern with complete accuracy because its attitudes and characteristics evolved from several sources of inspiration that even include changes in architectural design, resulting often in a pastiche of old forms that reject being guided by the function of a building. In the historical sphere, Arnold Toynbee refers to the postmodern phase that represents the fourth and final phase of history, which is characterized by no hope, anxiety, and irrationalism.[30] The term *postmodern* spread to literary criticism and other forms of cultural criticism. The French postmodernists draw their inspiration from Friedrich Nietzsche's call for an age of frivolity, a return of artistic creativity, eroticism, and playfulness and Martin Heidegger's vision of the end of metaphysics in his later works. There is evidence that Heidegger anticipated the term in his four-volume work on Nietzsche: "Western history has now begun to enter into the completion of that period we call the modern, and which is defined by the fact that man becomes the measure and the center of beings."[31] The postmodern theologian Mark C. Taylor designates, however, a historical ground for postmodernism: "Modernity ended and postmodernity began in Hiroshima on 6 August 1945."[32]

Lyotard, a leading postmodern thinker, thinks that the term *postmodern* is always implied in the term *modern* "because of the fact that modernity, modern temporality, comprises in itself an impulsion to exceed itself into a state other than itself."[33] According to Lyotard, the *post* of *postmodernity* suggests a matter of tone, style, experimentation, and multiplicity. Consequently, postmodernity is not a new epoch, but is rather better grasped as a rewriting of aspects of modernity, a writing again that makes modernity itself real. This type of experiment de-emphasizes the importance of grand theories or narratives, truth claims, and standards of valid argumentation. The postmodern writer does not operate within a set of rules, but rather creates rules that produce the event. If the product of the postmodern for Lyotard is the event, this means for him that postmodernism is a crisis of narratives, which are the quintessential forms of knowledge, a refined sensitivity to differences. Lyotard perceives a crisis of knowledge because it has become a commodity produced in order to be sold to consumers. The widespread embrace of the computer around the world strongly supports Lyotard's position about the commercialization of knowledge.

Selected Postmodernists on the Subject of Religion

Considering religion late in his career, Michel Foucault focuses his attention on how it is shaped by power, discipline, and regimen by examining how silence and confession operate. Silence operates within the structures of Christianity—Foucault's narrow model for a religious institution—to manipulate and control persons, whereas confession functions as a principle of coercion and power by subjugating, subjectifying, and forming a subject of knowledge. Operating through the said and unsaid, religion, fundamentally a mechanism of power, governs the self and nation-states. By stressing the mechanism of the coercive power of religion and its intention to establish structures of power, Foucault is able to develop his ideas about political spirituality. Moreover, Carrette shows how Foucault's engagement with theological themes radically transforms and destabilizes the field of religious understanding as when Foucault uses terms to disrupt traditional concepts.[34]

Jacques Derrida uses his nonmethod of deconstruction, which he defines as an event rather than a method, to disrupt and subvert the notion of religion that is defined as a response to the other person, before the other person and oneself in the form of an either-or rejoinder. As a response, religion—an ellipsis (mark of absence)—is both ambiguous and ambivalent. Just like everything else for Derrida, religion "begins with the presence of that absence."[35] The presence-absence of religion is also shared by God, an unnamable witness to the oath taken between parties. Derrida's comments from the margins of philosophy imply that we cannot grasp the essence of religion; nothing permanent or real is implied by the concept, or thought in a representational manner.

A similar line of argument is made by Hent de Vries when he asserts that religion does not reflect any cosmic, divine, human, or social nature because religion plays a role in a "house of mirrors" that eludes "all mimesis, all representations."[36] Because religion is difficult to grasp, it is akin to a semantic black hole of absence-presence from which nothing escapes. Besides this metaphor to express something about religion, a second metaphor is a blinding blaze of light forming a sensory overload that renders religion almost invisible, suggesting that it is too much to comprehend. Nonetheless, there is still something called religion in spite of some scholars wanting to dispense with it because the subject of its existence and essence are too difficult and imprecise to grasp.[37] Citing approvingly the position of Stanley Cavell that there is no proof, no epistemic certainty, no scientific paradigm, and no method that can determine the origin and end of religion, de Vries imagines religion as a *coincidentia oppositorum* (conjunction of opposites), which represents a name for something that transgresses domains consisting of discourses or disciplines, a horizontal or lateral transcendence, and a now centrifugal rather than centripetal movement. In short, religion is a saturated phenomenon in the sense of its complexity.[38]

According to de Vries, the various forms and elements of religion do not correspond to reality in a representational way; they also do not establish truth or objectivity. De Vries summarizes, "They neither mirror the world as it is, nor do they designate 'what is better for us to believe,' without any further reason given."[39] I discuss the problematic nature of representational thinking for postmodernists and its implications for religious studies more fully in chapter 6.

Because its nature is continually slipping from our grasp, religion is an elusive subject to understand, according to Mark C. Taylor. He traces this difficulty to the fact that it is always withdrawing from the seeker, rendering religion neither here nor someplace else. Taylor calls attention to what he sees as religion's tendency to disappear in its coming to be, while allowing appearances to emerge in this continual process. Its elusive nature makes religion difficult to find, a feature that makes it also difficult to define with any precision: "Religion is an emergent, adaptive network of symbols, myths, and rituals that, on the one hand, figure schemata of feeling, thinking, and acting in ways that lend life meaning and purpose and, on the other hand, disrupt, dislocate, and disfigure every stabilizing structure."[40] Taylor compares religion to a double-edged sacrificial knife that gives people a purpose in life and meaning, while simultaneously undermining the stability of human existence with its destructive power.

This line of thinking can be discerned in anthropology with a scholar such as Michael Lambek, who holds that postmodern or post-structural anthropology is more concerned with issues of power, discipline, and how religious people are shaped.[41] Lambek thinks that religions lack an autonomous essence and cannot be conceptually separate from the domain of power. Whatever theories of religion are devised by an anthropologist or someone from another discipline, they cannot have universal application no matter how clever.

From many of the postmodern perspectives, it appears that *religion* is a useless term because it does not bear the sense of applying to any objective reality, especially from a cross-cultural viewpoint when members of another culture do not use the term. There are scholars, however, who think that the term *religion* does not need to be abandoned because it can be refined instead of discarded. In fact, it is possible from a critical realist position to assert that a scholar can apply the term *religion* to another culture, even if this term is lacking in that culture's vocabulary. If religion represents patterns of behavior that are independent of a scholar, it is possible to differentiate between the conceptual effort to identify a practice and that of interpreting it. By using indigenous terms, it is possible to identify a practice and then to interpret it in nonindigenous terms.[42]

The Postmodern Challenge to Religious Studies

Because of its problematic nature, it is reasonable to ask whether or not we should abandon the concept of religion. Even though the term owes its origin to Western thought and cannot be applied cross-culturally without problems, it is possible to retain the term on pragmatic grounds. Martin Riesebrodt, a sociologist, makes the following argument: "It seems to me unnecessary to abandon the concept of religion, for the criticism of it, is insufficiently persuasive. Its critics overemphasize the Western origin of the concept and fail to consider all its definitions and modes of usage."[43] Riesebrodt proceeds to define religion as a particular complex type of meaningful social action within a web of meaning. He views religion as a system of social practices in relation to superhuman powers.[44]

Since religious studies is a product of the Enlightenment with its values and representational mode of thinking, it is threatened, or at least challenged, by postmodern thought. Postmodern philosophy is also a lure for scholars seeking a new approach to the study and interpretation of religion. Some scholars find postmodern philosophy attractive because it enables them to use it as a tool to ask new questions about religion, to methodologically subvert prior scholarship, or to attack the representational mode of thinking commonly used in religious studies. As will become evident in the following chapters, many postmodern thinkers seek to disrupt or more subtly to subvert the type of thinking common in a discipline like religious studies.

In each of the following chapters, the challenge of postmodern thinking will be evident. Chapter 2 discusses the theory of religion developed by Georges Bataille with respect to the themes of eroticism, violence, and sacrifice. Chapter 3 covers Bataille's notion of the gift and Jacques Derrida's inquiry about the possibility of a pure gift within the context of Marcel Mauss's theory. The fourth chapter considers the method of genealogy, concept of power, and theory of discourse of Michel Foucault as they are used by Edward W. Said and his notion of Orientalism, a style of scholarship that affects cross-cultural studies. Using Mircea Eliade, Wendy Doniger, and Jonathan Z. Smith as examples of scholars from the area of the history of religions, chapter 5 compares these figures with selected postmodern thinkers on the topics of hermeneutics, comparison, and difference. Because many scholars of religion use the representational mode of thinking to make sense of religious phenomena, chapter 6 explores the rationale for the subversion of this type of thinking by looking at the theory and method of Eliade as representative of a type of scholarship within religious studies. Finally, this examination of the postmodern challenge considers ways in which scholars in religious studies might critically respond to this test.

2

Eroticism, Violence, and Sacrifice

BEING FASCINATED BY the relationship between eroticism, violence, and sacrifice, Georges Bataille, who worked as an archivist at the Bibliotheque nationale, explored these aspects of religion in his writings, exerting a significant influence on postmodern philosophers in France. Jacques Derrida admitted being influenced by him because his own theory of general economy was formed by reading Bataille.[1] Michel Foucault was also influenced by Bataille, and Foucault characterized him as "one of the most important writers of his century."[2] Foucault was drawn to Bataille's speculative thoughts because "they connected with his own interest in abnormality and exclusion."[3]

Bataille was born in Puy-de-Dome in 1897 and converted to Catholicism in 1914 only to renounce his faith six years later after considering the priesthood as a possible vocation. The lives of his parents were tragic because his father—Joseph-Aristide—suffered from blindness and a general paralysis related to syphilis, and his mother lost her sanity and committed suicide later in her life. After turning away from a religious vocation, Bataille reverted to a life of debauchery devoted to gambling, excessive drinking, and sexual encounters in brothels on which he spent large sums of money. After his marriage to the much younger Sylvia Maklès, a woman of Romanian-Jewish descent born in France, his bacchanalian lifestyle did not change and even included a fascination with necrophilia, as is evident in some of his novels. Bataille's assiduous visits to brothels were akin to attending church for him because the brothel embodied truth, death, and eroticism, and served as a substitute church with the women functioning as its saints.

While working as a librarian, Bataille learned ethnology from Alfred Metraux, who had attended the lectures of Marcel Mauss. During the late 1920s and 1930s, Bataille was involved in the surrealist movement. After the release of the Second Manifesto of Surrealism in 1929–30, Bataille and other dissidents were expelled by André Breton, who criticized Bataille for devoting too much attention to vile and corrupt matters within the world. Bataille's novels, for instance, bordered on pornography, and some of his essays were concerned with discussing those things that were embarrassing, ignoble, filthy, deformed, and idiotic, much like his literary hero the Marquis de Sade. Accusing the surrealists of decadent aesthetics that made it impossible for them to grasp the plight of the lower classes, Bataille split from them.[4] He also argued that they refused to use de Sade's erotic works in the social realm because the surrealists wanted to maintain their own control over language, whereas Bataille wanted to use de Sade's writings in his attempt to call into question the role of language in society. From Bataille's perspective, the violence and excess in the language of de Sade undermined the ability of the surrealists to control, master, or describe language. Even though Bataille emphasized the ugly side of human existence, Julia Kristeva refers to him along with James Joyce "as emblems of the most radical aspects of twentieth-century literature."[5] Bataille took delight in delving into the vomit and dirt of life because the refuse of life and the heterogeneous, which possess an erotic value, cannot be neatly separated from philosophical and religious issues.

During the 1930s and 1940s, Bataille joined, cofounded, or himself established a number of organizations. After reading Marx and Engels in 1930, Bataille participated in Cercle Communiste Democratique and contributed to the review called *La Critique Sociale*, an anti-Stalinist Marxist publication founded by Boris Souvarine (a pseudonym for Lifschitz), from 1931 to 1934. Following his Marxist phase and a temporary reconciliation with Breton, Bataille helped to form a political group of intellectuals called Contre-Attaque, whose purpose was to counteract the spread of Fascism by means of agitation, force, and violence. Bataille's association with this group led some people to accuse him of being a Fascist sympathizer or a collaborator, charges disputed by Alan Stoekl.[6] By wanting to motivate others to action, Bataille in his writings demonstrates the influence of Georges Sorel and the violence associated with the mythic general strike. Along with other intellectuals between 1936 and 1939, Bataille founded a secret society and published four issues of the review *Acéphale*, which was named after a headless mythical figure connected to war and violence, and reflected the influence of Nietzsche rather than Marx on Bataille's thought due to Nietzsche's stress on the subversion of established society and stimulation of a rebirth of social values. Around the same time, Bataille was also connected to the College de Sociologie, which became a gathering place for avant-garde intellectuals and social scientists intent on replacing functionalist sociology with a discipline that would account for the various kinds of expenditure in society. In 1946 Bataille founded the review *Critique,* and served as editor-in-chief until his death in 1962. This less political journal was eclectic because of its broad subject matter and more intentionally international perspective after World War II, and it opposed existentialism and rivaled Sartre's journal *Les Temps Modernes.* Bataille's editorship of *Critique* secured his place in Parisian intellectual circles after the war. Bataille's editorship of an intellectual journal, scholarly work, pornographic novels, and personnel debauchery render him a perfect example of a postmodern saint, a blatant human contradiction.[7]

We can understand Bataille's thinking in part as a reaction against Hegel and an embrace of Nietzsche. As Jürgen Habermas observes, there is an anarchist trait that links Bataille and Nietzsche, and they are driven into close proximity by an "aesthetically inspired concept of freedom and superhuman self-assertion" that originates with the latter thinker.[8] Following the influential Alexandre Kojève's Marxist interpretation of Hegel, Bataille calls Hegel's work a philosophy of death or an atheism in which human beings take the place of God.[9] Just as Hegel's attention is absorbed in death and sacrifice, a negativity incarnated in the death of a victim, Bataille is also concerned with sacrifice in his own work as a response to the unreasonable claim of Hegel that suggests that human beings take the place of God.[10]

This chapter is concerned with Bataille's theory of religion and sacrifice because his theory and methodology represent a serious challenge for religious studies for the following reasons: his theory questions the role that language plays in society; he questions the constant homogenization of experience; his method of heterology emphasizes the material character of transgression; his profanation of the holy acts as a model for his concept of transgression; his method stresses excess; and if the heterological object is the other, the other cannot be an object of knowledge because the theory calls into question the identity of the subject, on whom knowledge depends. Moreover, his method of heterology and its examination of heterogeneous reality avoid presence and any scientific measurement. In order to grasp his theory of religion, it is necessary to examine his understanding of the human situation and his method. And to understand his theory of sacrifice, it is important to examine its connection to eroticism and violence. Finally, I will test his theory by comparing his insights with the Sun Dance of the Sioux and offering an alternative interpretation.

Human Situation

Bataille expresses two views of the human situation. In his earlier, obscene view he envisions human beings living in an earthly anus in his essay entitled "The Solar Anus" (1927). Although the earth might masturbate sometimes, the sea is continuously masturbating: "The terrestrial globe is covered with volcanoes, which serve as its anus. Although this globe eats nothing, it often violently ejects the contents of its entrails."[11] This means that molten lava represents the feces of the earth, and humans are those who have excrement dumped on them by the earth, giving us a rather anal view of the human situation. Just because humans may be stained by the excrement of life, this is not a hopeless situation. In an essay on a surrealist painting, *The Lugubrious Game* by Salvador Dali, Bataille calls attention to the little man in the lower right-hand corner of the painting who is wearing underwear with an excrement smear on them. Bataille interprets this stain as a vehicle for liberation, because he insists that we must embrace this human waste smudge and the anal obsession that goes with it.[12] By means of this twofold embrace, he argues, we will become free.

A much less anal view of the human situation is provided by a later understanding of the human plight that stresses violence and difference. On the most fundamental level, we find that one animal eats another within a world of immanence and immediacy. This animal world, which cannot transcend itself, is closed to us. Bataille thinks that the only thing that animals have in common is quantitative difference.[13] For human beings, an animal is a thing: "An animal exists for itself and in order to be a thing it must be dead or domesticated."[14] Humans are also like things because they have bodies of animals. Human beings are, however, different than animals because they use tools. By using tools, humans posit an object, which is opposed to immanence, is alien to the individual self, and is the self's thing. A tool changes both man and nature: "it subjugates nature to man, who makes and uses it, but it ties man to subjugated nature. Nature becomes man's property, but it ceases to be immanent to him."[15] The realm within which one lives is a world of things and bodies, and the individual also becomes a thing. This results in two things for the individual: one feels powerless and also feels a stranger to oneself because one loses immanency, immediacy, and intimacy.[16] This realm of things and bodies represents the profane world, which is different than the holy and mythical world of the sacred.

Theory of Religion

Bataille develops his theory of religion through his unusual methodology. We are given a hint of the type of method that he prefers when he writes: "My method, or rather my absence of method, is my life."[17] This quotation is suggestive because it implies his dislike for any kind of systematic or all-encompassing method. Bataille's insistence on using life as a mode of hermeneutics sets a limit on interpretation, an approach that is consistent with his use of a heterological theory of knowledge. Because of the basic contradiction of life, a heterological method is a necessity because it considers questions of heterogeneity and helps one deal with the contradictions of life that are beyond the view of scientific knowledge, which is only concerned with homogeneous elements, and the Hegelian dialectic, which tends to totalize everything or to give a homogeneous representation of the world. Instead of emphasizing sameness, heterology reverses the philosophical process and stresses differences. Because it is no longer an instrument of appropriation, philosophy must now serve excretion. Hence, heterology leads to the possibility of excess by introducing a demand for material gratification in a violent manner.[18] Bataille's heterology, a study of otherness, is also connected to scatology, a study of bodily waste at the overflow margins of the human body.

Heterology must not be confused with a science of the heterogeneous, because scientific knowledge can only be applied to homogeneous elements. Not only is heterology opposed to any philosophical system, it actually reverses the philosophical process because it functions in an excessive manner and does not strive to appropriate anything.[19] Heterology is an excessive method because it is connected to violence, transgression of norms, and wastefulness. This method gives Bataille's work a revolutionary and radical character and impetus, which represents a "mode of non-dialectical materialism where the primary goal is not collective social revolution, but individual sovereignty."[20] By stressing difference, otherness, transgression, and excess, the heterological method shapes Bataille's understanding of the nature of religion as a fundamental distinction between sacred and profane, forming a kind of microcosm of the greater macrocosmic polarity between heterogeneity and homogeneity. In this respect, the sacred is excessive, a radical form of alterity or otherness, and a spontaneous and free overflowing of life. This sacred heterogeneous vitality of life is located beyond rational and conceptual categories that are equated with what is static.

Bataille's method concentrates on heterological objects, which can take the form of excrement, tears, death and the cult of cadavers, religious ecstasy, and heedless expenditure. The continual expulsion of heterological objects by a person manifests an impossibility for a self to maintain its identity because its heterological nature is continuously transgressing the bodily barrier that separates and defines subjects and objects.[21] This suggests that the self, which normally makes knowledge possible, is called into question by the otherness of the heterological object that is itself not an object of knowledge. This transgressive nature of heterological objects connected to the self is also evident in the sacred.

The social customs, laws, and mode of governance of a particular culture are characteristic of the homogeneity of profane human society. This profane realm is a genuine order in which discontinuity, a lucid differentiation between contrasting subjects and objects, is common. In sharp contrast to the homogeneity of the profane realm is the heterogeneity of the sacred, a world of madness, violence, and general excess. The otherness of the sacred as compared to the profane is characterized by its unproductive expenditure of energy, whereas the profane is the realm of work, productivity, and reason.[22] Within the profane world, excessive action is limited and desire is repressed because of its inherent tendency to exceed social limits. The sacred, which represents a realm of immanence in contrast to the profane, is a dangerous threat because it continually tends to irrupt into violence: "The sacred is exactly comparable to the flame that destroys the wood by consuming it."[23] The threat that the sacred will break out into violence reflects its contagious character that is envisioned as dangerous.[24]

Bataille's distinction and definition of the sacred and profane is an exact parallel to Nietzsche's contrast between Apollonian and Dionysian opposition. The Apollonian represents order, light, reason, limitation, and the perfection of dreamland for Nietzsche, while the Dionysian aspect symbolizes a destructive force, chaos, fantasy, and limitlessness. The Apollonian element of Nietzsche becomes Bataille's profane world, whereas the sacred is equated with the Dionysian. In sharp contrast, the distinction between the sacred and profane in the theory of religion espoused by Mircea Eliade interprets this basic distinction the opposite way. For Eliade, the sacred represents order and the profane symbolizes chaos.[25] Bataille's work is, of course, influenced by the earlier distinction made by Emile Durkheim, who argued that the division between the sacred and the profane was the most distinctive trait of religious thought and that their distinction was indicative of their absolute heterogeneity.[26] This line of thinking was embraced by Marcel Mauss, who along with Henri Hubert identified sacrifice with the sacred in their classic work on the subject.[27]

The dynamic and violent aspects of the sacred for Bataille provoke a response of terror. Why is terror evoked in human beings by the sacred? The sacred, an effervescent aspect of life, is constantly threatening to overflow into violence.[28] There is the continual danger that human beings will be overwhelmed by the contagious violence of the sacred, a malefic force that destroys through contagion anything that comes close to it.[29] For Bataille, this indicates that the sacred itself is divided: "the dark and malefic sacred is opposed to the white and beneficent sacred and the deities that partake of the one or the other are neither rational nor moral."[30] Although the sacred possesses value, it is also vertiginously dangerous. Moreover, Bataille's heterological approach, which is not a genuine or systematic method, enables him to see that the sacred is different within itself and not merely distinct from the profane. Even though the sacred is equivalent to religion for Bataille, this simple equation does not give us a complete view of the nature of religion, a perspective that can only come by examining the interrelationship between eroticism, violence, and sacrifice.

Eroticism and Death

Without giving any historical proof for his position, Bataille asserts that the origin of eroticism can be traced back to a time before the division of humanity into free human beings and slaves in prehistoric signs of erotic life embodied by figures with large breasts and erect penises, but its foundation is the sexual act itself.[31] The knowledge of death plays an important role in the origin of eroticism. Although his claim cannot be refuted or proven, Bataille asserts that prehistoric beings were aware of death, an awareness that gave rise to an awareness of eroticism. The knowledge of death is essential because it gives rise to sensibility, which in turn stimulates eroticism, an extreme emotion that separates the sexuality of humans from that of animals.[32] The difference between humans and animals is more precisely defined when he asserts that "eroticism differs from the animal sexual impulse in that it is, in principle, just as work is, the conscious searching for an end, for sensual pleasure."[33] There is also anticipation by the participants in erotic play that it will culminate with sensual pleasure. In the pleasure of erotic play one does not gain anything or become enriched, unlike engaging in work, because eroticism is a realm of pure play, whose "essence is above all to obey seduction, to respond to passion."[34]

If humans are discontinuous beings who yearn for continuity as Bataille claims, eroticism gives us a foretaste of continuity because it strikes at the center of our being: "The transition from the normal state to that of erotic desire presupposes a partial dissolution of the person as he exists in the realm of discontinuity."[35] By participating in erotic activity, individual beings have their fundamental continuity revealed to them. In sharp contrast to discontinuous existence stands nakedness, a state of communication that reveals a search for a possible condition of existence beyond that of self-possession.[36] By stripping naked and standing in the open for anyone to see your flesh, the self becomes dispossessed by its nudity, which finds its consummation in a subsequent erotic act. Nakedness and the dispossession of the self are partially indicative of radical and antisocial aspects of eroticism that entail "a breaking down of established patterns... of the regulated social order basic to our discontinuous mode of existence as defined and separate individuals."[37] Eroticism is also antisocial by its very nature because it is a solitary activity done in secret that is outside the confines of everyday life.[38]

Eroticism must not be confused with an ordinary sexual act between two or more partners or with oneself. In other words, human sexuality is not by itself necessarily erotic. Eroticism, an aspect of an individual's inner life, represents a disequilibrium that stimulates a person to consciously call his or her own being into question.[39] By stressing eroticism as a part of a person's inner nature and as disequilibrium, Bataille wants to present eroticism as an essential part of a person's inner or religious life with an ability to disrupt an individual. Calling attention to the erotic images carved in stone on Hindu temples, Bataille confirms the religious aspect of eroticism by asserting that it is fundamentally divine.[40]

Eroticism must also not be confused with desire: "The object of desire is different from eroticism itself; it is not eroticism in its completeness, but eroticism working through it."[41] Desire suggests the transgressive nature of eroticism because within "eroticism is the desire that triumphs over the taboo."[42] The nature of desire and the impulse to transgression contribute to the apparently insane world of eroticism and render it unrecognizable by others. Transgression is violent and a principle that causes chaos, although it does help us to close the boundaries to a continuity of being, which Bataille equates with death.

It is death that represents the final sense of eroticism: "Eroticism opens the way to death. Death opens the way to the denial of our individual lives."[43] From our discontinuous way of life, death can return us to continuity by means of eroticism.[44] Even though life and death are opposites, Bataille seems to suggest that they can be reconciled and combined into a holy alliance or *coincidentia oppositorum*, an event that occurs by means of eroticism.[45] In his novel entitled *My Mother*, particularly its central theme of incest, the son, for instance, finally engages in sexual intercourse with the corpse of his mother, representing a union of the erotic and death. This helps one to understand that for Bataille, death exalts eroticism and eroticism renders death a desirable goal.[46]

Violence and Sacrifice

Human beings have never been able to reject violence—to utter a definitive "no" to it. The reason for this inability to discard violence is partially due to its origins in basic human emotions like anger, fear, and desire. The acceptance of violence causes humans to become dizzy, nauseous, and pass through an experience of vertigo.[47] Although human beings accept violence in the depths of their being, they still try to reject it, but they are not wholly successful in controlling the excessive urges to commit violence. Unlike René Girard, who thinks that violence can be controlled by ritual, Bataille argues that nothing can control it.[48] Violence is connected to animal or human flesh because it is the flesh that it transgresses and violates, a feature that suggests that sexual activity is a form of violence. Since violence is directly connected to the flesh, its relation to eroticism is also apparent: "In essence, the domain of eroticism is the domain of violence, of violation."[49] Moreover, the intimate connection between violence and sacrifice is even more apparent than that between violence and eroticism.

If violence reaches its culmination in the event of death, sacrifice is the ritual activity par excellence of destruction, its primary principle. This does not mean that the basic intent of sacrifice is annihilation: "The thing—only the thing—is what sacrifice means to destroy in the victim."[50] By means of the sacrifice, the victim is drawn out of the world of things into a realm that is immanent to it. This separation from the world of things is also true for the sacrificer: "The sacrificer needs the sacrifice in order to separate himself from the world of things and the victim could not be separated from it in turn if the sacrificer was not already separated

in advance."[51] Sacrifice is an inward form of violence, whereas war represents an outwardly directed form of violence.[52]

Even though violence is directed toward the victim, it is not necessary
to destroy the victim except as a thing in order for it and the sacrificer to
regain a lost intimacy, a realm that is antithetical to the real world.[53] Bataille
refers to the victim as the "accursed share" that is destined for violent consumption, a mode of communication for separate beings. The victim is
also "a surplus taken from the mass of useful wealth."[54] This tends to suggest that the intention of sacrifice is not necessarily to kill the surplus
victim but rather to give something. That which is given is ideally accomplished in a selfless spirit without any expectation of receiving an economic
or personal benefit. The violence perpetrated on the sacrificial victim calls
attention to the violation of its flesh, which indicates a connection to the
sexual act.

Both the sexual act and sacrifice are similar because they both reveal
the flesh.[55] In the calling of attention to the flesh, the external violence of
the sacrifice becomes evident, and the internal violence of the subject is
revealed. Sacrifice and sexual-erotic intercourse also share violence in
common: The lover strips the beloved of her identity no less than the
blood-stained priest his human or animal victim. The woman in the hands
of her assailant is despoiled of her being. She is brusquely laid open to
violence.[56]

Thus eroticism is like sacrifice because the female partner, either
within or outside marriage, plays the role of the victim, especially when
she is a virgin whose blood flows, with the male assuming the part of the
sacrificer, while both participants lose themselves in the continuity
established by the violence. This suggests that the continuity of life is not
affected by death, but is rather proven by death, a reflection of its ability to
illuminate the meaning of sacrifice and life:[57] "Death reveals life in its
plenitude and dissolves the real order."[58] This implies that the intimacy of
life is not revealed until the last possible moment when death becomes a
sign of life. In the final analysis, sacrifice brings life and death into
harmony.

Bataille's theory of religion and sacrifice enables us to see its interconnection with eroticism, violence, and death. By showing their intimate
relationship, Bataille is then able to stress themes that are important to
him like separation, difference, transgression, and excess. It is also important for Bataille to reintroduce eroticism into a theory of religion and
ritual. His rationale is that "in casting eroticism out of religion, men

reduced religion to a utilitarian morality. Eroticism, having lost its sacred character, became unclean."[59] By nature of its connection with eroticism, violence, and death, sacrifice is excessive and creates differences.[60] Its transgressive nature, which is grounded in eroticism and violence, necessarily means that sacrifice stands in sharp contrast to morality.[61] Having defined the nature of sacrifice for Bataille, I can test his theory by comparing it to an actual sacrifice, which is something that he fails to do with his theory by failing to refer to actual examples of sacrifice in the religions of the world. For this purpose, I have chosen to examine the Sun Dance of the Sioux in order to show the shortcomings of Bataille's theory of sacrifice. And I will conclude by offering a reasonable interpretation of the Sun Dance by concentrating on its symbolism.[62] My account of the Sun Dance will rely on the work of J. R. Walker because his information was gathered from several different sources, and it represents the most authoritative account available to us of the rite in one period of its history.[63] My approach presupposes that the rite and its meaning have continued to change in response to new circumstances for the Sioux. By selecting this rite, I am being eminently fair to Bataille, from one perspective, because the erotic and violent features of the Sun Dance could be used to prove the validity of his theory, assuming that one neglects contrary features.

Bataille's Theory and the Sun Dance

The complexity of the Sun Dance makes it difficult to interpret. Although he does not consider the Sun Dance of the Sioux, Joseph Jorgensen interprets, for instance, the Ute and Shoshone rite as an acquisition of power that transforms the person and allows him to gain power, status, and autonomy.[64] From another perspective, another scholar interprets the Sun Dance of the Sioux as a commemoration of tribal virtues expressed in the dance, a celebration of the people, an acknowledgment of the generative power of the sun, and a celebration of renewal.[65] The rejoicing over renewal of the world is close to Ake Hultkrantz's interpretation of the rite as a recreation of the cosmos.[66] According to R. B. Hassrick, the Sun Dance represents a socially unifying activity and a chance to resolve a conflict between an individual ego and adjustment to physical and social forces.[67] Another scholar interprets the Sun Dance in terms of its various functions: unifying force, maintaining tribal traditions, ensuring tribal well-being in hunting and warfare, offering a dancer perpetual prestige.[68] I propose offering a different interpretive approach for the Sun Dance that will critically reflect on Bataille's theory. We will see that the Sun Dance of the Sioux exhibits a threefold significance: existential, social, and cosmic. In other words, if we examine the many symbols associated with the rite, we will see that this sacrifice enables a successful participant to attain three levels of being.

While the sacred pole was being painted, for instance, instructors and students sat in a circle around the black painted figures of a buffalo and man, each depicted with exaggerated genitals in order to impart the potency of Iya, patron god of libertinism, to the man and the potency of Gnaski, the crazy buffalo and patron god of licentiousness, to the buffalo. According to Black Elk's nonrisque interpretation of the images, the buffalo represents all the four-legged animals on the earth, and the figure of the man signifies all people.[69] In contrast, Bataille would be quick to seize on the erotic connections of the patron gods of libertinism and licentiousness. If the erotic is a quest for sensual pleasure, represents a realm of play, and reveals a foretaste of continuity, it cannot be used to interpret the meaning of Iya and Gnaski because within the context of the Sun Dance they more powerfully suggest the renewal and recreation motifs of the rite. Bataille's concept of eroticism also would not fit into an insightful interpretation of the Sun Dance as a dominant theme of the rite because of its antisocial character as a solitary activity accomplished in secret.

The heterological method of Bataille is intended to alleviate the contradictions of life and free the individual from the homogeneity of the world. In contrast to Bataille's insistence on a search for radical difference, the worldview of the Sioux embodied in the symbolic aspects of the Sun Dance, an offering of body and soul to Wakan-Tanka (the Great Spirit), suggests a homogeneous view of the cosmos. The universe is, for instance, represented by the round form of the ceremonial drum, whose steady beat is the throbbing at the center of the cosmos.[70] Within the context of the Sun Dance, the cosmic pillar of the universe is represented by the cottonwood tree, which represents the enemy that is symbolically killed and transported back to the center of the camp using sticks because human hands are not allowed to touch it. The ritual participants consecrate the tree with the stem of the sacred pipe, another symbol of the earth, the buffalo, and everything that lives and grows on the earth. Once the tree is trimmed of its branches and its sides and branch tips painted red, the rawhide effigies of a man and a buffalo are suspended from the crosspiece of the sacred tree, and it is placed into a hole at the center of the camp. The sacred tree not only suggests a universal pillar but also represents the way of the people.[71] Other cosmic symbols are the sun and earth signified by a red circle, symbolic of all that is sacred, and in the center of the circle that represents the sun a blue circle that suggests Wakan-Tanka, the center of the cosmos and all existence.[72] Moreover, the lodge of the Sun Dance is composed of twenty-eight poles that each signify an object of creation, forming a circle that represents the entire created world.[73] It is difficult to find anything excessive or transgressive in these cosmic symbols of the Sioux that would support Bataille's position.

Rather than achieving the differentiation that Bataille's theory advocates, the sun dancer symbolically acquires the cosmos. According to the ethnological report of J. R. Walker, the candidate who dances the most excruciatingly painful form of the dance with the intention of becoming a shaman is given a small hoop by his mentor. This hoop is symbolic of the sky, the four winds, time, all things that grow, and all circular things made by the tribe.[74] After his successful completion of the dance, the sun dancer is allowed to place this symbol on his tepee. This privilege suggests that he attains all that the hoop symbolizes. The highest aspiring sun dancer does not find that the cosmos becomes other for him, and he does not stand as an individual sovereign within the cosmos. He rather becomes part of the whole and thus acquires the cosmos.

Instead of perceiving the cosmic symbolism associated with the most painful performance of the rite, Bataille's writings suggest that he would stress the sadistic and masochistic aspects of the rite. Sadism, an excessive violation of modesty and a violent excretion, is not only an eruption of excremental forces, but it also forms a limitation by subjugating whatever is opposed to such an eruption.[75] If masochism is an enjoyment of pain, the violence exercised on the flesh of the sun dancers is viewed by Bataille as a transgression and violation of the participants' flesh, which also calls attention to the flesh itself and connects it to the erotic. Bataille also thinks that violence against the flesh is an external manifestation of the internal violence of the sacrificial participant, which is perceived as a loss of blood and as various forms of ejaculations.[76] Moreover, the cutting of the flesh is suggestive of the discontinuity of the self for Bataille.

Unlike the solitary activity of eroticism for Bataille, the sun dancer of the Sioux rite does not distinguish or divorce himself from his society, because he represents the people and suffers on their behalf during the rite. After purifying themselves, their clothing, and equipment to be used in the rite, the participants cry at the center of the camp and adopt the suffering of the people, which enables other tribal members to gain under-

standing and strength.[77] If the discontinuity characteristic of Bataille's profane human society is present among the Sioux, the Sun Dance is intended
to bridge any social divisions by uniting the social bonds of a particular
tribe and uniting them with different Indian tribes. By means of an invitation from the tribe initiating the rite prior to its beginning, other Indian
tribes are invited to participate in the rite, even though some of the visitors
are hereditary enemies.[78] This scenario is intended to enhance the social
solidarity of the Indian nation and build a closer relationship with the
things of the universe, and the sacred center created by the dancers is
alleged to always be with them throughout the remainder of their existence.
There is no evidence of transgressive or excessive social behavior by the
sun dancers in Bataille's sense. Moreover, the dancers have acquired a
sacred power during the rite that they may then share later with other
members of their society. The acquired power of the sun dancers may be
invested in those who are sick by the dancers placing their hands on the
less fortunate.[79] The intention of this practice is to share the sacred power,
cure the sick, and enter into communion with others; in comparison to
Bataille's theory, the intention of the sun dancers is not to differentiate
themselves from their society. It is rather to share a sacred power that can
benefit every member of the tribe. Bataille's heterological method and its
stress on finding radical difference prevent him from seeing the socially
unifying possibilities of a rite like the Sun Dance.

According to Bataille, violence is inevitable because human beings
cannot totally reject it. As I previously noted, the Sun Dance represents a
threefold sacrifice of which the initial two sacrificial actions are symbolic:
the cutting down of the cottonwood tree, which is symbolic of the enemy;
the shooting at the effigies of a man and buffalo suspended from the crosspiece of the sacred tree; and the final action, the actual sacrifice of human
flesh, which takes place on the fourth day of the rite. The second symbolic
killing of the effigies of a man and buffalo, amid much rejoicing by the
participants, represents the hope for future success in hunting and victory
in war.[80] These symbolic killings typical of the Sioux rite violate Bataille's
assertion that violence cannot be controlled. The symbolic nature of the
Sioux killings suggests rather a limiting and eventual termination of violence and not a promoting of any cycle of violence. Although Bataille is
right to emphasize the importance of violence in sacrifice, there does not
appear to be any danger that the contagious violence of the sacred will
overflow and overwhelm the Sioux and other tribes. There are certainly
martial features to the Sun Dance, but their symbolic nature suggests a

containment of violence rather than any overflowing of it. Bataille's theory does make clear, however, that the Sioux accept violence, even though they try to reject or control it.

Within the drama of the Sun Dance, there is a hint of an inherent prestige associated with victims choosing to perform the sacrifice in the most painful and violent manner. The actual sacrificial victims, for instance, can choose to dance in any of four ways: gazing at the sun from dawn to dusk; having wooden skewers inserted into their breasts, which are tied to rawhide ropes secured about halfway up the sacred pole; having wooden skewers inserted into their breasts and then being suspended about one foot off the ground; or having wooden skewers inserted, to which thongs are attached to one or more buffalo skulls, which they must drag along the dance area.[81] The Sun Dance is not completed until the flesh of the victim has been torn through, representing the death and rebirth of the victim. It is permissible for others to assist by pulling on the ropes to end a victim's agony.

It is not too difficult to image the pain, a bodily sensation associated with human tissue or bone damage, being experienced by the dancers. The sun dancers are examples of a voluntary type of pain that involves self-inflicted or contextually accepted pain for the most part. Overall, pain operates to enhance the social bond, establish a relationship with one's deity, transform a person, provide insight into the meaning of life, and gain salvation for one in some cases.[82] Moreover, pain can produce powerful feelings that affect a person's capacity to perceive and know reality, along with psychological dissociation that can trigger overwhelming emotions. From another perspective, the pain associated with the Sun Dance occurs within the context of a social drama in which the dancer plays the roles of both sacrificer and victim. Many of these features of pain are evident during the Sun Dance for its practitioners, and tend to confirm Bataille's notion about the role of violence in rites.

The multiple numbers of sun dancers contradicts, however, Bataille's assertion that a victim represents a surplus of communal wealth and substitutes for other members of the community.[83] Neither is the victim an accursed share destined for violent destruction. Bataille is right, however, to emphasize the importance of death in sacrifice, which possesses the power to return one to continuity by means of eroticism. What he fails to see is the connection between death and spiritual rebirth. And because of his notion of eroticism, which represents a disequilibrium that stimulates a person to consciously call his or her being into question,

Bataille is not able to recognize that the sun dancer is able to find his identity.

The Sun Dance adheres to Bataille's theory of sacrifice to some extent because it calls attention to the flesh, reveals external violence, and makes clear the internal violence of the subject. The violation and breaking of the sun dancer's flesh does suggest the correctness of Bataille's observation about the intimate connection between human flesh and violence. By giving pieces of their flesh, the sun dancers, however, act contrary to Bataille's claim that the violation of the victim's flesh connotes a connection to a sexual act. At this point, Bataille's theory is problematic because it lacks consistent sense in the context of the Sun Dance. Bataille's need to reintroduce eroticism blinds him to the facts or drama of an actual sacrifice. The flesh of the sacrificial victim in the Sun Dance represents ignorance,[84] and not the dispossession of the self, an antisocial aspect of eroticism for Bataille. From an existential perspective, to be freed from the ropes tied to the skewers symbolizes freedom from the bonds of the flesh and not some erotic urge. The lack of an erotic emotion is evident in the inner intentionality of the victim symbolized by the donning of rabbit skins on his arms and legs. The rabbit is a symbol of humility, a virtue with which one must approach Wakan-Tanka. The victim is also equated symbolically with the sacred pipe that stretches from heaven to earth.[85] In this context the sacred pipe indicates the transcending of earthly flesh. The dancer becomes the center of the world in which the four directions meet when he is tied at the center of the four poles, so that the four directions converge in his body.[86]

Within the drama of the Sun Dance, elements of eroticism, violence, and death are evident. This does not mean, however, that these features of sacrifice necessarily involve stressing separation, difference, transgression, and excess. Although it is possible to find these features in the Sun Dance to some degree, the Sioux rite stresses finding one's identity within a religious and social tradition. By successfully completing the rite, a sun dancer does not separate himself from the group or become distinct from other things, but he rather often assumes a position of leadership within the tribe. And I have already noted how the sun dancer is intimately related to his mentor, ritual assistant or second, and other members of the tribe who play various roles in the rite, which suggests the socially unifying nature of the rite. Moreover, within a tribal society like the Sioux, the individual's identity is socially defined, even though one's visions and dreams help one to define oneself and one's place within a wider social context.

Besides being a form of human sacrifice, the Sun Dance also functions as an initiation rite. The dancer attains a totally new existential status of enlightenment and responsibility, having died to his former ignorant condition. The ordeal that one endures is often accompanied by visions of the divine. And the successful completion of the rite is a prerequisite if one aspires to become a shaman. Walker notes that after the successful completion of the Sun Dance the victim is eligible for leadership of a war party or for chieftainship.[87] The candidate receives new meaning and status, symbolized by the red design, a symbol of all that is sacred, drawn on his chest by the shaman. Furthermore, the victim is equated throughout the rite with the moon, which waxes and wanes, lives and dies, like all things.[88]

Concluding Remarks

The significance of the Sun Dance enables us to see that there is an alternative interpretation to Bataille's theory that is more faithful to the actual evidence and is not simply imposed on the ritual activities by the creative imagination of a theorist. This interpretive analysis of the Sun Dance is suggested by the patterns exhibited by the rite itself and reflects more accurately the actual rite and its religious and symbolic context, whereas Bataille includes a personal agenda because he wants to reintroduce the erotic back into religion. In other words, Bataille's theoretical speculation about eroticism shapes his theory of religion and sacrifice, and he assumes that the erotic left religion, an inaccurate assumption based on evidence located in the Sun Dance. Thus his theoretical worldview takes precedence over the religious phenomena that he examines or that he fails to consult in the first place.

With his involvement in the surrealist movement, his emphasis on embracing bodily waste, his anal and erotic obsessions, the role of the ambiguous pineal eye in his works, and composition of excessively obscene novels, all this suggests an explicit advocacy of decadence by Bataille. The themes of excess and decadence are evident in his novels. In *My Mother*, for instance, the socially excessive theme is incest. His novel *The Blue of Noon* focuses on the nauseous and squalid aspects of human life when its characters engage in endless orgies, vomiting, and urinating. The erotic and death are continually united in the *Story of the Eye* when, for example, the two leading libertines of the novel have sexual intercourse next to the cadaver of a young girl they have driven to death; another dramatic example is the rape of a priest by the female protagonist and his death by strangulation and simultaneous sexual orgasm; and another is the death of the distracted matador gorged through his eye by the horn of a bull as he is distracted and blinded by the obscene antics of the female protagonist. Moreover, Bataille's hermeneutical method of heterology is designed to lead to excess and decadence. Trying to explain his *méthode de méditation*, used in his book on religious experience, Bataille writes, "I think like a girl takes off her dress. At its most extreme point, thought is immodesty, obscenity itself."[89] This kind of statement seems to suggest de Sade or Mephistopheles becoming Faust. In his work on heterology, Julian Pefanis summarily asserts that the works of Bataille are "a theater of the excremental in whose scenes one may glimpse golden threads."[90] Fredric Jameson, a self-admitted American adherent of postmodern literary criticism, affirms that decadence is a characteristic of postmodernism: "'Decadence' is thus in some way the very premonition of the postmodern itself, but under conditions that make it impossible to predict that aftermath with any sociological or cultural accuracy, thereby diverting the vague sense of a future into more fantastic forms, all borrowed from the misfits and eccentrics, the perverts and the Others, or aliens, of the present (modern) system."[91] And if decadence originates in political despair,[92] Bataille's hermeneutical program is a political manifesto and not an apt tool for interpreting religious phenomena.

From a more positive perspective, Bataille's theory of religion does call our attention to neglected elements in the study of religion in the form of bodily waste: excrement, saliva, tears, urine, mucous, dirt, skin, and so forth. Although his distinction between the sacred and the profane cannot be applied consistently as a useful hermeneutical device in regard to the religious phenomena or worldview of American Indians, his emphasis on the difference within the sacred itself is suggestive. Moreover, he is right to stress the violent aspects of sacrifice and their sexual implications.

Although violence is certainly present in the Sun Dance, the Sioux rite appears to move in the direction of nonviolence by symbolically killing an enemy, for instance, represented by the tree, which tends to undermine Bataille's opinion that violence cannot be contained. By offering his body and soul, the Sioux sun dancer points to a renewal and continuance of cosmic generative forces. The Sun Dance also joins Indian societies together and provides for social continuity by allowing others to share in the sacred power engendered by the rituals. Moreover, the rite enables the sun dancer to become ontologically transformed by being reborn and being set free of his mortal flesh. Although there is a sense in which the sun dancer is distinctive, the emphasis of the rite is unity with society and social well-being rather than the differences between the sacrificial victim and society. Nonetheless, Bataille does help us to see that violence chews up humans, digests them, and turns them into fecal waste.

While a dynamic and dramatic performance that affirms the significance of the human body, the Sun Dance serves as a vehicle for the highest symbolic truths.[93] This rite enables the sun dancer to locate himself in the cosmos and to explain to the body its place within the cosmic order, nothing short of a revelation of a way of being located in the universe. This rite enables the sun dancer to realize true personhood and community, because it reveals his personal uniqueness and his uniqueness in relationship to others. By the community coming together to share and act out a worldview that assures a sense of unity, this rite strengthens the individual, reunites the communal bonds, and binds together anew the threads that hold together the cosmos.

3

Excess, Time, and the Pure Gift

ALTHOUGH IT IS unusual for a book to be so widely revered among a scholarly audience for any length of time, the work entitled *Essai sur Ie don forme et raison de l' échange dans les sociétés archaiques* by Marcel Mauss, first published in *L' Année sociologique* in 1924 and republished in 1950 by the Presses Universitaires de France, is generally considered a classic in anthropology and religious studies. This exemplary paradigm of scholarship is not given, however, the same respect and acceptance by some postmodern thinkers because it fails to address in part the significance of difference. Two of the best examples of such postmodern critics of Mauss's theory of the gift are Jacques Derrida and Georges Bataille.

Within the context of discussing the philosophy of Martin Heidegger, Derrida thinks that the German philosopher elucidates that giving (*Geben*) and the gift (*Gabe*) lack any ontological status because it is impossible to think of them in terms of Being: "Because they constitute the process of propriation, the giving and the gift can be construed neither in the boundaries of Being's horizon nor from the vantage point of its truth, its meaning."[1] Since they amount to nothing without a subject being or an object being, Derrida concludes that the gift or giving does not possess any essence. He also playfully claims that "to give" does not involve exchange. In fact, a pure gift is without exchange, without return.[2] Derrida's deconstruction of the notion of gift necessarily implies that there is no need for any party to feel any obligation toward the other. Deconstruction is the experience of the impossible, which is an aporia (meaning "a way to go"), but aporias are made to be broken by means of deconstruction.[3] This position is in sharp contrast to that of Emmanuel Levinas and his emphasis on obligation. Having nothing to do with Being, a thing, an act, exchange, or an obligation, the gift is more akin to an excess that overflows language.

The excessive nature of the gift is especially emphasized by Georges Bataille, who is fascinated by the practice of the potlatch among tribal societies. If Mauss perceives a necessity for a harmonious reciprocity among parties in the act of exchanging gifts, Bataille's emphasis on the excessive nature of the potlatch, a unilateral gesture of expenditure (*dépense*), allows him to stress its disruptive nature and undermines the homogeneity implied by the evidence used by Mauss. Bataille calls into question Mauss's theory of the gift by utilizing a modified version of the potlatch for the general economy, undermining Mauss's view of a gift exchange without loss or gain. Not only does the potlatch disrupt the established social-economic order, it also enables us to encounter death, which is symbolized by the dramatic destruction of goods. The ultimate form of expenditure for Bataille, however, is eroticism, an ambiguous social phenomenon connected to a vacillation between attraction and repulsion.

Before I develop further some of the insights of Derrida and Bataille on the nature of the gift, it will be useful to review some of the major highlights of Mauss's classic theory of the gift to better grasp more accurately the position to which the postmodern thinkers are reacting. After examining the positions of Bataille and Derrida on the phenomenon of the gift, I place their theories within the context of theoretical work completed on the Hindu notion of the gift in order to test their reflections about the nature of the gift within the context of a particular tradition and to discern any insights that they might offer when reconsidering the Hindu notion of the gift. This approach is suggested by the work of Mauss because of the central role played by the Hindu conception of the gift in his work, even though J. P. Parry indicates that the Hindu understanding of the nature of the gift is inconsistent with the basic thesis of Mauss.[4] Finally, I compare some aspects of the work of Bataille and Derrida with Mauss in order to demonstrate some of the problems associated with the respective positions of each side and to briefly compare some aspects of their respective positions with respect to such issues as time, presence, and rationality.

Gift and Obligation

From the scholarly perspective of Mauss, a gift can be any object or service, possessing a uniqueness that is given within a web of social interrelationships, which suggests that a gift is more pervasive than simply a present because it can include labor. It is rare for a present to assume the form of labor. Mauss's theory of the gift concentrates more on circulation and consumption and not on productive consumption and consumptive production as did Marxian theory. Mauss wants to identify the social significance of a gift and what gift exchanges inform us about people doing the giving and receiving, the objects given and received, and what this practice tells us about social relations within a given context. The uniqueness of a gift is related to the people involved in an exchange and the precise moment of the exchange, whereas a commodity type of relationship is characterized by the lack of an enduring connection between the people and object in a more alienated and fungible type of relationship. It is possible to summarize the uniqueness of the gift in this way: "In gift relations people are thought of or identified in terms of their fundamental, inalienable attributes and relationships, and hence are unique."[5] This does not necessarily mean that gifts, which are inalienable objects, and commodities are exclusive categories because there are gift transactions that embody elements of alienation and individualism.[6] It is possible for a utilitarian or superfluous gift to be a commodity, although Mauss's use of the term *gift* does not specifically identify the exact object or service exchanged.

According to Mauss, the giving of a present to someone is not a voluntary action because any gift involves obligation and economic self-interest. A person gives to another person because one is obligated to act in this way, and the person receiving a gift is then involuntarily obligated to return the gift. The obligations of this fundamental exchange system are imposed on both parties by social groups and not by the individuals themselves.[7] The obligatory nature of gift transactions is dissimilar to those of buying and selling in which a buyer is only obligated to pay for what is purchased from the seller, a transaction that terminates any further obligation or relationship. The obligatory nature of the gift does not mean for Mauss that a gift is never free; it does, however, suggest that in fulfilling the obligation to give a gift, one recreates that obligation by reaffirming the social relationships of which the obligation is a distinct part from the commencement of the exchange.[8] Mauss conceives of the process of exchange in a rather broad way because the exchange goes beyond mere economic goods; it includes social acts of politeness conceived in a liberal way that encompasses such activities as rituals, dances, festivals, banquets, and military services and can even involve the exchange of women and children, which represents an example of Mauss's tendency to place greater stress on a more active role for humanity in social phenomena than his mentor Durkheim.[9] Mauss does, however, draw a distinction between gift exchange, which is associated with tribal cultures dominated by kinship and group relations, and commodity exchange, which is evident in industrial types of societies characterized by social class and division of labor in which self-interest, independence of both giver and recipient, and frequent impersonal relationships predominate.

When a person presents a gift to someone else that person is not merely giving some inert or neutral object, but is rather giving an active part of him- or herself, which suggests that a gift is inalienably connected to the giver. Mauss is suggesting that a gift is something personal and alive with a special power that not only generates itself but also possesses the power to renew the relationship between the giving and receiving parties. The recipient of the gift receives something very special: "one must give back to another person what is really part and parcel of his nature and substance, because to accept something from somebody is to accept some part of his spiritual essence, of his soul."[10] Thus, the gift possesses a vitality, which often includes individuality for Mauss. By giving part of oneself in the gift, one not only participates in the gift but also creates a lasting spiritual bond between persons.

Throughout his theory, Mauss emphasizes the importance of obligation, which he stresses is threefold: to give, to receive, and to reciprocate. The threefold sequence of obligation forms a never-ending cycle of exchange, a cycle that suggests an orderly system. Whether the receiver is a large social group, a small group, or a lone individual, they are all obligated to receive. The group or individual with whom they enter into an exchange relationship is in turn obligated to give, an obligation that can have dire consequences if it is not fulfilled by the group or person. The potentially serious political and social consequences of meeting the demands of the obligation to give are lucidly made by Mauss: "To refuse to give, to fail to invite, just as to refuse to accept, is tantamount to declaring war; it is to reject the bond of alliance and commonality. Also, one gives because one is compelled to do so, because the recipient possesses some kind of right of property over anything that belongs to the donor."[11] And upon receiving a gift one is under pressure to reciprocate in order to complete the cycle of giving, which then continues in the cycle of exchange. This cycle of giving forms a structure that constrains both the giver and the recipient because of the obligations imposed on both parties. Moreover, the cycle of exchange suggests the binding effect of the gift by linking different kinship groups. The binding effect of the gift is destroyed, for instance, when a recipient rejects the gift because one is also rejecting the social relationship enhanced and reinforced by the gift and the giver's concern for the recipient. In other words, the gift for Mauss is too personal and very integral to the identity of the giver, unlike an impersonal commodity, for someone to just reject it.

Two other features of the gift identified for their importance by Mauss are ownership and certainty. The former feature means that when one receives a gift one necessarily gains ownership over it and does not merely possess it.[12] As gifts circulate in certain indigenous societies (Mauss refers to Melanesian and Polynesian groups in his classic work), they create certainty that they will be eventually reciprocated, a feature that Mauss finds within the gift itself.[13] These two features of a gift emphasize the obligatory and economic self-interest aspects of the nature of the gift. According to one authority, the core of Mauss's model is represented by the distinction between gifts and commodities, a dual distinction that can be applied to the social identity of objects, to types of transactions between parties, and to kinds of societies. This type of categorization leads Mauss to distinguish between what he calls gift societies (e.g., Melanesian societies) and commodity systems (e.g., Western societies). In the former type of society the gift influences all aspects of social life, whereas in the latter type of society it is alienation that is prevalent. This type of distinction is an example of the Occidentalism of Mauss that is connected to his Orientalism.[14]

The dynamic nature of the gift is evident in the phenomenon of the potlatch, a kind of orgy of generosity in some tribal societies. This system of gift exchange can become violent, exaggerated, and antagonistic, features that have special appeal to someone like Bataille. The effect that is produced by a potlatch is all encompassing from the perspective of Mauss: "In certain kinds of potlatch one must expend all that one has, keeping nothing back. It is a competition to see who is the richest and also the most madly extravagant. Everything is based upon the principles of antagonism and rivalry."[15] This competition revolves around honor and prestige for the participants in a reciprocal pattern that creates obligations among the parties. The competitive nature of the potlatch is similar to a game that one risks losing. If one loses within the context of the potlatch, one loses social rank and status and even one's personal persona. It is the obligation to reciprocate that Mauss identifies as the essence of the potlatch.[16] And the destructive quality of the giving resembles a sacrifice.

The potlatch is structured and constrained by obligation because no one can refuse to participate or refuse to be a recipient of a gift, which is indicative of the burden that accompanies any gift. If one refuses to participate, this is indicative of one's fear of having to reciprocate and losing in the exchange, a dramatic proof that one is unequal to the giver and unable to meet the challenge offered by the gift. It is very easy to be captured by the power of the items exchanged, a power that causes the things exchanged to be circulated, given, and returned. During the potlatch, the power inherent within the things exchanged becomes manifested: "Each one of these precious things possesses, moreover, productive power itself. It is not a mere sign and pledge; it is also a sign and a pledge of wealth, the magical and religious symbol of rank and plenty."[17]

Excessiveness of the Gift

If Mauss wants to strip the irrational from the notion of gift and emphasize its harmonious reciprocity, Bataille thinks that the potlatch disrupts the homogeneity of Mauss's theory and dramatically magnifies the difference between his notion of *dépense* and the *don* of Mauss's theory. Unlike Mauss, Bataille wants to examine the irrational, disruptive, destructive, and excessive aspects of the gift. The examination of these types of features enables Bataille to also stress its powerful, paradoxical, absurd, and erotic aspects. In order to accomplish his objective, Bataille examines the potlatch of the American Indians of the Northwest (e.g., Tlingit, Haida, Tsimshian, and Kwakiutl tribes), in which he finds a circulation of wealth without bargaining. Within these tribal cultures, the giver challenges, humiliates, and obligates the receiver, who must in turn respond to erase the humiliation, assume the challenge, and satisfy the obligation created by accepting the excessive gift. Within this context, the demand for dépense originates from within the person, although it cannot be asserted that there is a reason for it other than the desire a person may possess for it.[18]

Alluding to Mauss's theory and the phenomenon of the potlatch, Bataille agrees that the act of giving represents the acquisition of a power. In fact, the giver surpasses himself in the act of gift giving because he acquires a power, which is connected with contempt for the riches that one gives away. Thus, there is a relationship between power, a surpassing virtue of gift giving, and renunciation, a feature that Bataille identifies with the essence of the gift that he specifies as "the prohibition of immediate, unreserved, animal gratification."[19] The power closely associated with the gift is interrelated with the paradoxical nature of the gift because the gift becomes reduced for Bataille to the acquisition of power. There is no power, however, associated with the gift if one's act is done in silence or solitude. The excessive giving must be done in a public manner: "But if he destroys the object in front of another person or if he gives it away, the one who gives has actually acquired in the other's eyes, the power of giving or destroying."[20] The power that the giver gains over the recipient manifests the absurdity of gifts. Bataille explains more fully the absurdity:

> Not only does he have the power over the recipient that the gift has bestowed on him, but also the recipient is obligated to nullify that power by repaying the gift. The rivalry even entails the return of a greater gift: In order to get even the giver must not only redeem himself, but he must also impose the "power of the gift" on his rival in turn. In a sense the presents are repaid with interest. Thus the gift is the opposite of what it seemed to be: To give is obviously to lose, but the loss apparently brings a profit to the one who sustains it.[21]

This intertwining of power, obligation, and absurdity helps Bataille to show that the gift is not some homogenous pattern of exchange, but that it is rather more akin to a heterogeneous and irrational phenomenon. Bataille's position also renders individual givers and their social organization ambivalent because there can be no unilateral response to the demand to give.[22]

According to Bataille, the giver gains rank, and this acquisition depends on one's capacity for bestowing gifts. From the fact of acquisition, Bataille enumerates a number of what he calls laws. The first law is that appropriation reflects the squandering of surplus resources. By squandering the surplus, it is prestige that is acquired by the giver, a determinate of one's rank. If social rank can be gained like any other commodity and represents a source of profit, it is still dependent on the wasteful expenditure of resources, which theoretically could have been acquired in some other way. The final law expresses the ambiguity and contradictory nature of the gift. Bataille elaborates that the giver "must waste the excess, but he remains eager to acquire even when he does the opposite, and so he makes waste itself an object of acquisition."[23] And long after the loss of resources, the acquired prestige gained by excessive and impulsive giving remains with the giver. The final so-called law isolated by Bataille affirms that any individual accumulation of wealth is doomed to destruction because the individual does not genuinely possess the wealth and the social rank that accompanies it. Wealth is analogous to a pipe bomb for Bataille because it can destroy the builder just as readily as its intended victim. The giver lies, for all intents and purposes, to him- or herself and others because the giver never really possesses the wealth that he or she dispenses.[24]

Bataille connects the potlatch to sacrificial action, but he does not view it in the same way as Mauss. Although the potlatch is not equivalent to a sacrifice, it does function in a complementary way by withdrawing wealth from productive consumption. Bataille elaborates further that "in general, sacrifice withdraws useful products from profane circulation; in principle the gifts of potlatch liberate objects that are useless from the start."[25] Within the context of discussing the theory of religion and the role of gift in the theory of E. B. Tylor in contrast to Bataille, Mauss and his coauthor Henri Hubert in their classic work *Sacrifice: Its Nature and Function* think that Tylor gives too much weight to the notion of gift in his theory of religion. Mauss and Hubert think that there is a sense in which a sacrifice is a gift, if one considers that a sacrifice gives a worshipper rights over his or her deity, but this is not sufficient reason with which to build a theory of religion.[26] In her discussion of the Great Sacrifice in Moroccan culture, M. E. Combs-Schilling, for instance, denies that the sacrifice, a vigorous attempt to have sexual intercourse with the sacred, is a gift because it is more physically active than a gift and is structured to attract biological power exemplified by sexual intercourse and human birth.[27]

Within the context of discussing the gift of women and their distribution by male kin, Bataille connects the exchange of women, a form of potlatch, with eroticism, an extreme, solitary, human emotion that is rooted in the alternation of affirmation and denial, of fascination and horror, attraction and repulsion.[28] The gift of women is unnatural because to renounce a coveted object represents a kind of inner revolution within the giver. Bataille attributes the erotic value of the given object (a woman in this case) to the prohibition against incest, which calls attention to the covetous nature of the object or to the sexual value of it by the process of prohibition itself.[29] Bataille speculates that the gift of a woman may be a substitute for a sexual act. There is, however, no disputing the fact that both the sexual act and gift provide a relief for the initiator.[30] Since eroticism is excessive by its very nature, Bataille wants to stress the excessive and heterological nature of the gift by linking it with eroticism. Moreover, eroticism represents the most extreme form of dépense: "the sacrifice of the self is the most complete gesture of communication."[31]

Sexual excesses include a wide variety of social transgressions (incest, homosexuality, necrophilia, and sadomasochism) that exceed normal social boundaries. Both sexual excess and violence associated with sacrifice are symbolized by the Acephalus—a headless body holding the decapitated head with a skull's head in the groin area of the body. The decapitated head marks the loss of reason and end of the Hegelian system of philosophy, whereas castration represents sexual prohibitions and taboos and punishment for transgressing socially prescribed norms. With its symbolic union of beheading and castration, the Acephalic man represents a coincidentia oppositorum.

The Gift within the Flux of Time

According to Derrida, if the phenomenon of the gift is examined within the context of time, the gift becomes impossible due to the predominance of time. The gift and time share a relationship to the visible, although time, a manifestation of invisibility, does not give itself to be seen, withdrawing itself continuously from visibility. In contrast, the gift calls attention to itself by announcing itself and giving itself to thought as that which is impossible.[32] Within the temporal context of the gift, there is a weaving together of feelings of indebtedness, gratitude, and congratulations that encompasses both donor and recipient. From Derrida's perspective, the web of relationship and feelings commences to annul the gift from the very start of the exchange. In a recorded dialogue at a conference with Jean-Luc Marion, Derrida says, "as soon as a gift is identified as a gift…then it is canceled as a gift. It is reintroduced into the circle of an exchange and destroyed as a gift."[33] Derrida continues to assert that he wants to extricate the gift from the circle of economy and push it to its absolute impossibility. For purposes of clarification, Derrida is not arguing that there is no gift, although he does want to stress that it lacks presence and cannot be intuitively identified as such.

In order to think the gift one must not think of it in relation to giving, the circulation of an economy, or exchange. Derrida wants to think that aspect of the gift that is strange or foreign to an economy. The gift is only possible at a paradoxical moment when time is torn apart because the present is related to temporal synthesis, which makes it impossible to think the present moment of the gift.[34] In an essay that discusses the philosophy of Emmanuel Levinas in his book *Psyché: Inventions de l'autre*, Derrida imagines a time prior to the gift, a time before the attempt to give prior to desire, before obligation, prior to contract, and before gratitude.[35]

Derrida develops further the theme of the impossibility of the gift by isolating three elements of the gift: donor (intention to give), gift (giving of something), and donee (someone other than donor). By assuming that these elements are essential to the notion of the gift, a person demonstrates a precomprehension of the nature of a gift. The three conditions of the gift—donor, gift, and donee—simultaneously designate the conditions for the impossibility of the gift. In other words, Derrida uses the very conditions or elements of the gift against it in order to show its impossibility. These three conditions produce the "annulment, the annihilation, the destruction of the gift."[36] The reciprocity of the gift, its return or exchange, annuls the gift. Derrida is attempting to think the nature of the gift devoid of reciprocity, return, exchange, or debt. For the gift to be truly what it is there must be absolutely no returning of a gift and the donor must not expect any restitution. Derrida pushes this line of thinking to its limits by emphasizing that simply recognizing or identifying something as a gift is sufficient to annul it. If we push the gift to its limits, Derrida argues that it will not appear as a gift to either the donor or donee.

For a gift to be itself, it must not even give itself to someone's field of perception. If it does not appear, the gift cannot be grasped as a gift. Therefore, it is best if the donor and donee forget it in a radical sense that includes the total loss of memory or consciousness of it.[37] Derrida is suggesting an absolute form of forgetting that makes the gift itself a condition of forgetting: "Forgetting and gift would therefore be each in the condition of the other."[38] Derrida thinks that the gift accords with the experience of the trace in the sense of a cinder.[39] From Derrida's perspective, traditional views of the gift represent a transcendental illusion. Thus we need to rethink the gift and its impossibility in order to push philosophy to its limits.

Rather than the traditional transcendental illusion of the Western philosophical understanding of the gift, Derrida wants to be able to see the event of the gift, which is described as irruptive, unmotivated, and disinterested. Derrida argues further that "this word *Ereignis*, which commonly signifies event, signals toward a thinking of appropriation or of de-propriation that cannot be unrelated to that of the gift."[40] This event of the gift, which only adheres to principles of disorder and is thus devoid of rules or concepts, is prior to any relationship to a single subject or to more than one subject. This implies that the event (*ereignis*), a heterogeneous aspect of the gift, is prior to any relationship of donor and donee that taints the gift of its purity. Within the flux of time, the moment of giving and receiving are two events that cannot exist simultaneously in time because they are separated in its flow. Derrida also uses the term *khora* (an event) to refer to a place of the nongift that makes the gift possible. The khora, a possibility of taking place, is a spacing, a place of nondesire, a point that does not give anything away.[41] If we look for the gift, we are seeking the impossible, which is a form of madness: "To desire, to desire to think the impossible, to desire to give the impossible—this is obviously madness."[42] Derrida connects this madness to the previously discussed practice of forgetting and does not intend to suggest that madness, a double ligature of reason and unreason, is a negative experience.

According to Derrida, Mauss does not concern himself enough with the incompatibility of the gift and its exchange, whereas Derrida wants to problematize and interrogate their connection in order to call attention to their difference. Agreeing in principle with Bataille's emphasis on the excessive nature of the gift, Derrida argues that "the problem of the gift has to do with its nature that is excessive in advance, a priori exaggerated."[43] Any gift that is moderate or ordered is not strictly speaking a gift. In his work *Glas*, Derrida equates exchange playfully to castration, the basic principle of exchange: "It castrates, equalizes or lops off [*lague*] the pleroma; it tends to maintain two forces, two erections, two pressures at the same height."[44] As the principle of exchange, castration is the difference, which is within the gift itself. For Derrida, the gift and exchange represent a gift and countergift, a kind of giving-taking.

It is this difference that Mauss neglects in his theory, according to Derrida: "The difference between a gift and every other operation of pure and simple exchange is that the gift gives time."[45] The gift not only gives time, but it also demands and takes time. Derrida wants to concentrate on and think about the thing, the gift itself, in time. If one mistakenly reduces the gift to an exchange as in the theory of Claude Lévi-Strauss, one terminates the very possibility of the gift. Derrida seeks a thinking that can think about and do the act of giving in an excessive sense, to give beyond the proper norm, to give excessively. In fact, it is only the excessive gift, a giving without calculation and measure, that is truly speaking a pure gift, which is one without borders.

The excessive aspect of the gift can also be witnessed in the relationship between the other, the gift, and violence. By accepting a gift, the other is caught in a trap because the exposed donee places him- or herself at the mercy of the donor. This point is exemplified by Derrida's characterization of the gift as an annulus, which suggests a ring, collar, necklace, or the chain of the gift.[46] The irreducible violence of the gift is a manifestation of its excessive nature and its very condition. Within the process of circulation, the violence of the gift represents its impurity.[47]

The excessiveness of the gift and its place within the context of time suggest its apocalypse. By moving toward its end, the gift reveals that "the truth of the gift unveils only the non-truth of its end, the end of the gift. Times are (no longer) near, there is time no more."[48] Therefore, it is time that destroys the gift, and it is time that operates as the deconstructive agent.

If the gift moves inexorably toward its apocalypse, its beginning, which is prior to any exchange, represents a holocaust (a term that Derrida substitutes for Hegel's *Opfer* or sacrifice). In contrast to Hegel's sacrificial holocaust that manifests the presence of the otherness of the holocaust, Derrida's use of the term *holocaust* is nonpresent, totally other, and beyond the borders of ontology, leaving only the traces of ashes. For Derrida, both the gift and holocaust share the "not" in common. Therefore, the pure gift is the holocaust, a gift that burns or annuls itself before it even exchanges anything.[49] The gift is pure in the sense that it is without exchange or expectation of return.

The Gift within the Time of Hinduism

What does Bataille's and Derrida's notion of the gift share with a traditional cultural view of the gift? This type of question can be answered by examining an actual religious tradition in which the gift plays a central role. It is also possible to test the theories about the gift in Bataille and Derrida by comparing them to a particular cultural tradition. Thus it is useful to consider the forms of the gift in Indian culture, where it plays a significant role and provides insights into the behavior and values of that culture.

The Hindu religious tradition makes a distinction between a gift called *daksiṇā*, an exchange for ritual services rendered by Brahmin priests, and another type of gift termed the *dan*, a giving vital to village life because the donor gets rid of danger (*sankat*), various kinds of afflictions (*kast*), and evil or sin (*pap*). Although there are some features that overlap, these two kinds of gifts are conceptually different. Without going into great depth, I examine the notion of daksiṇā before examining the significance of dan.

With respect to dakṣiṇā, I focus on the scholarly work of P. V. Kane and Jan Gonda besides considering some relevant primary source materials, and examine the more recent work of Gloria Raheja and Jonathan P. Parry on the notion of dan.

The early Hindu tradition emphatically emphasizes the importance of giving and the necessity of being generous. According to the ancient Rig Veda (RV), the Vedic god Indra embodies the spirit of giving and serves as a paradigm of the generous ruler. Indra is called the giver (RV 1.54.8), and he is the divine force that gives impetus to liberality (RV 5.30.7). The Vedic poets express a dual expectation of Indra: he is expected to be generous by virtue of his position as king of the Vedic pantheon (RV 3.14.6), and he is expected to punish those who are excessively parsimonious (RV 1.176.4). An earthly king is expected to emulate the heavenly king or Indra to the extent that the generosity of both must overflow in a visible manner. There are also Vedic hymns or stanzas (e.g., 5.27.4, 5.33.9, 8.5.37, 8.19.36) praising patrons of the arts who give to poets that Louis Renou and Jean Filliozat refer to as "captationes benevolentiae."[50] Gonda does not think that Renou and Filliozat do justice to the Vedic poets because their supposition appears to be that "liberality was a natural and inalienable quality of their patrons, that these people could not but be conceived as generous because they were wealthy and it behooves the rich to distribute their possessions to others."[51]

The merit of the gift itself is tied to the mental attitude of the giver, the manner in which the gift is acquired, the worthiness of the giver and recipient, and the humble way in which they are given to another.[52] According to the Manusmṛti (4.186), even if all these criteria are met, the gift embodies a danger to the recipient because he or she could become attached to the habit of receiving gifts because there is a danger of losing one's spirituality. The giving of dakṣiṇā is not merely for religious services performed, but also establishes beneficial partnerships (RV 8.79.5; 10.151.2). The giving presupposes that gifts are offered within the context of auspicious times and places. In his study of the topic, Gonda demonstrates the close connection between dakṣiṇā and śraddhā (faith) that manifests a mutual trust between the god and his devotees.[53]

Gonda conceptualizes an identity between the giver and the gift, citing a passage from the epic Mahābhārata (13.76.13) where the donor talks of giving oneself. Gonda thinks that giving involves placing "oneself in relation to and then … participat[ing] in a second person by means of an object, which however is not actually an object, but a part of one's own self."[54] In order to support his position, Gonda refers to Gerardus van der Leeuw, the Dutch phenomenologist of religion, who supports his own position by referring to Mauss. Bataille and Derrida reject this kind of monistic identity between the giver and the gift.

The French postmodernists would also object to Gonda's argument that the reciprocity between the giving and receiving parties is equivalent to a circular process of mutual giving and receiving that not only maintains the world but is also something on which the continuance of life depends.[55] Moreover, they would be critical of Kane's assertion that "a gift once completed by acceptance is irrevocable."[56] Kane wants to emphasize that once a gift is accepted this is equivalent to ownership of it. And this acceptance can be mental, verbal, or physical.[57] From the perspective of Bataille and Derrida, Kane misses the heterological element within the gift itself. This is not entirely true of J. C. Heesterman, who perceives a risk in giving because the priest must accept the evil and impurity (*pāpman*) associated with the performance of death rites and acceptance of the patron's death impurity, or pollution.[58] There is a conspicuous absence of obligation on the part of the priest to return the gift. Kane and Gonda also appear to miss the sacrificial feature of the gift that is textually supported by the *Manusmṛti* (1.86) for a degenerate age and the work of Madeleine Biardeau and Charles Malamoud on ancient Indian sacrifice.[59]

From the perspective of Bataille and Derrida, Kane and Gonda carry on the legacy of Mauss by essentially agreeing with him that groups participate in exchanges and not merely individuals, those who exchange are moral, and the gift contains something of the spiritual essence of the donor, which prompts the recipient to return the gift and establishes an enduring bond between persons. Kane and Gonda also agree with Mauss that a gift commands a gift in return that flows from the giver to the recipient and back again from the receiver to the donor. Moreover, the gift possesses a powerful binding force that unites two parties.

Kane and Gonda do not appear to find anything excessive about the gift during the Vedic period that would confirm the position of Bataille. This is not true of Romila Thapar, who appears to support in part Bataille's theory of the gift by stressing the element of the potlatch in Vedic sacrifice. Thapar does not think that the reciprocity between the major castes of givers is balanced because the Kshatriya caste assumed the greatest burden of giving, whereas the Brahmin caste played the role mostly of recipients. Thapar thinks that the use of wealth tended to transform the sacrifice into a kind of potlatch.[60] Thapar and Bataille agree that the potlatch is a series of countergifts that creates a debt encountered in a subsequent ritual context that tends to maximize the compulsion of giving in ever greater amounts.

In a similar spirit and in reaction to the theory of Mauss, Heesterman argues that ancient Vedic priests deconstructed sacrifice, a multifunctional, pivotal, broken world that hovers dangerously on the brink of collapse, and renders problematic any gift theory of sacrifice because such a theory does not function within a context of a ritual killing followed by a communal meal. Heesterman finds the three major elements of the sacrifice—killing, destruction, and feast—paradoxical because the killing of the sacrificial victim and gift to the gods are necessarily destroyed by fire, a distinctive feature that separates the sacrifice from the gift.[61] Within this context, Heesterman perceives a secret connected to the burned oblation and destruction, which possesses nothing in common with a gift or offering of food to the gods, but rather represents an original absence of gift and "abandonment in self-abnegation" by the sacrificer.[62] From a different perspective, Derrida grasps the insights of Heesterman as evidence of the sacrifice sacrificing itself because the sacrifice is inherently a supplement of itself.[63]

In comparison to Kane and Gonda, Heesterman is more sensitive to the heterogeneous nature of sacrifice and gift because he sees an inner tension in sacrifice, which embodies on the surface order but internally threatens catastrophic disorder. The gift of food is not a harmless exchange because the sacrificer makes a gift of his dead self to his guests and gets rid of his burden of death, a scenario that indicates a tension in the exchange that is an antithetical and potentially agonistic mode of acceptance. Whereas Kane and Gonda have a tendency to see harmony and stability in the gift, Heesterman views it as characterized by tension, instability, and conflict due to the onus of death, although the elements of contest and conflict are mitigated by the countervailing features of alliance between host and guest.[64] Embodied within the notion of gift for Heesterman is its inherent deconstructive feature, a potential to replace the sacrifice itself within an alternating context of conflict and alliance.

As noted previously, the other major type of gift is called dan in Hindu cultures, which embodies more of an obligation to accept than any right to claim a gift. In her study of the Hindi-speaking region of northern India in the village of Pahansu, Raheja emphasizes the importance of auspiciousness (śubh) and inauspiciousness (naśubh), which both vary with the context, with relation to dan. Assuming that conditions are proper and participants are appropriate, the donor possesses an opportunity to transfer inauspiciousness to the donee and create the advent of auspiciousness. From the viewpoint of the Brahmins, there is a poison in the gift because it embodies the sin and evil of the donor.[65] Jonathan Parry criticizes Raheja's position because his own fieldwork in Banaras indicates to him that the poison in the dan is not inauspiciousness as Raheja asserts, but it is rather sin and pollution that form a seamless source of misfortune.[66]

Parry discusses the gift given to a priest by pilgrims for rendering funeral services for the deceased in the city of Banaras. According to Parry, it is important for a pilgrim to be a unilateral giver and not to accept any gifts from another person. In fact, the best form of a gift is secret and without a recipient. A good example of a secret kind of gift is money that is surreptitiously thrown into the Ganges River.[67] Parry also indicates the contradictions and problems associated with giving. If a gift is, for instance, to be given only to a priest of unimpeachable moral character, the giver cannot know for certain if the recipient possesses such character. The recipient also functions as a retainer for the sins and moral filth of the donors, which places a tremendous burden on the priest.[68] Moreover, these priests of death are not worthy vessels for the acceptance of gifts, which taints the quality of all gifts.[69] And if the Brahmin priest attempts to approximate the lifestyle of a world renouncer, the priest's acceptance of gifts compromises by definition the ideal of an ascetic because the priest loses any semblance of ascetic autonomy by immersion into the material and social world of exchange of gifts. In contrast to Raheja's claim that the dan is not a hierarchical representation. Parry finds evidence for a preeminently hierarchical conceptualization of dan within the context of the gift exchanges associated with death in the city of Banaras.[70] Parry and Raheja do agree, however, that there is a poison in the gift within the respective social contexts that they studied.

With respect to the work of Parry, Derrida helps us to see that the phenomenon of the gift can be another way to help us apprehend death. Derrida suggests that death is essential to the process of exchange because "it is only on the basis of death, and in its name, that giving and taking become possible."[71] If the gift itself for Derrida is inaccessible, unpresentable, secret, and not present, it is death that cannot be removed from the donor or recipient, and it is something that cannot be given or received by another. Death is a feature of life that one can only take upon oneself for Derrida, whereas Parry wants to insist that the priest accept the burden from the pilgrim by accepting the latter's gift. From Derrida's perspective,

Parry does not account for the element of time, a feature also neglected by Raheja in her study. This is exactly the element that Pierre Bourdieu calls scholars to recognize in his work: "To restore to practice its practical truth, we must therefore reintroduce time into the theoretical representation of a practice which, being temporally structured is intrinsically defined by its tempo."[72] The countergift, for instance, must be deferred and different in order to avoid any resemblance to swapping or lending. The time element—the interval—in the exchange of gift and countergift is ultimately exposed by misrecognition (*méconnaisance*) of the limits and constraints of the practice of exchange.[73] Following the suggestion of Bourdieu, Catherine Bell also warns us that by abstracting the act of giving from its temporal situation and reducing its convoluted strategies to a set of reversible structures, one's theoretical analysis will misconstrue the real dynamics of the practice.[74]

The Possibility of a Pure Gift

From the perspective of Bataille, Kane and especially Gonda are captive to the theory of Mauss, although they are able to witness that giving represents the acquisition of power as stressed by Bataille. Raheja and Parry are at least able to perceive a poison in the gift. At times, there are hints that Raheja and Parry can also see the irrational and excessive aspects of the gift. There are suggestions that the scholars of the Indian notion of gift recognize, along with Bataille, the role of power in the practice of giving, the giver surpassing him- or herself in the act of giving and establishing a relationship between giving and renunciation. Kane and Gonda do not, however, stress or appear to recognize the absurdity of gifts that Bataille emphasizes in his work, although Heesterman is aware of the gift's paradoxical nature. None of the scholars of Indian culture seems to recognize the potential erotic nature of the gift, which for Bataille is indicative of its heterological nature.

From Derrida's perspective, Gonda, Parry, and Raheja do not really think the gift because they do not think that aspect of it that is strange. The Indian theorists try to think the gift in the present moment, which Derrida thinks is impossible. Derrida is also the only one who attempts to imagine a time prior to the gift. The four examiners of the Hindu notion of gift manifest their precomprehension of the nature of a gift by isolating the three elements of a gift (e.g., donor, donee, and the gift itself). What appear to the four theorists to be the bases of the possibility for a gift are indicative of its impossibility for Derrida because of the destructive nature of these elements, which Derrida identifies with its reciprocity, an invitation to give. The genuine or pure gift is devoid of the notion of reciprocity or expectation of restitution. If one pushes the gift to its limit and looks for its nonpresence, it will not appear as a gift to either a donor or recipient. From Derrida's perspective, Kane and Gonda represent traditional views of the nature of a gift. And even though Parry and Raheja perceive a poison in the gift in their respectively different ways, they are not prepared to totally rethink the heterological nature of the gift. Parry and Raheja are also not ready to rethink the gift prior to its relationship of donor and recipient that steals it of its purity. The scholars mentioned cannot imagine the gift within the flux of time and the impossibility of two events—giving and receiving—existing simultaneously in time that suggests the giving and taking of time by the gift.

With respect to rethinking the gift within time, Derrida wants one to risk madness when attempting to think the impossible. Derrida wants us to look at and consider the difference within the gift itself, which he identifies with castration, whereas Bataille perceives something erotic in the exchange of gift and countergift. The emphasis on the excessive nature of the gift by Bataille and Derrida manifests its violent nature, which for Derrida represents its impurity. This indicates that Derrida connects the excessiveness of the gift with its apocalypse and subsequent holocaust, a pure gift. But this pure gift is an impossibility because it is annulled before it is ever exchanged. To be devoid of exchange or expectation of return reflects the paradoxical characteristics of the pure gift. Derrida seems to ironically suggest that a pure gift is an impossible possibility.

This is evident, for instance, in Derrida's reading of the story of Abraham from the Hebrew Bible, which represents a secret between a man of ardent faith and his God. All communication between the two unequal parties must be suspended to enable the sacrifice to become a pure gift. Derrida elaborates Abraham's position: "Abraham is in a position of nonexchange with respect to God, he is in secret since he doesn't speak to God and expects neither response nor reward from him."[75] The exchange of gift and countergift are put at risk in the sense that Abraham expects nothing in return. And yet he is aware that God offers recompense at the exact moment of renunciation. Abraham's son is given back to him because "he renounced calculation."[76] The situation of Abraham indicates the "not" of the gift—its "aneconomy," in Derrida's term—which represents in the story a gift of life or, from another perspective, a gift of death.

The four scholars of Indian culture that I have considered in this chapter are not necessarily wrong about what they write concerning the gift in Indian culture. But from the perspective of Bataille and Derrida, they fail to see the heterological aspect of the gift. Derrida would go even further by stressing that they fail to push the notion of the gift to its limits. If the four scholars did push the notion of the gift to its limits, they would have discovered that the context of gift giving is indeterminate and full of ambiguities. Not only do the positions of the postmodernists give us something to think about when reconsidering the notion of gift, they help us to grasp the more radical implications of the gift and enable us to see that the notion of gift is not simply about exchange, obligation, and receiving. Bataille and Derrida make the excessive and irrational potential of a gift more lucid in contrast to the theory of Mauss and those he influenced. By examining the notion of gift within the context of time, we are more likely to grasp its powerful, paradoxical, ambiguous, contradictory, absurd, and erotic aspects.

Concluding Remarks

From the postmodern perspectives of Bataille and Derrida, the Maussian theory of gift giving is static, even though the theory is developed within the context of the perspective of evolution. Mauss's approach to his subject seems to imply that it is possible to view the practice of gift giving as an unconditioned observer from a privileged vantage point outside the flux of time. Mauss does not take the process of time very seriously from the perspective of the postmodernists because the explanation of gift giving does not require a sequence, although Mauss does not explicitly deny development and change.[77] Since history is continuous and transitive for Mauss, present time develops out of the past, which implies that the past continues to exist in the present. Because the past shapes and influences the present, there is no discontinuity between these two moments of time, whereas Bataille and Derrida stress the discontinuity of moments of time. From the perspective of the postmodern thinkers, Mauss cannot account for historical disruptions and discontinuity very easily in his theory. With Bataille's embrace of and emphasis on the potlatch, he wants to stress the significance of periodic disruption of the orderly sequence of time. Furthermore, if Mauss had given the process of time more attention in his theory, he would not have assumed the ontological presence of the act. From the postmodern viewpoint, by placing the phenomenon of gift into historical flux, it cannot be made into a universal and timeless category. Moreover, if Mauss had placed his notion of gift giving within the flux of time, his theory would not have also assumed that gift giving is an objective social fact because within the flux of time there are only traces, from the perspective of Derrida, for instance.

Mauss is also interested to show that the worldwide practices of gift giving can be reduced to their elementary forms and that human nature is fundamentally social, whereas Bataille and Derrida tend to stress heterogeneity over homogeneity. Mauss attempts to get at the simplest forms of gift giving in order to discern the unconscious mental teleology of the practice. This is a good example of Mauss's attempt to uncover unconscious and conscious meanings of gift giving from a cross-cultural perspective that would shed light on common features, a procedure that is consistent with his attempt to correct a shortcoming of Durkheim's theory by bringing into closer proximity the disciplines of sociology and psychology.[78] Nonetheless, this procedure assumes that the best way to approach the study of gift giving is by finding the simplest and earliest examples of society that one can.[79] This is not, however, the best way to proceed because there is no reason to accept the evolutionary viewpoint that assumes that religions develop from simple to more complex forms.

Mauss's theory of gift giving is an example of a twentieth-century form of rationalism, which borrows elements from empiricism and Kantian a priori thinking. But this is a rationalism that is socially grounded, a product of social groups. Within the Kantian scheme of thinking and by each step of analysis, unity is always presupposed by the philosopher, which Kant calls the synthetic unity of apperception. Thus, Kant argues that it is thinking that unifies, forming a unity of a particular kind. According to Derrida, the principle of reason is not simply reason. Derrida wants to heed Heidegger's call in *Der Satz vom Grund* to respond to the call of the principle of reason. When we obey the call of the principle of reason we ask about its grounding principle. By following this track of thinking, we find ourselves in a circle because we are trying to account for reason by means of reason. Another possibility is to encounter an abyss, which is defined as "the impossibility for a principle of grounding to ground itself."[80] Derrida calls into question whether or not it is permissible to account for the principle of reason by using reason itself. Accompanying the modern dominance of the principle of reason for Derrida, there is also an interpretation of the essence of beings as objects, a representation that is encountered by a subject. Although the principle of reason is dominant in Western philosophy and its corollary representational thinking assures the subject doing the thinking of its own presence, Derrida asserts that we never encounter, scrutinize, or interrogate the origin of the principle of reason itself. Derrida concludes by arguing that reason is a single species of thought, which does not mean that we can conclude that thought is irrational.[81] In contrast to the rationality that grounds the work of Mauss, the postmodern modes of thinking of Derrida and Bataille are antifoundationalists, radically skeptical of any theory, and distrustful of any possible universal claims of reason. Although it is not necessary to accept any transcendental claims for reason, there is a real danger of disparaging reason in this way or embracing the irrational as Bataille tends to do in his writings.

Calvin Schrag points, for instance, to the purposelessness of the postmodern mode of thinking: "With the subversion of a logos-grounded episteme, all that remains is a succession of *hetero-doxa* in which each prevailing opinion is countered by a new opinion within a conflictual rhapsody of 'rhetorical agonistics' that has neither goal nor purpose."[82] Not only is there a danger of being left with rhetorical opinions that are as relative as other opinions, there is also a danger of undermining the solidity of one's own starting point by questioning the foundations of rational thinking. It is not necessary to assume that thinking is grounded in reason or that the foundation of reason is problematic because it is possible to ground thinking in valuation, an axiological hypothesis, according to Robert Neville, that is part of his call for a reconceiving of the foundations of thinking.[83] Mauss would agree with Neville's argument for the social character of thinking and its demand of responsibility. It is important to be aware that thinking is conditioned by history and the social and cultural milieu in which it finds itself. There is also a danger in Derrida's position of undermining his own claim to truth(s) by deconstructing the rational distinctions between subject and object.

Mauss's work on the gift is an excellent illustration of the importance that he placed on classification in order to enhance human understanding by connecting ideas and unifying knowledge. Mauss views classification as a "first philosophy of nature" that is rooted in social relations which provide the distinctions for such a system.[84] Mauss envisions a social hierarchy along with a logical hierarchy and unity of knowledge. And the resemblances and differences uncovered by a process of classification are due to affection more than intellect "because they affect the sentiments of groups differently."[85] Bataille and Derrida are opposed to hierarchies of all sorts. From Derrida's perspective, Mauss creates a metaphysical and social hierarchy that is a result of representational thinking. Derrida's method of deconstruction does not destroy preexisting structures from the outside, but it rather subverts them from the inside, which is another way of overturning hierarchies and subverting representational thinking.[86]

From the postmodern perspective, Mauss's theory presupposes an ontological presence of people engaged in gift giving over a continuous period of time. No such claim to ontological presence can be asserted by Mauss with absolute certainty from the postmodern perspective, because one cannot make the assumption that what is real is so by virtue of the fact that it is simply present. According to Derrida, the philosophical presuppositions behind Mauss's gift theory are indicative of what the postmodernists call logocentrism, a type of ontotheology characteristic of Western philosophy and its metaphysics of presence. By presupposing this ontological presence, Mauss tends to emphasize anthropomorphism as a primary characteristic of much of the religious context of gift giving, whereas Derrida tends to stress difference and absence in his philosophy in order to demonstrate the bankruptcy of the philosophical tradition of the Enlightenment. By assuming that metaphysics is the basis of Western culture, Derrida's attempt to undermine the metaphysical tradition of Western thought results, nonetheless, in giving metaphysics an exaggerated importance.[87]

An important aspect of Mauss's work is his intention to strip the notion of gift of any irrational elements, whereas Bataille embraces the disorder of the Dionysian aspect of the gift by emphasizing the potlatch. Bataille wants to undermine the harmonious reciprocity that Mauss tends to stress in his work. Rather than the homogeneity that is emphasized by Mauss, the heterological method of Bataille stresses the heterogeneous aspects of knowledge, which are beyond the purview of scientific knowledge because it is only concerned with homogenous elements. If Mauss tends to stress the homogeneous aspect of gift giving, Bataille and his heterological method, which he borrowed from Nietzsche, is strictly opposed to any orderly, homogeneous representation of the practice of gift giving. For Derrida, knowledge is not merely objective, as Mauss suggests in his theory, because that which we know occurs within a historical, relational, and personal context. What we can know is relative, indeterminate, and participatory, which suggests that our knowledge is forever incomplete. Although it is not necessary to embrace the radical skepticism of this particular postmodernist, it does appear wise and prudent to include both the homogeneous and heterogeneous elements of this fascinating practice when rethinking the notion of gift giving.

4

Genealogy, Power, and Discourse

IN HIS WONDERFUL, award-winning novel entitled *Midnight's Children*, Salman Rushdie has his main character, Saleem Sinai, open the narrative by reflecting on the moment of his birth. He tells the reader that he was born in the city of Bombay at midnight on August 15, 1947, at the precise instant of India's independence. Outside the nursing home of his birth, there are large crowds celebrating the momentous moment as fireworks explode in the sky. Saleem humorously confesses:

> Soothsayers had prophesied me, newspapers celebrated my arrival, politicos ratified my authenticity. I was left entirely without a say in the matter. I, Saleem Sinai, later variously called Snotnose, Baldy, Sniffer, Buddha and even Piece-of-the-Moon, had become heavily embroiled in Fate—at the best of times a dangerous sort of involvement. And I couldn't even wipe my own nose at the time.[1]

In a sense Rushdie's character is calling attention to the moment of transition between the colonial period and the postcolonial era in India.

According to some scholars, colonialism was a time of subjugation by Western political powers, whereas postcolonialism is a period during which those formerly subjugated critically respond to their trials. According to Homi K. Bhabha, postcolonial criticism emerges from the former colonial context and testimony of Third World countries. They interrupt and interact with modern ideological discourses that attempt to make hegemonic interrelations the norm. Moreover, postcolonialists "formulate their critical revisions around issues of cultural difference, social authority, and political discrimination in order to reveal the antagonistic and ambivalent moments within the 'rationalization' of modernity."[2] In addition, postcolonialists examine issues like loss of meaning, hopelessness, and other kinds of social pathology. Finally, postcolonial theory reminds us of the persistent neocolonial relations with the present.[3]

Adding to points made by Bhabha, Gayatri Chakravarty Spivak draws a useful distinction between internal and external colonization. If the latter represents the colonization of other space, internal colonization refers to patterns of exploitation and domination of disenfranchised groups within a country like the United States or Britain. Spivak draws another distinction between colonialism and neocolonialism. The former is a European creation stretching from the mid-eighteenth century to the mid-twentieth, whereas neocolonialism represents a dominant economic, political, and cultural development in the twentieth century in the aftermath of the disparate dissolution of the territorial empires. Finally, postcolonialism describes the present global condition.[4]

If economic interests motivate colonialism, postcolonialism is a result of reaction to and resistance to colonialism and imperialism, which is a deliberate, state-sponsored policy. By intermingling the past (colonialism) and the present (imperialism), postcolonial theory focuses on the active transformation of the present from the domination of the past.[5] Besides engaging in acts of historical retrieval, postcolonial theory also attempts to dislocate, undermine, and displace Western knowledge about the Oriental other. According to Robert Young, the basic presupposition about the operation of postcolonial theory is that "intellectual and cultural traditions developed outside the West constitute a body of knowledge that can be deployed to great effect against the political and cultural hegemony of the West."[6] In addition to replacing the heritage of colonialism, postcolonial theorists want to also decolonize the West.

In this chapter I adopt a critical attitude toward the notion of Orientalism as defined by Edward W. Said and two writers of postcolonialism he inspired. In the first instance, I briefly review the contribution of Said. With regard to postcolonialism, I will review the contributions of Bhabha and Spivak. In addition to considering the political nature of their work, this chapter focuses on problems associated with their methods and especially the issue of representational thinking. Lurking behind the work of Said, there is the influential, theoretical shadow of Michel Foucault and his radical agenda shaped by the philosophy of Nietzsche that also needs to be critically addressed.

This type of critical analysis is necessary for a book on religious studies because many scholars in the discipline do their research within the context of Eastern religions, and those scholars have become part of the heritage surrounding the negative aspects of Orientalism that casts suspicion on their scholarship about indigenous peoples of the East and also on their academic leaders. The critical, negative, threatening aspersions cast on the scholarly work of Western academics such as Jeff Kripal, Paul Courtright, Wendy Doniger, and James Laine are part of what Eastern critics see as the continuing Orientalism practiced in the West.

Said and Orientalism

As part of his method, Said empties the term *Orientalism* of its previous content and revises it to suggest scholarly work that is unsympathetic and hostile toward Oriental people. If we examine the historical meaning of the term, we find that it represented a school of painting mostly in western Europe, and was later a branch of scholarship composed mostly of philologists focusing on the recovery, examination, interpretation, and publication of original texts. During the summer of 1973, the term was discarded at the Twenty-ninth International Congress of Orientalists in Paris. The term was, however, retrieved from the garbage heap of history by Said to be used for polemical abuse and the demonization of Western scholars.[7]

According to Said, the intellectual creation of the so-called Hindu or Muslim is a social and mental construct of Western scholars that can be called Orientalism. By this, he means that Orientalism is a created body of theory and practice that represents a style of Western scholarship that has been used by it practitioners as a tool to dominate, restructure, particularize, and divide Oriental things into components that can be more easily managed and manipulated. This is done with the intention of exerting hegemony based on the assumed superiority of European ideas over the backward ideas and practices of the orient. This style of scholarship is directly connected to a long history of Western domination and exploitation of Oriental cultures. From the perspective of the present moment, this helps to explain the current plight of these denigrated cultures. Said expresses it this way: "The relationship between Occident and Orient is a relationship of power, of domination, of varying degrees of a complex hegemony."[8] This kind of scholarship embodied within itself racism, ethnocentrism, imperialism, and convictions about /Western superiority. The guilty Western scholars did not objectively describe what they witnessed in the Orient, but rather recreated the Orient, which assumed the guise of an unchanging entity.

His basic criticism is that this creation is a representation that does not accurately reflect the reality in cities, towns, and villages throughout the

Orient of real people. The representation of people living in the Orient is a product of a representational mode of thinking that is fundamentally flawed, derogatory, and illusory. Moreover, the caricature of the Oriental person is designed to socially and political control such a person. Said correctly calls attention to a past tradition of racism, ethnocentrism, and imperialism of Western scholars. Thus, we are in his debt for correcting deficiencies within Western scholarship.

Unfortunately, Said is guilty of the same crime by creating a false caricature of Western scholarship by means of his own representations that he calls Orientalism. Why would he fall prey to the transgressions of some Westerners and create a false representation of the work of all Western scholars working on Eastern cultures? The answer to this question can only be discerned by looking at his adoption of the post-structural methodological approach of Foucualt and the French scholar's political agenda. Viewing Foucault from a historical perspective, it is possible to affirm that just as Foucault's work is a reenacting of Nietzsche's methods, Said's notion of Orientalism is a reenacting of Foucault.

Texts, Power, and Discourse

Said's understanding of the nature of texts and power has been shaped by his reading of Michel Foucault's work. From the perspective of Said, it is significant that Western scholars have described the Orient in books. According to Said's understanding of Foucault's notion of a text, a book assumes over time a greater authority and utility than the actual phenomena that it allegedly describes.[9] This scenario creates a crisis for those being described because the readers are shaped by what they have read, forming a reinforcement and determination of a reader's experience. Not only does the reader become what he or she reads, the books themselves create the knowledge and reality that they allegedly describe. This produces a tradition or way of looking at foreign cultures that establishes a set of constraints on thought, and sets limitations on what thought can be examined in an unprejudiced way. According to Said, Orientalism is a political vision of reality that promotes difference between the common and the foreign that degenerates into an antihuman attitude on the part of its practitioners.

Once the vision of Orientalism is accepted and embodied within a text, it is extremely difficult to change the picture of the East created by Westerners because the vision contained within the text constrains any subsequent interpretation. Said asserts, "This means that a text has a specific situation, placing restraints upon the interpreter and his interpretation not because the situation is hidden within the text as a mystery, but rather because the situation exists at the same level of surface particularity as the textual object itself."[10] Joining what he considers the perspicacity of Nietzsche on this subject, Said concludes that texts are basically instruments of power that represent a process made by an author, critic, and reader.[11] Within the context in which the phenomenon of Orientalism developed, texts served the hegemonic interests of Western political powers that further promoted an unequal relation between them as the colonizers and oppressors and the unfortunate colonized and oppressed Orient. The lives of texts, for Said, are not in any sense real, but are rather matters of force and conflict: "Texts incorporate discourse, sometimes violently."[12] Implied in the argument of Said is the point that a text, although it is an instrument of power and can keep one in bondage, can also be used as a power to free the oppressed. And this assumes, of course, that the texts have readers, a point that Said does not mention.

Intertwined with Foucault's notion of text is his understanding of discourse, which Said also borrowed. Theory of discourse does not concentrate specifically on language because it is more concerned with a discursive type of knowledge. This means that discourse is concerned, for instance, with social subjects and consciousness created by ideologies, which are grounded in economic or class relations. This process occurs by means of a circulating power that shapes the social subjects by means such as regulation, construction, and exclusion. These forms of knowledge render possible what can be said and what cannot be said.[13] Even though Foucault's notion of discourse undermines the Marxist's notion of ideology, it is inseparable from the formation of a discipline and the shaping of the object studied by a particular discipline.

Said also adopts Foucault's assertion that discourse always involves some kind of violence. What this means is that discourse imposes its linguistic order on the world, functioning as an instrument of power. Because Foucualt's notion of discourse is concerned with social subjects and types of consciousness shaped by ideologies that are based on socioeconomic differences, discourse always involves violence and a circulating power that shapes people. Just as Foucault's work seeks to overcome common binary oppositions with a structuralist's modes of thinking, the distinction between East and West forms the political context for Said's theory to prove his basic presupposition: there has never been any neutral, unbiased, objective scholarship on the Orient. By operating with Foucault's grasp of the relationship between culture and power, Said is unable to acknowledge the power possessed by the subjugated because he insists on their being victims without agency, although Foucualt would disagree with him because of his understanding of agency as a form of resistance by an oppressed person or group against cultural forces.[14]

For Said, Orientalism is a violent form of discourse that represents a kind of Western projection onto the Orient in an attempt to govern it.[15] In short, discourse is a form of knowledge utilized to control the other by creating representations of the Orient that depend on Western institutions, traditions, social conventions, and accepted modes of understanding to be effective. Said understands the creation of Orientalism as a repetitive process of representations that take their reality from the authority embodied within textual repetition. Thus Said cannot and does not want to claim that there is a real or true Orient because it is a construction by the Orientalist that stands for an ideological representation without genuine reality.[16] Nonetheless, representations are connected to violence against what is represented, "as well as a contrast between the violence of the act of representing something and the calm exterior of the representation itself, the image—verbal, visual, or otherwise—of the subject."[17]

Said and His Critics

Said is convinced that culture is a repressive means to power, a position he shares with Foucault.[18] It is certainly true that a particular culture can become oppressive and even tyrannical. Said's view is, however, too one dimensional because he neglects the way in which a culture can act as a bearer of symbols, values, customs, institutions, and meanings for its adherents. Since there is an inevitable tyranny built into the fabric of any culture for Said, it is impossible for any group to legitimize its cultural identity. John McGowan indicates the advantage of taking such a stance because it "has the advantage of undermining (delegitimating) all existent social forms but points only to an anarchic 'politics of difference' as an alternative."[19] Nonetheless, Lisa Lowe questions Said's assumption that Orientalism monolithically constructs the Orient as the other of the Occident.[20] Along similar lines of criticism, David Smith argues that there is no evidence that Orientalists doing linguistic and textual study served colonial purposes, since the conquerors and exploiters did not have any interest in or sympathy for such scholarly work.[21] Moreover,

Rosane Rocher criticizes Said for creating a single discourse that is undifferentiated within time and space, and social and intellectual identities.[22] The postcolonial scholar Homi K. Bhabha shares Rocher's concern with the totalizing aspect of Said's argument and his assumption about an unequivocal intention by the West realized through its discursive representations.[23] According to Robert Young, the totalizing effect of Said's Orientalism keeps him from offering an alternative to the phenomenon that he criticizes, or solving the problem about how he can separate himself from the coercive structures of knowledge. The result is that Said repeats the structures that he censures, and he does not offer any alternative forms of knowledge, which is a reflection of his inability to rigorously tackle the problem of method.[24]

Bernard Lewis, who shows that Said gives his reader a restricted version of the Orient, undermines the impression that Said gives of presenting a totalistic picture. According to Lewis, Said reduces Orientalism to the Arabic Middle East. Furthermore, Said neglects to include the Germans among the practitioners of the discipline, and his work reveals a "lack of knowledge of what scholars do and what scholarship is about."[25] Besides demonstrating contempt for modern Arab scholarship, Said is accused by Lewis of composing science fiction history and lexical Humpty-Dumptyism (i.e., it means what I say it does). Said is also charged with incompetence with respect to his treatment of Islam that manifests an ignorance of its history and spirituality.[26]

In addition to these types of criticism, others criticize Said's notion of discourse. Bhabha, for instance, finds his notion of discourse too determining, univocal, and uniform because it undermines the complexity of the writers he covers.[27] Young does not like the way that Said examines a restricted number of mostly literary texts and then makes broad historical generalizations based on this limited number of texts. Young also thinks that Said's approach creates a problem for historicity because it dehistoricizes texts and treats them synchronically and ahistorically, which undermines history as a field of objective research. This scenario suggests all knowledge is relative, a result of relying on the theoretical work of Foucault. Said also contradicts himself with his notion of discourse when he claims that the Orient is a misrepresentation of the real but also acknowledges that it is impossible for anyone to accurately depict other cultures in any case.[28]

There are other scholars who have criticized Said on more epistemological grounds. Wilhelm Halbfass cannot understand how it would be

possible for a Westerner to study another culture without certain precon-
ceptions, and to eliminate all nonindigenous categories of understanding
another culture.[29] And if an Oriental culture were freed of Eurocentric
presuppositions and constructs, would it have an identity free from all
constructs? Halbfass does not think that an Oriental culture could be freed
of all constructs, because of the internal superimpositions that tend to
derive from different forces, within any culture.[30] From a different perspective, Catherine Gallagher describes succinctly the epistemological
impasse Said encounters: "He writes of distortions of reality while denying
the existence of a reality beneath the distortions. He notes that knowledge
is always bounded by place but insists that there is an epistemological
locus of displacement called exile."[31]

In sharp contrast to Said, J. J. Clarke finds a wide range of attitudes
embodied within Orientalism that are often affirmative and demonstrate
an attempt by the West to integrate eastern thought into its intellectual
concerns. Unlike what Said might claim, Clarke thinks that these more
affirmative attitudes toward the Orient cannot be explained as matters of
"power" and "domination." If one views Orientalism as simply a ruling
imperialist ideology, this means to miss its role in the Western context as
"a counter-movement," a subversive entelechy, albeit not a unified or consciously organized one, which in various ways has often tended to subvert
rather than to confirm the discursive structures of imperial power.[32] Clarke
acknowledges that the reaction of Westerners to the East was patronizing,
chauvinistic, and racist. And yet Westerners also exhibited a fascination
with the East that manifested itself in a tendency to romanticize the East,
and contributed to a systematic misrepresentation and oversimplification
of it. Clarke criticizes Said for the narrowness of his explanation, for a tendency to reductionism, and for ignoring the complexity of the motivations
for Orientalism. What Said fails to acknowledge is that "Eastern ideas
have been used in the West as an agency for self-criticism and self-renewal,
whether in the political, moral, or religious spheres."[33] Clarke goes on to
argue that Orientalism has served as a corrective mirror in the West that
"provides a conceptual framework that allows much fertile cross-referenc-
ing, the discovery of similarities, analogies, and models; in other words,
the underpinning of a productive hermeneutical relationship."[34]

Clarke goes astray, however, when he agrees with Said that all human
knowledge is political. This is a universal type of assertion that is not supported by common sense and ordinary experience. It is only necessary to
call attention to the apolitical nature of mathematics and scientific discov-

eries in DNA research, for instance, to refute such an argument. Of course, mathematical and scientific knowledge can be used for political purposes. But this is another issue. If Said is quite rightly opposed to broad generalizations about the Orient, it is inconsistent of him and Clarke to claim that all human knowledge is political.

Without mentioning him specifically, Hugh Urban points to a deficiency in the work of Said, who depicts those who are colonized as passive, unreflective, and submissive subjects. Referring to the Indian colonial context, Urban argues that Indians did not simply accept the imaginary representations projected on them. Indians could appropriate and subvert representations and transform them into anticolonial uses. Citing the mimetic use of the image of the goddess Kālī, Urban observes:

> Within the colonial imagination, the native is often represented as the negative antitype of the colonizer: conceived as savage or feminine, the native embodies the irrationality and backwardness against which the colonizer imagines himself. Yet particularly in cases like the terrifying goddess Kālī, this image often becomes a frightening mirror that reflects back the colonizer's own deepest fears, fantasies, and dangerous desires.[35]

For critics like Urban who assert that his analysis of Orientalist discourse does not leave sufficient room for genuine dialogue and constructive interaction, Said responds in his more recent book *Culture and Imperialism* with his notion of "discrepant experiences," which are experiences that expose the limitations of such abstract concepts as "East" and "West." "Discrepant experience" suggests the possibility of recognizing a world order that respects differences of all kinds.[36] Nonetheless, Said's reaction is more of a beginning than a guideline for a real constructive interaction between the parties.

Arguably, the most complete book-length critique of Said's notion of Orientalism is provided by Daniel Martin Varisco, who criticizes Said on literary and historical grounds.[37] Varisco criticizes Said, for instance, for supporting his theory with material from novels and neglecting their satirical and theatrical function as a way for a writer to criticize his or her own culture. He also accuses Said of selecting only authors who manifest racist and ethnocentric biases, using quotations out of their context, lacking any appreciation for irony, and overrelying on fiction as an example of an instrument for creating imperialist ambitions. Varisco characterizes Said's method as historically flawed because it neglects the complexities of history, being at times ahistorical, being inattentive to historical detail, denying the relevance of historical context, being guilty of conflating the ideology of imperialism and historical reality of colonialism, projecting contemporary attitudes and prejudices into the past, and ignoring the historical and social context of the authors cited. Finally, by ignoring historical logic, Said falls into a methodological antinomianism.

A Critical Look at Said's Political Agenda

There is a certain irony contained in Said's discussion of Orientalism. Said, a Palestinian and member of the so-called Third World educated in the West, uses some of the philosophical notions of Michel Foucault and Nietzsche to develop his own theory. After he spends considerable effort criticizing Western scholarship, it is ironical that Said would use some of the philosophical theories of Foucault and Nietzsche, members of former European colonial powers. According to Said's philosophical hero Foucault, knowledge is power and it tends to be coercive in order to gain control.[38] Said's intention is to use his knowledge to control Western views of the East. What we have in Said's book is a clever attempt, by a self-portrayed powerless person, to turn the tables on the powerful. By using Western philosophy to construct his argument, and not something from the East, Said indirectly confirms the prejudice of practitioners of so-called Orientalism about the East, that it possesses nothing of enduring intellectual value to offer to the Western mind. Moreover, Said's characterization of Orientalism functions in his work as a kind of evil bogeyman, which reminds one of religious fundamentalism in America and its polemic against secular humanism for its alleged godlessness and divinization of human beings.

The adoption of Foucault's notion of power presents Said with additional problems. Foucault conceives of power as a force that circulates like an air-conditioning system. In contrast, Said understands power as hierarchical and as something imposed from above by a superior person, institution, or nation on inferiors. If Said were to truly adopt Foucault's notion of power, Said would have to admit that members of the Orient do possess power. In fairness to Said, I think that he comes around to this position in *Culture and Imperialism* when he discusses the active resistance by non-Western natives that he admits to having left out of his book on Orientalism.

Bsides the problematic use of Foucault's notion of power, another problem with Said's post-structualist-postmodern approach to comparative studies is his concept of culture, which is for him a system of discrimination and evaluations. Said tends to conceptualize culture in terms of power relationships. When a particular group in a given country identifies itself with the prevailing cultural milieu, that culture tends to become tyrannical, "and it also means that culture is a system of exclusions legislated from above but enacted throughout its polity, by which such things as anarchy, disorder, irrationality, inferiority, bad taste, and immorality are identified, then deposited outside the culture and kept there by the power of the state and its institutions."[39] By a continual process of differentiation of itself from what it perceives to be different from itself, culture protects and conforms itself and gains hegemony over its society and state. Thereby, it vindicates its power over everything different.[40] Again, we witness the influence of Foucault on Said in Foucault's view of culture as a repressive means to power.[41] Although it is true that a given culture can become oppressive and even tyrannical, Said's view is too one dimensional because, as I pointed out earlier, he neglects the way in which culture can act as a bearer of symbols, values, customs, institutions, and meanings for its adherents. Since there is an inevitable tyranny built into the fabric of any culture for Said, it is impossible for any group to legitimize its cultural identity.

Within the context of his argument about failings of Orientalism, Said's use of spatial metaphors (e.g., distance, exile, margins) is instructive because it indicates that he favors models of escape, and believes that criticism should take place between culture and system in individual consciousness, which is distanced from both of them. These spatial metaphors are problematic in association with the notion of the other: "To put it another way, to imagine the other as distant and separate is profoundly undialectical."[42] It also places oneself outside social relations, whether they are Western or Eastern.

Said's Children

Along with the work of Frantz Fanon in books like *The Wretched of the Earth*, published in 1961, which analyzes the relation between violence and national consciousness, and *Black Skin, White Masks*, published in 1963, which studies the effects of race within colonial and postcolonial contexts, Said's work has given impetus to the development of postcolonial studies. Within the context of this field, there is not a single postcolonial theory or a single person that speaks for the entire field. This lack of consensus creates a situation that tends to be confusing to those outside of the discussion when different authors offer diverse definitions of the nature of notions like imperialism, colonialism, and postcolonialism. The "postcolonial situation" is a reference, for instance, used to describe a global condition. After we examine and compare different nations and cultures, this condition may reflect an unequal distribution. Because of the diversity of postcolonial studies, I intend to survey just two figures as representative examples of the children of Said and Fanon. These scholars are Homi K. Bhabha and Gayatri Chakravorty Spivak, although there are others who could have also been chosen.

In his work *Location of Culture*, published in 1994, Bhabha utilizes a methodological combination of deconstruction, psychoanalysis, and literary and historical criticism. He views the present moment as characterized by transition, disorientation, lack of direction, and restlessness.[43] He seeks transition moments in between locations of time and space where one can develop new strategies for individual and communal selfhood.

Without replicating or inverting its character, Bhabha wants to create alternatives to the prevailing culture. He introduces his notion of "vernacular cosmopolitanism," which originates with his insistence on a continuation of an anticolonial struggle, which unifies local concerns with international political relevance.[44] Bhabha's notion of cosmopolitianism, which is paradoxically formulated, envisions the postcolonial subject gaining real political power from a complicit relationship between colonial and neocolonial discourses. This process renders the postcolonial subject a historical person. In addition, the postcolonial subject also becomes contemporary with others, and his or her local situation starts to exert an international influence.

Bhabha's vision also includes a perception of a subaltern secularism, which emerges from the limitations of liberal secularism and "keeps faith" with those communities and individuals that have been denied by and excluded from the egalitarian and tolerant values of liberal individuals. Furthermore, Bhabha argues, "such secularism does not assume that the value of freedom lies within the 'goodness' of the individual; freedom is much more the testing of boundaries and limits as part of a communal, collective process, so that choice is less an individualistic internal desire than it is a public demand and duty."[45] His stress on subaltern studies is an attempt to displace the West from the center of theoretical knowledge. This can only be accomplished by shifting the writing of history away from its traditional representational mode of thinking.

Spivak shares many of the same concerns as Bhabha, but she uses a different set of methodological approaches that combines deconstruction, feminism, and Marxism. By using this combination of approaches to the subject of postcolonialism, Spivak confesses to being a *bricoleur* (using what is at hand). This suggests that a reader will not discover a master discourse or critical taxonomy in her work. Much like Derrida, Spivak does not assume or promote a philosophical position that she would defend against critics. By using a combination of feminism, Marxism, and deconstruction, she intends to retain the discontinuities and complexities that she discovers and exposes.

In what sounds very Daoist, Spivak argues that postcolonial intellectuals must "unlearn" theoretical and privileged positions. Such a call suggests that postcolonial intellectuals must initially rid themselves of biases, prejudices, and preunderstandings that they might bring with them to their work.[46] A problem with such an argument in the case of Spivak is that the notion of intellectual "unlearning" exposes a basic contradiction within her position because her anti-individualism conflicts with her assumption about the fundamental homogeneity of the subject. Moreover, her call for the intellectual to "unlearn" is rather utopian.[47]

Another problem arises with Spivak's assertion that history is a process of epistemic violence.[48] By "epistemic violence," she means the construction of a specific representation of an object of study. Any object can be constructed without any existence or reality beyond its specific representation. Such a representation usually consists of a historical narrative from a Western perspective. To counteract the Western representation, Spivak wants to produce a new narrative about how the Third World was itself created as a representation for the West and for itself. Within the context of such a discussion and using her feminism, Spivak claims that the Third World woman cannot speak. There is a danger in this claim because Spivak suggests that she is constructing herself as a spokesperson and representative for the Third World woman. Moreover, Spivak idealizes, essentializes, and turns the Third World woman into an icon that she intends to contest from the start.[49] If this is the case, she is also rather presumptuous because she possesses an elitist status by virtue of her position at an Ivy League research institution like Columbia University, even if we consider her origins. In short, Spivak is not a Third World woman, and it is presumptuous for her to claim to speak for "all" of them, although her empathy for them is certainly commendable.

If her feminism does not mesh easily with her use of the deconstructive method of Derrida, this is equally true of Spivak's Marxism, which is invoked in part for political effect and renders her method inconsistent. Her use of Marxism makes her approach inconsistent because Spivak wants to use essentialism and universals in certain situations in a strategic way. This approach conflicts with her use of the deconstructive method that seeks to undermine essentialism and all universals. In the final analysis, deconstruction, Marxism, and feminism do not go together comfortably. By trying to use all three approaches, she shows an ambivalence to give up all "isms" on her part, and this approach essentially contradicts her deconstructive method. Does this make her a "halfway" deconstructionist? I do not think, based on the position of Derrida, that it is possible to be a "halfway" deconstructionist.

There is also a certain amount of irony associated with Spivak's use of Marxism because it possesses a long history of involvement in anticolonial struggles. And yet Marxism is itself the historical ideology of political imperialism used by the former Soviet Union as it colonized the countries of eastern Europe. Of course, Spivak would want to distinguish her brand of Marxism from its orthodox European type. She suggests using Marxism as a means of critiquing the objective material conditions in former colonial countries with an analysis of the subjective effects of the material conditions. Nonetheless, postcolonial thinkers like Spivak do little to expose the causes of the poor material conditions of former colonial subjects and do not offer ways to bring about change.[50]

By means of her three-pronged approach, Spivak joins political company with the subaltern from her perspective. In fact, she attempts to create a literary insurgency that is highly political. Moreover, she wants to create a crisis within historiography in order to counter its hegemonic tendency. I am impelled to ask the following question: Is her Marxist politicization of postcolonialism an improvement over the representations that she seeks to deconstruct? With her revolutionary rhetoric, she talks in a Marxist political spirit, but she does not walk with the subalterns from her ivy perch at Columbia University. With her heavily laden, dense, and obscure deconstructive, Marxist, and feminist jargon, it is highly unlikely that she could adequately communicate with any subaltern subject. In contrast to scholars like Spivak, there are others such as Ashok Malhotra and his students in upstate New York who join the subalterns and build homes and schools for them in rural India.

Representations and Representational Thinking

Said, Spivak, and Bhabha share a common concern. They stand opposed to Western representations of the East in part because the representations created by Western scholars possess no reality, according to their perspective. Post-structural-postmodern thinkers, such as Foucault and Derrida, influenced the thinking of such postcolonial figures. In this section of the chapter, I want to critically examine the genealogical approach of Said and Foucault. Then, I want to turn critical attention to Derrida's method of deconstruction and its use by Bhabha and Spivak because these methods represent a challenge to religious studies and its general conduct of inquiry into religious phenomena and history.

With respect to Said, a person can ask the following question: Has he created a concept, representation, or "ism" with his notion of Orientalism? I raise this question within the context of the writings of a person who informs us that he is opposed to representations and the type of thinking on which it rests. Said's adoption of Foucault's notion of genealogy represents an attempt to overcome the representational mode of thinking. In order to response to the question raised, I propose to briefly review Nietzsche's method of genealogy and then its use by Foucault.

According to Nietzsche, it is important to grasp the origin of something by means of the method of genealogy, a nonscientific type of history that is unrelated to dates and facts. In contrast to the historical method with its sweeping narratives, genealogy is more akin to an illustrative sketch. It is possible that the importance of philology in the eighteenth century inspired Nietzsche to develop his method of genealogy with its connection to etymology, which can be traced by philologists in the absence of precise historical data and dates. Much like philologists, Nietzsche demonstrates a conviction that shifts in words and values can be traced independently of detailed historical evidence.[51] With respect to values, genealogy is an excellent way to demonstrate their plurality and differences from other values of diverse cultures, although Nietzsche insists that discerning the origin of something settles nothing. Robert Soloman interprets genealogy as an ad hominem argument: "Genealogy is not mere history, a search for origins, verbal or material, but a kind of denuding, unmasking, stripping away pretensions of universality, and merely self-serving claims to spirituality."[52] Thus genealogy is a means of exposing what is hidden and secret.

Because the history that we inherit is not a body of facts for Foucault but rather a collection of interpretations of various kinds that continue into the future, it is not possible to reach primal, untainted material using scientific or research tools. Why is this view of history accurate? Even the most primary historical data is a product of interpretation for Foucault.[53] Since we possess merely signs of an object that already represents the interpretation of another sign, there is not only no foundation to interpretation, but it is also a never-ending task.[54] A scholar must also be aware that history is made difficult because it stands within an interconnected web of power relations. It thus cannot find a place outside this interconnection by which to make an accurate analysis. An aspiring historian is also unable to account adequately for the paradoxical nature of the discontinuity of history because such a historian describes what he or she perceives from his or her perspective.

In order for a historian to grasp what is occurring, Foucault turns to Nietzsche and his notion of genealogy to complement his earlier archaeological method, with the purpose of developing a new theory of discourse. In contrast to his earlier use of archaeology, that of genealogy widens one's analysis of a particular topic by concentrating "on the forces and relations of power connected to discursive practices; it does not insist on a separation of rules for production of discourse and relations of power."[55] This position implies that a purely descriptive history is useless, as Nietzsche contends in his work *The Gay Science*. Nietzsche is primarily interested in appreciating and defending interesting differences that are found by demonstrating the plurality of human histories. Nietzsche, Foucault, and Said agree that genealogy is not a mere search for origins. It is more akin to a process of unmasking and stripping away pretensions of universality. According to Foucault, genealogy focuses on emergence, origin, descent, and birth.[56] For Foucualt, genealogy is more of a diagnostic approach that focuses on the interrelations of power, knowledge, and the human body. Foucualt adopts this method because he is concerned with discontinuity, differentiations, dispersion, and mutations that are neglected and forgotten aspects of history.

As the genealogist attempts to discern the punctuating gaps of history, Foucault refers to an effective history (*wirkliche Historie*) that is not associated with metaphysics, acknowledges no absolute, does not claim to be objective, and is without constants. This type of radical history makes no truth claims and recognizes that all knowledge is relative theory. Within the Nietzschean spirit, Foucault's adoption of genealogy suggests that he wants to abandon objectivity and any vision of truth.

Moreover, genealogy allows Foucault to emphasize differences, discontinuities, and divisions within history and culture, which makes it a heterological approach that discovers the weak points of rationalism, separates history from metaphysics, and acknowledges no absolutes.[57] Foucault focuses on the interrelations of power, knowledge, and the human body by standing within the interconnected web of power relations at the current moment and acknowledging the relative nature of all knowledge, which is interrelated with social institutions and practices. Consequently, knowledge is never something neutral because it is always connected to power relationships. Foucault's ultimate goal is to question the given established order. The impetus of his approach is to subvert hermeneutics by attempting to collapse the distinction between theory and practice, rendering the act of theorizing "the uncovering of the hidden sources of truth in specific power interests."[58]

Using Foucault's notion of genealogy, Said explores patterns, traces developments, and sketches values in transition. At the same time, Said constructs a representation of the West that he calls Orientalism. This construction stands in sharp contrast to his attempt to overcome the representational mode of thinking. As I have argued in another work, Foucault also does not overcome the representational mode of thinking, and the same can be affirmed for Said.[59] Said gives us an unbalanced, distorted, incomplete, and highly politicized construction that is only partially real. In addition, his adoption of the method of genealogy from Foucault gives his reader something more akin to fiction than historical analysis. Of course, the use of genealogy presupposes that historical objectivity is impossible and that historians are really constructing fiction anyway. Therefore, there is an indefinite multiplicity of interpretative possibilities. This approach results in either a fictitious relationship to the truth or a dismissal of it and any notion of what is.[60] Foucault admits to doing this, but I am not certain that Said is as publicly honest as Foucault. Hans G. Kippenberg asserts that such postmodern thought is reminiscent of the crisis of historicism about a hundred years ago. Both crises are connected to the insight that historical descriptions contain a strong subjective aspect and are thus handicapped. This calls into question any distinction between correct and incorrect representations of the past and its distant data.[61] This possesses important implications for representational thinking.

Like Foucault, Said claims to be opposed to representational modes of thinking. However, his creation of the notion of Orientalism is a product ironically of a kind of representational thinking. Said is opposed to the Western creation of the Orient. Yet he creates a caricature of the West grounded in a representational mode of thinking, a kind of cognitive process from which postmodern philosophy strives to break free.

In contrast to Said's adoption of the method of genealogy from Foucault, Bhabha and Spivak use Derrida's notion of deconstruction. Derrida admits to following and continuing the work of Martin Heidegger, although Derrida wants to bring the efforts of Heidegger to completion by deconstructing the presence of the present because the representational mode of thinking is shaped by presence. *Deconstruction* is an ambiguous term that suggests the disarranging of the construction of terms in a sentence and disassembling the parts of a whole.[62] Thus, *deconstruction* refers to the disassembly of texts that attempts to exceed the sphere of its conceptual totality. Derrida denies that deconstruction is a particular event, a human act, or an operation. However, its goal is to locate an instance of otherness within a text that reflects a logocentric conceptuality and then to deconstruct this conceptuality from the standpoint of alterity. This is a procedure that suggests obtaining a position of exteriority with respect to that which one is deconstructing. This position of alterity is a form of writing that is accomplished on the margin of the text. Without waiting for any conscious deliberation by a person, deconstruction does occur as an event that enables it to deconstruct itself.[63] Derrida suggests that deconstruction is not a method because it is not reductive like an ordinary method; it is also not a nonmethod because it does not advocate uncontrollable free play.

According to Derrida, deconstruction is like an *exergue*, which is an inscription on the face of a coin or at the beginning of a book. It suggests functions associated with making something evident, a bringing forth, or displaying. Similar to an inscription, deconstruction possesses value within a context or in a series of possible substitutions of inscriptions.[64] Since whatever is inscribed is located within a chain related to other items, any external difference is also part of an internal process in which the interval or difference between items divides the items within the process. Whatever differences and contradictions are encountered by means of the process of deconstruction, the person using the method does not attempt to overcome these internal differences, but wants to maintain these heterogeneities. Therefore, deconstruction functions in Derrida's works in a parasitic manner because it preys on other readings or interpretations in an endless process.

Because deconstruction erases positions as they are immediately established, it is antidialectical in the sense that it destroys any progress of the dialectic, whereas Marxist philosophy is fundamentally dialectic and akin to Hegelian philosophy. If Marxism does not truly exist without its dialectic, this raises the following question: Can a person using a Marxist analysis continue to be a deconstructionist without contradiction? This is precisely the conundrum facing Spivak. Although the deconstructive approach of Spivak does a good job of disassembling colonial categories, her usage of the method does not result in newer or more adequate categories. This is partly a shortcoming of the method of deconstruction and its parasitic nature and tendency to repeatedly prey on a text. The notion of deconstruction, which is not truly a method or a nonmethod for Derrida, is subject to other types of criticism.

Deconstruction leads, for instance, to a radical skepticism that refuses to recognize the common world that everyone shares in order to create a better world.[65] There is also an exaggerated importance placed on metaphysics by postmodernists, which it falsely assumes forms the basis of Western culture. In turn, the deconstructive stance suggests that the destruction of its metaphysical basis would result in the collapse of Western culture.[66] Moreover, the attempt by deconstructionists to obliterate old hierarchies tends to upset the traditional distinctions between different subjects like philosophy and literature and disrupt such distinctions as equal-unequal, community-discord, uncoerced-coerced, and other such distinctions. Potentially creating a fluid cultural situation does not mean that anything worth affirming would emerge from this flux other than deconstruction itself and subjectivity.[67] Thus some critics perceive a loss rather than any worthwhile gain to be made by using deconstruction.

Concluding Remarks

Even though Said exposes the false ideas, presuppositions, and stereotypes that Western scholars formed of the Orient, his work exemplifies his own prejudices. The West is depicted as responsible for the current problems of the East because Western ideas and attitudes have undermined traditional Eastern cultures by enslaving them and making them feel inferior. To turn his own postmodern perspective against him, one can argue that Said's work becomes an artifact or an episode in the history of Eastern responses to Western views of the Orient. Thus the stereotypes and prejudices of Western scholars of the Orient are supplemented in Derrida's sense of the term—an addition to, a surplus—by Said's equally stereotypical, prejudicial, and political work.

Nonetheless, Said's work makes an important contribution by exposing the shortcomings of a nonscholarly style of Orientalism. Thus Said teaches us lessons about how not to do cross-cultural scholarship. His work should not, however, intimidate those doing research on the East, even though his political objective is to accomplish just that condition and to deter scholars from doing cross-cultural studies. We can, however, agree with him when he wants to stop scholars from doing cross-cultural studies in a stereotypical fashion. We should recall that an author, for Said, always writes against or in opposition to something or someone. Certainly, scholars should avoid perpetuating cultural stereotypes that have no basis in reality. As I have argued, however, Said is just as guilty of using hermeneutics for political purposes as those figures he discusses in his books. Unfortunately, he neglects to mention those Orientalists who made important contributions to our knowledge of the Orient and who embraced elements of Oriental culture in their personal lives because they recognized its enduring value. Both sides—East and West—need to make new beginnings.

Because Said contributes to exposing the wrong ways for Eastern and Western cultures to encounter each other, we owe him a debt of gratitude. We can repay him by doing work that is more self-conscious of our biases and strives to be fair with the treatment of the subject of our study. But we must also be aware that Said's work is a clever attempt to turn the tables on Western scholars and intimidate them with the power of his own text. Said confesses to the personal nature of his work when he writes, "In many ways my study of Orientalism has been an attempt to inventory the traces upon me, the oriental subject, of culture whose domination has been so powerful a factor in the life of all Orientals."[68] Since he is convinced that a text is an instrument of power, Said attempts to use this power against the West in spite of his claims to be a marginal person caught between two cultures.[69] In his attempt to repay the West for injustices inflicted on the East, Said reveals the political agenda of his work, which serves as an excellent example of hermeneutics used for political purposes. In the case of postcolonial thinkers, they are caught between a politics of structure and fragmentation.[70]

And although Bhabha and Spivak call for a fuller appreciation and acceptance of differences, their use of deconstruction leads to similar problems with respect to method and politics. Like Said, Bhabha and Spivak adopt methods from Western thinkers and not Third World thinkers. In other words, Bhabha and Spivak claim to speak for the non-Western other, but they use methods devised by Westerners, which gives the impression of contradicting and undermining their purposes. Bhabha tells his reader that he wants, for instance, "to rename the postmodern from the position of the postcolonial."[71] But he is using Western methods to do the renaming, which necessarily implies that he is not using the discourse of the Third World to rename the postmodern.

In summary, many Westerners reacted to the East in patronizing, chauvinistic, and racist ways, while others were also fascinated with the East, which manifested itself in a tendency to romanticize it.[72] This latter tendency contributed to a systematic misrepresentation and oversimplification of it. Thus it is important to avoid narrow explanations and a tendency to reduce complex issues and ignore the complex nature of the motivations for Orientalism. Said's position and those of Bhabha and Spivak tend to neglect the role of Eastern culture in the process of renewal and self-criticism for those in the West. Possibly, Rushdie's main character sums it up best when he refers at the end of the novel to immortalizing his memories by sharing his tale with readers, even though distortions are possible. He summarizes the situation in the following way: "We must live, I'm afraid, with the shadows of imperfection."[73]

5

Hermeneutics, Comparison, Context, and Difference

IN THE PREFACE to his work entitled *Thus Spoke Zarathustra*, Friedrich Nietzsche discusses the tightrope walker who performs on a rope stretched between two towers over the market square of a town. As the tightrope walker reaches the center of the rope, a brightly attired buffoon arrives and rapidly traverses the rope. With a devilish cry, the buffoon leaps over the tightrope walker, who is disturbed by this occurrence, loses his balance, plunges into the market square below, and lands near the prophet. When the fallen man regains consciousness the prophet tells him that there is no devil or hell to fear because the soul of the tightrope walker would be dead before his body. The man thinks that if the prophet is right he would leave no legacy. Zarathustra replies that danger has been the calling of the tightrope walker, and he has been faithful to his calling. The riskiness of walking a tightrope is also shared by someone engaged in hermeneutics.

The hermeneutist runs the risk of misinterpreting his or her subject. Sometimes, the interpreter runs the risk of distorting his or her subject by using inadequate, deficient, or inappropriate hermeneutical tools. In the second chapter of this book, I considered Georges Bataille's theory of religion and sacrifice, and found it to be inadequate as an overall theory of sacrifice that could advance our understanding of the subject. As the chapter demonstrates, Bataille's theory of religion is ahistorical and devoid of any relationship to evidence from any religious culture or based on any such data. What Bataille does give his reader is a discourse on discourse, a kind of metatheory. Bataille's discourse on discourse does not fit the data of the Sun Dance in chapter 2, but his new discourse does reflect his anal view of life and his decadence, which tends to obscure the subject of religion. Since Bataille's theory does not fit the data, it can be concluded that he is writing a book of fiction or book on religion as pornography. The pornographic charge is evident when one compares themes (e.g., excessiveness, waste, economy, eroticism, union of desire and death, and difference) in his theory of religion with his pornographic works. This does not mean that his insights are totally without some merit, but his theory of religion needs to be grasped within the existential context of his life. This necessarily means that his work on religion and other postmodern thinkers needs to be used with care and extreme caution. It is easy to jump on the theoretical bandwagon of the latest trend and ride it until it fizzles out, but it is another matter to be a discerning consumer.

In this chapter I propose to examine the postmodern challenge to hermeneutics by using the hermeneutical methods of Mircea Eliade, Wendy Doniger, and Jonathan Z. Smith as three examples that have been used in religious studies scholarship. I compare these hermeneutical methods to the postmodern approach of Gilles Deleuze and focus special attention on the importance of difference among postmodernists.

Eliade's Heremeneutics

Eliade understands himself as a historian of religion, although such a scholar must exceed the intellectual grasp of an ordinary historian who attempts to reconstruct a historical event. The intellectual reach of the historian of religion surpasses the common historian because the former "must trace not only the history of a given hierophany, but must first of all understand and explain the modality of the sacred that that hierophany discloses."[1] Thus, Eliade's approach is not merely concerned with historical accuracy but also with understanding and explaining the material. Besides being historical, the methodological approach of the historian of religion must be as encyclopedic and as all-encompassing as possible in its scope, which renders the discipline impossibly difficult because a practitioner has to know everything, refer to other disciplines for help, and always seek genuine sources.[2] Although one needs to consult a specialist on a given topic that one is investigating, Eliade strongly emphasizes going back to the original sources such as primary texts.[3] Wanting to ground his method on the historically concrete, Eliade thinks that it is necessary to examine all the manifestations of a religious phenomenon, not merely to discern its message, but also to attempt "to decipher whatever trans-historical content a religious datum reveals through history."[4] Any attempt to interpret a transhistorical message has been problematic for some of Eliade's critics.[5]

Where Eliade sees unity within archetypes that he finds in history, Deleuze recognizes instead a metaphysical position and need for a multiplicity of difference.[6] In place of archetypes, a single universal principle, and the multiple because of their abstract, static, or all-encompassing natures, Deleuze wants to stress the specific, particular, and singular because no words, phenomena, or events have a multiple sense for him. From the Deleuzean perspective, the most common feature of phenomena is difference, which refers to differences that are incapable of identifying their nature except by means of differentiation, a focus on difference to the extent of excluding any possible unity between sameness and difference common with representational thinking.

In sharp contrast to representational thinking, Deleuze proposes to think difference, which he envisions as both a positive and disruptive process. By thinking difference, one affirms surfaces or planes not as something derivative or secondary but as surfaces constituting a fluctuating series that forms them. Deleuze wants everyone to conceive of concepts as a series of waves on a plane of immanence that lacks depth.[7] According to Deleuze, concepts are concrete, whereas a plane is both abstract and a horizon of events. The plane, an indivisible milieu, is populated by concepts that it continuously links together. There are no pure concepts devoid of empirical content, which allows Deleuze to stress immanence without any foundation beneath it and to reject all forms of transcendence. In summary, Deleuze thinks from the surface in order to think difference, which necessarily involves thinking on and affirming the surface, becoming a primary rather than s secondary mode of focus for a thinker.

Nonetheless, the history of religions represents a total hermeneutics for Eliade because it is "called to decipher and explicate every kind of encounter of man with the sacred."[8] This total hermeneutics reaches beyond understanding and interpreting religious phenomena because it is concerned with thinking about religious facts in a potentially creative way, which can lead to the creation of new cultural values. This creative hermeneutics possesses the potential to change us, to stimulate us, to nourish us, and to revitalize our philosophical thinking. By creative hermeneutics, Eliade means more than a method of interpretation, because it is also "a spiritual technique that possessed the ability of modifying the quality of existence itself."[9] Thus, hermeneutics, a never-completed task, is creative in a dual sense: It is creative for the particular interpreter by enriching his or her mind and life, and it is creative because it reveals values unavailable in ordinary experience. This type of awareness is liberating for Eliade. Besides its potential ontological implications for the individual interpreter, the study of unfamiliar religions more than broadens one's horizon of understanding because one encounters representatives of foreign cultures, which results in culturally stimulating the interpreter.

For Eliade, hermeneutics is also a risk and an adventure because the historian of religions is confronted with numerous strange situations during the course of her or his studies that are extremely complex and need to be interpreted in order to be understood. The various boundary situations opened before our hermeneutical gaze often challenge us to rethink our own ontological situation. By learning as many boundary situations as possible from different religious cultures, interpreters are able to abstract the structure of the different kinds of behavior encountered. Eliade understands this search for symbolic structures as a form of integration into a larger whole or system and not a form of reduction. But it is insufficient to discern the structures of religious phenomena or behavior; it is also necessary to understand their meaning. If religious phenomena reveal new and unexpected perspectives by means of which they can be grasped and articulated into a pattern or system, Eliade argues that "[t]his makes possible not only the intuition of a certain mode of being, but also the understanding of the 'place' of this mode of being in the constitution of the world and of the human condition."[10] Eliade implies that he followed this type of approach because the dialectic of the sacred, a tendency to indefinitely repeat a series of archetypes, demand it. Because of the fact that hierophanies repeat themselves and inherently seek to reveal the totality of the sacred, it is possible for us to distinguish religious facts and to understand them.[11] This process implies a comparative approach to the study of religious phenomena.

If meaning becomes obscured, it is possible to restore it by means of comparison and exegesis.[12] Moreover, Eliade asserts in his journal the following: "[I]n the history of religions, as in anthropology and folklore, comparison has as its function to introduce the universal element into 'local,' 'provincial' research."[13] With respect to the use of comparison, Eliade makes a distinction between the historian of religions and the strict phenomenologist. According to Eliade, the phenomenologist rejects using comparison because such a scholar confines him- or herself to finding the meaning of a particular phenomenon: "The historian of religions does not reach a comprehension of a phenomenon until after he has compared it with thousands of similar or dissimilar phenomena, until he has situated it among them; and these thousands of phenomena are separated not only in time but also in space."[14] This does not mean that the historian of religions is content to compare elements in her or his typology or morphology, an apparent invention by Goethe around 1795. The historian is also aware that religious phenomena are not exhausted by history, although she or he needs to remember that religious phenomena develop within and reveal their meanings within history.

Eliade's use of phenomenology, history, intentionality, intuition, morphological classification, rationality, and the necessity of order are all rejected by Deleuze as aspects of representational thinking. By adhering to his representational mode of thinking, Eliade subsumes religious phenomena by means of resemblance, a procedure that falsely presumes a continuity between a sensible intuition in a concrete representation and an archetype. According to Deleuze, this type of taxonomic categorization of religious phenomena cannot possibly capture differences between phenomena. What Deleuze perceives Eliade doing is imposing a system of organization over phenomena that are dynamic and different, transforming these phenomena into something static. Deleuze proposes to substitute a plane of experimentation on which a person can map an immanent plane with its extensive relations and intensive capacities, an experiment that rejects Eliade's assumption that a scholar can find essences.

Eliade and His Predecessors

In order to more fully grasp the hermeneutics of Eliade, or any such scholar, it is important to place that person within the appropriate scholarly context by reviewing the contributions to the study of religion from earlier thinkers and to distinguish what Eliade attempts to accomplish with the theoretical intentions of prior scholars. The historical aspect of religious phenomena was often neglected, for instance, by some of his predecessors. The embrace of the theory of evolution, along with its concomitant scientific aura, by scholars such as Herbert Spencer, Edward Tylor, Claude Lévy-Bruhl, James G. Frazer, and Emile Durkheim obscured the historical nature of religious phenomena. And their own approaches to the study of religion were ahistorical, an approach that was consistently criticized by Eliade. Furthermore, the quest for origins was a misguided endeavor because there was no way to investigate primordial religion accurately, from the perspective of Eliade.[15] If the human mind simply responded to the laws of nature as Tylor claimed, there was no place for human creativity, from the viewpoint of Eliade.

The embrace of the theory of evolution also led to a tendency among many scholars before Eliade to reduce the origin of religion to a particular phenomenon such as the souls of deceased humans developing into supreme beings, according to Spencer; identifying animism as the basis of religion, as did Tylor; the argument by Frazer that religion developed from magic; and the single-minded focus on the social aspects of religion by Durkheim. To these examples of a tendency to reduce religious phenomena by some scholars, Eliade emphatically reacted:

> Indeed, there is no such thing as a "pure" religious fact. Such a fact is always also a historical, sociological, cultural, and psychological fact, to name only the most important contexts. If the historian of religions does not always insist on this multiplicity of meanings, it is mainly because he is supposed to concentrate on the religious signification of his documents. The confusion starts when only one aspect of religious life is accepted as primary and meaningful, and the other aspects or functions are regarded as secondary or even illusory. Such a reductionist method was applied by Durkheim and other sociologists of religion.[16]

Another danger to which the theory of evolution contributed in the scholarship, for instance, of Tylor and Frazer was that of gathering material from all around the world and arranging it into a sequential pattern that accorded with a preconceived plan. Tylor, Frazer, and Spencer shared a tendency to view religious phenomena and actions as natural phenomena that developed out of human reason and not supernatural intervention. From the perspective of Eliade, there are three problems with such tendencies for the study of religion: the illegitimate use of scientific models; a misuse of primary sources; and the danger to overemphasize rationality, found in such scholars as Tylor, Lévy-Bruhl, and Max Weber. Eliade elucidates the problematic nature of relying on scientific paradigms: "Neither the history of religions nor any other humanist discipline ought to conform—as they have already done too long—to models borrowed from the natural sciences, still more as these models are out of date (especially those borrowed from physics)."[17] Thus, a fundamental premise of the philosophy of positivism associated with Auguste Comte was a logical and methodological unity between the natural and social sciences, which for Eliade resulted from confusing what German scholars called *Naturwissenschaft* and *Geisteswissenschaft*, respectively disciplines of the natural science and humanistic studies, Eliade was convinced that no humanistic discipline should conform to models taken from the natural sciences. The positivistic aversion to metaphysical thinking was an obstacle to grasping the nature of religion, and its claim that science was focused on empirical facts irrespective of the human subject was anathema to Eliade's method and personal philosophical convictions, although he perceived a structural analogy between the scientific method and literary imagination in which the human mind is free to play outside the process of logical thinking.[18]

With respect to the second problem associated with the use of sources, Eliade's emphasis on focusing on primary sources has already been mentioned. Moreover, he thought that the history of religions, an empirical method for the study of religion, represented a multitude of past messages waiting to be deciphered and understood by the scholar.

Late nineteenth-century theorists concerned with the quest for the origin of religion used the method of comparison in an illegitimate way from the perspective of Eliade because they used it to attempt to prove the theory of evolution and to support their contention that earlier forms of religion were inferior to Christianity in some cases or Western modes of thinking in other instances. If earlier forms of religion were discovered to have survived to the present moment, these were labeled modes of superstition by Tylor or said to expose weak points of modern society by Frazer—to cite just two examples. This line of argument manifested a cultural and religious arrogance by Western scholars. With respect to surviving beliefs and practices from an earlier period of religious history, Eliade referred to these things as camouflaged in the banality of the modern world.[19] There were also numerous examples of mythical survivals in the modern world that could be discovered in the notion of Aryanism in Germany; the adoption of eschatological myths by Marxists; the figure of Superman in comic books; the exodus to suburbia, which reflected a nostalgia for primordial perfection; and the modern embrace of the novel, which represented a desire to hear desacralized but mythological narratives, whereas reading itself suggested to Eliade an escape from time.[20] The hermeneutics of Eliade demonstrated a sensitivity to the use of Western categories when interpreting archaic religious beliefs and practices in sharp contrast to most of the scholars reviewed in this book, with the possible exception of Joachim Wach. Moreover, although Eliade has been criticized for his use of the comparative method, his use of it represented an important improvement over that of most of his predecessors. If it is possible to agree that Eliade's use of the comparative method represented a significant or even a small improvement over its use by his predecessors, this single example, although other examples could be cited, begins to refute any exaggerated and scurrilous assertion that Eliade's scholarly career was an abject or grandiose failure.[21]

Eliade's use of the comparative method is devoid of the positivistic and behavioristic slant of Spencer's method, which tended to exclude meaning and human subjectivity. Eliade seems to have scholars like Spencer in mind when he asserts, "It is impossible to imagine how consciousness could appear without conferring a meaning on man's impulses and experiences."[22] For Eliade, meaning is intimately linked with what it means to be a human being. Eliade's work also counters the penchant for using comparison to demonstrate the inferiority of primitive religion, as in the work of Tylor and Frazer, or using it to prove that primitive mentality is prelogical because it lacks the rigor and rationality of Western thinking. Unlike Max Müller, Eliade did not compare religions to determine which one is the best, as if comparison is a means of testing one's own faith and religion against others or assumes the guise of a game with a winner and a loser. Although Eliade attempts to avoid Durkheim's reductionism, they agree that comparison helps to demonstrate that religions share common features. And Eliade thinks that the use of comparison is more helpful than just sharpening the focus of the scholar, as did P. D. Chantepie de la Saussaye. Eliade is, however, closer in spirit, regarding the use of comparison, to the scholarship of Cornelius Tiele, Weber, and Wach with their respective emphasis on historical research to pave the way for classification, empathetic understanding, and advocacy of an impartial and objective approach, the need to avoid insufficient or distorted conclusions, and using comparison as an aid to understanding, although Eliade is a bit leery of the emphasis on rationality found in the methods of Tiele and Weber.

For the most part, Eliade and his predecessors avoid the individualizing type of comparison used to "contrast specific instances of a given phenomenon as a means of grasping the peculiarities of each case."[23] With the exception of Weber and Wach, they also neglect the variation-finding type of comparison intended "to establish a principle of variation in the character or intensity of a phenomenon by examining systematic differences among instances."[24] Many of Eliade's predecessors engage in the universalizing type of comparison because its overall aim is to "establish that every instance of a phenomenon follows essentially the same rule."[25] Eliade's method of integrating elements into his system of morphological classification and his emphasis on an encyclopedic approach to the history of religions suggest that he uses the encompassing type of comparison that operates by placing different instances of a phenomenon "at various locations within the same system, on the way to explaining their characteristics as a function of their varying relationship to the system as a whole."[26] This suggests that the encompassing type of comparison commences within a large structure or process, and Eliade's morphological classification of myths and symbols in his work the *Patterns in Comparative Religion* is a good example of the use of this type of comparison.[27] When using this type of comparison, the scholar can select particular locations or phenomena within the structure or process and explain similarities or differences between them as a result of their relationship to the entire structure. If the encompassing type of comparison is historically grounded, it can help the scholar explain large structures or processes, connect these explanations to the temporal and spacial context, and enhance our understanding of the overall structures or processes and help us better understand their particular parts. Thus, whatever type of comparison a scholar chooses to employ, it possesses the potential to enhance our understanding of religious actions and phenomena.

Smith, Maps, and Territory

After presenting a paper on Eliade and Deleuze at a panel at the annual convention of the American Academy of Religion some years ago, I stayed on for a second panel focusing on the work of Eliade because I wanted to hear Charles Long's presentation on his former friend and colleague. In a vigorous and animated style, Long defended Eliade against the criticism of Jonathan Z. Smith over his method of comparison by saying in part that Smith would not have had a career if Eliade had not existed. This inflated assertion about Smith was an exaggeration by Long that the listeners received with laughter and in a spirit of levity, but it was truthful to the extent that Smith has been very critical of the way that Eliade used the comparative method, although Smith does not reject the importance or usefulness of comparison in the study of religion. Instead of the broad generalizations made by Eliade, Smith intends to circumscribe comparison by providing some reasonable guidelines for its use.

Smith makes judicious use of the metaphor of a map (worldview) that he playfully claims is not territory (experience). By using this metaphor, he wants to offer a locative strategy to map the world in order to overcome all incongruity. Smith proceeds by presupposing the interconnectedness of all things, the usefulness of symbolization, and the power and possibilities of repetition. The maps of religion are myths and rituals, which are significant only in the sense of creating a sense of territory. It is axiomatic for Smith that maps negotiate territory, which means that there are endless ways to perform rites and apply myths in an effort to construct meaning in life.[28] Smith disagrees with Eliade that religious meaning can be gained by endless repetition of sacred narratives. Religious meaning can instead be gained by manipulating and negotiating myths and rites, applying them to situations of life, adjusting life to these maps, and being continuously re-created.

Smith identifies two inseparable mapping strategies: locative and utopian. Both of these strategies are intended to overcome the separation between map and territory. The locative approach makes the map correspond perfectly with the territory, whereas the utopian way operates by eliminating map.[29] Consequently, religion is a mapmaking and map-using process grounded in the difference between maps and territories, and it enables us to see that religion is an ongoing process. This means that religion is more about application and not essence. Rather than being defined by essential structures, religion, as Smith views it, is a mode of creating meaning, which calls for students of religion to expand their understanding of it by applying, reshaping, and challenging aspects of the academically constructed concept of religion.

Since humans not only discover their place within the world, which Smith connects with human experience (territory), and also create it by means of maps that reflect their worldview, Smith has decided to look at the dynamic relationship between maps and territories instead of Eliade's morphological classification as a way to organize evidence found in the cross-cultural study of religions. To this interplay between map and territory, Smith applies a hermeneutics of suspicion, an exploratory device intended to explain away.[30] Moreover, Smith stresses the importance of place because he is opposed to Eliade's notion of the center, arguing that what makes something sacred is its place and not its centeredness. According to Smith, culture defines its notion of place through its language, symbols, and social structure, which is equivalent to creating and discovering webs of meaning.[31] This position implies that the importance of place is revealed by a culture's locative vision.

Instead of Smith's locative metaphor of the map, Deleuze stresses the metaphor of the rhizome, which stands opposed to the paradigm of the tree that is hierarchical and centralized. The roots of the rhizome proliferate in many directions, and function by means of the notions of connection and heterogeneity. Intending to create a new image of thought in contrast to the binary subject-object structure of traditional Western thinking, Deleuze introduces the rhizome metaphor, which is a multiplicity, because it gathers together fragments and other elements that defy the logic of the representative mode of thinking and common sense.

In contrast to Smith's notions of map and territory, Deleuze also emphasizes a plane of immanence, which contains concepts, events, and singularities similar to a single wave that rolls and unrolls multiple waves of concepts.[32] The plane of immanence, a driving force of his philosophy, is paradoxical because it is a plane of consistency and its opposite because it is continually changing. From Deleuze's perspective, Smith's map is a vast plane of immanence. And because the scholar of religion is captive to a process of becoming based on Deleuze's thought, that scholar cannot know anything definitively, which includes even what she or he thinks. "The activity of thought applies to a receptive being, to a passive subject which represents that activity to itself rather than enacts it."[33] By implication of this type of position, the self (that thinks or exists) is undermined and unfinished for Deleuze in the sense that the individual scholar ceases to be a self-conscious self, because the scholar becomes a location where thoughts take place.

Difference, Repetition, and Comparison

Because the process of negotiating and manipulating the incongruities of life represents alternating for Smith between the exigencies of life and expectations of tradition, his method runs counter to Deleuze's notion of repetition, whose "for itself" is difference that underlies all identities and makes them unstable. It is difference that inhabits repetition.[34] Identities are illusions that obscure pure differences with repetition, operating as the alteration of relations between differences. In the final analysis, differences turn all representations into illusions.

Instead of repetition and its implications for difference typical of Deleuze's thought, Smith uses juxtaposition, a methodological operation that implies relationship. What this means is that Smith places side by side two things, which can be, for instance, interpretations, quotations, ideas, or approaches to one's subject of investigation. It is the difference between the two juxtaposed things that motivates their interplay and leads by necessity to comparison. Smith juxtaposes, for example, a locative map, a centered one, with a utopian map, a chaos-generating map that is artificial, constraining, and threatening, forming an antimap. This type of juxtaposition enables Smith to link the sacred and chaos rather than reflect Eliade's distinction between the sacred and the profane.

From the perspective of a historian of religions, Smith recognizes the need for comparison that is motivated by the existence of difference in the world. He isolates four modes of comparison: ethnographic, encyclopedic, morphological, and evolutionary. Each of these types of comparison used by scholars is flawed, according to Smith for various reasons. The ethnographic approach lacks a systematic mode of application and tends to be impressionistic, while the encyclopedic arranges items cross-culturally but does not explicitly compare or explain topics. Originating with romantic *Naturphilosophie*, the morphological approach arranges topics into a hierarchical series in a logical fashion, but it ignores the space and time context, although its discovery of archetypes is accomplished in a sudden and intuitive leap that simplifies everything. The evolutionary method of comparison includes change and continuity over time, emphasizing adaptation to a particular location, and arranges data from the simplest to the more complex, with the former being chronologically prior. Smith also rejects statistical, structural, and systematic description and comparison because the first provides no rules for evaluating comparisons, whereas the structuralist represents a subset of morphology with Marxist presuppositions, and the systematic approach focuses on a worldview that forms an unconscious deep structure that tends to ignore difference.[35] According to Smith, it is Ludwig Wittgenstein who reminds us that comparison is never about identity, but is rather about the postulation of difference.[36]

In contrast to these modes of comparison, Smith thinks that the method of comparison is built on contagion, in which one recollects similarity to the neglect of difference, which tends to get forgotten. Comparison is not merely a subjective experience, but is also an invention and not a discovery, which is a means of finding something. In distinction to discovery, invention is the realization of novelty that a person did not intend to find. Comparison is impressionistic, closely associated with memory, and not very methodically rigorous. These comments do not mean that Smith completely rejects comparison, although he does stress the importance of difference, though not to the extent of Deleuze.

Smith thinks that without comparison thought would be impossible, suggesting that it is unfeasible not to compare things. It is as if humans are condemned to compare because of the way our thought processes operate. Smith identifies four moments of comparison: description, comparison, redescription, and rectification. The double description refers to historical and ethnographic aspects of comparison. The first mode of description is to locate a subject in its social, historical and cultural context, whereas the second task of description is "reception-history," a taking account of the second-order scholarly tradition in order to elucidate how something became important.[37] The moment of rectification refers to the process of rectifying categories in relation to the way that they have been imagined.[38] Smith's emphasis on a double description strongly suggests creating a representation of a subject being studied, an outcome contrary to the spirit of Deleuze's thought.

Nonetheless, Smith agrees with Deleuze about the need for a discourse of difference that Smith thinks invites negotiation, classification, and comparison.[39] Not only does comparison bring differences together, but it also informs us how things might be conceived instead of telling us the nature of things. Comparison, a controlled exaggeration for the purpose of knowledge, calls attention to features of difference, and enables us to reimagine "phenomena as our data in order to solve our theoretical problems."[40] Smith conceives of comparison as a playful and active venture that breaks phenomena down only to reconstitute them, whereas Deleuze is more concerned with subverting phenomena in order to create uncertainty.

Smith and Deleuze agree that the language of difference is relational and relative, and accounts for meaning. The relative relation and relative nature of difference are evident in the notion of the other, suggesting relative and not absolute difference. Deleuze agrees with the spirit of Smith's following assertion: " 'Otherness' blocks language and conceptualization; 'difference' invites negotiation and intellection."[41] Moreover, language surrounding the other leads easily to misunderstanding that suggests an ontological cleavage rather than a state of being.[42] Otherness is a situational category because "something is 'other' only with respect to something 'else.'"[43] Otherness is also transactional, a matter of being "in between" one thing and another.

Deleuze argues that the other, which has three distinct and inseparable aspects that he identifies with a possible world, a face, and language, is a surface that pushes up against the individual. There is a danger that the other could be reduced to an object or a subject. Nonetheless, the other distorts one's field of perception, an event that Deleuze thinks is necessary for the structure of the perceptual field, on the one hand guaranteeing a temporal distinction between consciousness and its object, and on the other meaning that without the other, consciousness coincides with its object, which means that it is then impossible to account for what is unthought, outside, or different.[44] According to Deleuze, the other is an unusual object that it is impossible to think and cannot be thought by any mode of representation.

From Deleuze's perspective, despite Smith's calls for attention to difference, he is still engaged in representational thinking because he continues to use the conceptual tools of representation, such as identity, oppositions, analogy, and resemblance. These aspects of representational thinking are opposed by repetition, which opposes singularity to the general, a new universality to the particular, a distinctive to the ordinary, and instantaneity to permanence. Deleuze associates repetition with humor, irony, and something transgressive.[45] Instead of a world characterized by representations and solutions that privileges identity, analogy, opposition, and similarity, Deleuze envisions a world of movement that leaves us with problems and questions and thought that leaps and dances on a plane of difference and repetition.

This playful view of life espoused by Deleuze is shared by Smith through his references to the metaphor of map and territory, a metaphor hiding the comic. Thereby, as do numerous postmodernists, Smith invites his readers to share in a simulacrum instead of reality. This aspect of his work and his juxtapositioning of things, persons, and events are evidence of Smith playing the role of *homo ludens.*[46]

When Smith asserts that maps are all that we possess when we engage in the study of religion he suggests that the academic study of religion is limited to the analysis of texts. Sam Gill expands on this point by asserting, "He confines academic work to the comparative study of maps without regard to territories, all the while admitting that such territories at least exist."[47] Recognizing an advantage to Smith's approach, Gill calls attention to restricting the work of scholars to texts, which he views as an advantage because it provides a measure of objectivity. In a similar mode of approach, Alf Hiltebeitel, a scholar of Hinduism, and Gregory Schopen, a Buddhist scholar, both believe that textual work can be enhanced respectively by anthropological and archaeological data.[48] These scholars have combined textual studies and fieldwork with excellent results, and have proven that we need not be necessarily confined to texts. In fact, anthropology and archaeology can enhance the understanding of texts by verifying or negating assertions in texts.

Doniger and the Comparative Spider

The use of comparison, as one scholarly tool or method among others, is suggested by the very nature of myth, which is itself an inherently comparative form of narrative from Wendy Doniger's methodological perspective. This is true in a twofold sense because not only does myth itself compare items embodied within it, but it lends itself to comparison by its very nature. Since difference possesses the potential to alienate us from our world and each other, comparison can serve to assist us to discern differences and provide a rationale for them. Thus there is something very fundamental about comparison and the attempt by human beings to comprehend their surroundings: "Indeed, comparison of things acknowledged to have something in common is the basis of our entire way of making sense of the world, our intellectual taxonomy, our survival system."[49] In short, comparison helps us to cope with the incongruities of our existence and helps us to make sense of the world within which we reside. Doniger suggests that comparison is a useful and practical tool because "to understand what a thing is like is to understand what it is."[50]

Like many scholars before her, Doniger uses comparison to cross-examine diverse cultures, enabling a scholar to utilize the narratives of a foreign culture to reveal elements not present in one's own stories. Besides it revelatory potential, comparison opens our eyes to new possibilities and enriches us. The sage use of comparison can enable us to see ordinary things or events in a new light because it "defamiliarizes what we take for granted."[51] Not only does the method of comparison enable us to become more fully aware of the ordinary, it even forces us to see truths of which we may not have been aware but that then seem obvious.[52] Moreover, by exposing ourselves to the mythical narratives of the other, it is possible for us to reconceive our own sacred stories and to reevaluate long neglected aspects of them.[53] Doniger suggests that she enters into dialogue with the myths of the other, recognizing that verbal and textual utterances are ultimately intertextual. Moreover, the encounter between the scholar and the other is intersubjective.

From an interrelational perspective, comparison also forces us to confront the other in a meaningful way by recognizing that the other is "both different from and the same as us."[54] If we encounter a fellow American or someone from a completely different culture, Doniger thinks that we begin with sameness or similarity. In fact, she gives priority to similarity over difference, unlike many postmodern thinkers, for the following reason: "The similarity must be established before we can go on to the difference; we must acknowledge that there is something to compare before we can compare it."[55] But this does not mean that we must stop or be satisfied with finding likeness. We must conclude our encounter with the other with difference. Dongier offers a warning:

> Moreover, similarity must not be allowed to be normative: to assume one's original stance, to begin by assuming the self in the Other on some level, to say that the Other is "like me" is to an extent inevitable. But it must immediately be qualified by both difference and the shift of center: one must go on to say, "I am like," "I will be able to understand you because I am like you," and then, later "I see ways in which you are in fact not like me."[56]

Doniger is arguing for two things at this point. She wants to embrace both sameness and difference and to maintain them in equal balance, unlike many postmodern thinkers who want to just emphasize difference and neglect similarities. She also wants to stress the basic triangular nature of comparison.

The so-called triangle of comparison includes comparing a single other with another other with the understanding of the scholar forming the third angle. Doniger acknowledges the criticism of the deconstructionists about the inevitable subjectivity associated with interpretation. She turns the criticism of the deconstructionists into something positive when she writes: "Deconstructionists see this subjectivity as inevitable in any interpretive position, and in a sense it is. But it is also a strength for anyone engaged in explicitly cross-cultural work: the observer, the one who compares the stories, stands at the intersection of cross-cultural paradigms and the unique events of history."[57] From Doniger's perspective, the subjective and invisible third aspect of the triangle of comparison is real. In order to support her position of turning the postmodern criticism of the subjective nature of understanding into strength, she cites Jonathan Z. Smith, who depends on the insights of Charles Sanders Peirce and that philosopher's contention that when we compare two things we accomplish this task by means of our intellectual reason. Many postmodernists, of course, call into question the nature of reason and the semiotic realism of Peirce.[58]

Deleuze advocates, for instance, that desire, an antirational force, replace the role of reason. From Deleuze's philosophical perspective, the hidden metaphysical aspects of Doniger's position are an example of arboresent thinking shaped by arboreal metaphors.[59] By using his pragmatic method of rhizomatics, Deleuze is concerned with what one can do, representing an intertwining of unity and difference that concentrates on the surface and the connections between diverse fragments. Deleuze borrows the notion of the rhizome from biology to oppose origins and foundations and to emphasize that the rhizome is both proliferative and serial, and functions according to principles of connection and heterogeneity. Since the rhizome represents a multiplicity, it seeks to overcome the binary subject-object structure of Western thought.

Doniger and the Web of Context

It is axiomatic with Doniger that comparison be executed in a responsible manner. For her, this means to know the language of the primary sources in at least one of the religious traditions being compared. Moreover, it means that the comparative scholar must also know the context in which the myths occurred.[60] Possessing necessary language skills and sensitivity to context, scholars work not from the apex of some hierarchical structure that they impose on the material being studied, but rather begin from the ground and work upward.

By working from this direction, the scholar considers numerous materials in order to arrive at generalizations. This approach suggests that "the bottom-up argument is more numerological than logical, more inductive than deductive: it seeks to persuade by the sheer volume of its data rather than by the inevitability (or falsifiability) of the sequence of its assertions."[61] Thus Doniger disagrees with scholars like Ivan Strenski and Russell McCutcheon,[62] who advocate the necessity of falsifiable theories, because she is convinced that unfalsifiable theories are difficult to avoid. It is, however, possible to ameliorate any damage caused by unfalsifiable theories "if they are not followed unconsciously or reductionistically but are invoked explicitly and in groups."[63] It is assumed that the sheer volume of evidence and the direction to which it points will be convincing enough to the reader, and this overwhelming evidence will function to prove one's theory. From Doniger's perspective, it is possible for the comparativist to utilize more than a single theory and to juxtapose them against each other and presumably to let the shortcomings of each support the other. Doniger admits that this approach is eclectic.[64] An important consequence of Doniger's eclectic approach is made lucid by Brian Hatcher when he writes that "the very diversity of the tools precludes the chance of one claiming her ultimate or unquestioning allegiance."[65]

Another way to examine her advocacy of eclecticism is to review what she means by the toolbox approach to the study of religious phenomena. Doniger imagines a toolbox of methodologies from which a scholar can select an appropriate method for a specific mode of interpretation. It is possible for one's toolbox to possess such methods as psychoanalysis, literary criticism, history, ethnology, structuralism, philosophy, or sociology. In addition to these methods, she utilizes such disciplines as zoology, feminist theory, legal theory, and queer theory in her book entitled *The Bedtrick*.[66] By selecting an appropriate methodological tool, we will be able to discern patterns within the myths, for instance, that can also be discovered within particular fields of scholarship. Doniger offers a rather pragmatic suggestion to overcome potential problems with this type of eclectic approach: "Although this pattern is not derived from indigenous views of the material, it is not imposed inappropriately if it arises from the data, is applied only when and if it fits, and is abandoned when it becomes inadequate."[67] This type of methodological approach is intended to encompass the perspectives of both the scholar and the person or group responsible for the composition of the myth. If the perspectives of both parties are taken into consideration, it is unnecessary to decide which viewpoint is more valid because the perspectives of both sides are valid. Therefore, the toolbox approach suggests an acceptance of indeterminacy with respect to the study of religion. In other words, we cannot be absolutely certain about our knowledge about religion. This type of approach gives priority to hermeneutics over epistemology.

Although Doniger's multidisciplinary approach is admittedly eclectic and attempts to take into consideration the viewpoints of both the scholar and subject being studied, it is guided by an informed pragmatism that is intended to act as a guide to test one's theories about the patterns that manifest themselves during the course of one's examination and interpretation of the myths. A good example of this approach is Doniger's comparison of myths of the mare in Indian, Greek, and Irish literature.[68] Or the comparison of Daksha (Hinduism), Pentheus (Greek), and Jesus (Christianity) in a later work that finds that each is a victim of violence. Even though Daksha is both victim and the sacrificer, Pentheus and Jesus share the status of the victim with the Indian figure, but Jesus is distinct from the other two figures because he is both a divine victim of violence and human substitute for the surrogate victim, constituting a new religious paradigm in the history of religions.[69] This line of argument suggests that the study of religion is a very complex endeavor, and it cannot be reduced to a conceptual abstraction in the mind of the scholar.

Doniger's advocacy of her toolbox approach is suggested by the very nature of myth itself because "myth is the most interdisciplinary narrative."[70] Such a statement suggests that the method that one chooses to study and interpret myth must fit the nature of the religious phenomenon. There is thus a need for a multidisciplinary approach. It is possible to witness this need when Doniger compares dreams and myths and uses Western psychological insights to elucidate the Indian material for both epistemological and ontological purposes, serving to help us understand how we grasp Indian texts and "to help us understand the actual problem set by the Indian texts."[71] Doniger explains the relationship between myths and dreams in the following way: "A myth is a private dream that has gone public. But dreams are also made out of myths, for people tend to dream not only about their lives but also about the myths they have been taught. Dreams incorporate into personal fantasy elements of traditional, shared mythology."[72] Even though the connection between dreams and myths might suggest approaching such narratives using psychological tools, it is still important to remember that one must view the myth from a variety of angles in order to avoid the conundrums associated with reductionism. If one admits that any interpretation of a myth will reduce it to some degree, it is possible to reduce the danger of reductionism by looking at it from several angles and using different tools while attempting to draw as much insight and meaning as possible from the narrative without being "terrorized by the accusation of reductionism."[73] What Doniger's approach implies is that different methods are suited to different purposes and results, and a complete understanding is not grasped by any one method.

Doniger's toolbox approach becomes a means of exclusion from Deleuze's perspective, and is undermined by what it attempts to exclude, which he identifies with the simulacrum.[74] The simulacrum replaces the Platonic opposition of appearance and essence for Deleuze, and overcomes the dominance of identity established by Plato. The functioning of the simulacrum, a Dionysian machine, a phantasm itself, subverts the same or a representative model and renders it false. Being constructed on a difference, the simulacrum internalizes dissimilarity, but this does not mean that it is a degraded copy.[75] Deleuze's philosophical position manifests an anti-Kantian perspective that is nonconceptual and nonrepresentational.

Potential Methodological Problems

To her credit, Doniger anticipates many of the methodological problems created by her approach to the study of myth. I have already alluded to the issue of falisifiablity of theories. But there are also other potential methodological problems that gravitate around issues of the very nature of the comparative effort, the importance of context, the equality of methodologies, politics, and the approach of Claude Lévi-Strauss. The problematic nature of the structuralism of Lévi-Strauss is connected to Doniger's early book on the erotic and ascetic Hindu god Śiva and her ardent embrace of this method to the exclusion at that moment in her scholarly career of other possible methods, and it is tied to attacks on structuralism by many postmodern thinkers.

The comparative approach to the study of religious phenomena is often criticized for its lack of rigor.[76] This lack of methodological rigor is often exemplified by general hypotheses that are impossible to falsify. The comparative approach is also criticized for being impressionable and not resulting in new knowledge.[77] From within the context of her theory of myth, Doniger replies to such criticisms by arguing that myth itself suggests a comparative approach because of its fragmentary nature, a position shaped by the theory of Lévi-Strauss. Since myths are fragmented, they need to be supplemented by the fragments discovered in other myths in order to enhance our understanding of them. In addition, the supplement is necessary "because of the fragmentary nature of our understanding of the myths, especially those embedded in ancient texts."[78] Thus the fragmentary nature of both myths and of our understanding of them contributes to the necessity of a comparative approach. The issue of fragmentation is important enough for Doniger to publish a book about it and to probe the issue of duality as it pertains to genders and bodies.

This approach leads to a discussion of stories about seduction, guilt, innocence, virtue, sexual license, themes of wifely steadfastness and faithfulness, transposing male heads, splitting of androgynes, and bisexual transformation.[79]

This double fragmentation of myth and understanding also calls for grasping the cultural and historical context in which myths are composed, reworked, and retold. The importance of context is emphasized by the metaphor of the implied spider: "The implied spider generates, and is therefore implied by, the stuff that myths are made on."[80] This suggests that the author of a myth is implied by what the myth reveals about the author's experience. Although it is not possible to witness the creative action of the author of a myth, it is possible for the scholar to witness the webs of significance, meaning, and culture that the author leaves behind in the form of myths. The web itself represents the shared experience, which is already narrative, of human beings within the culture.[81] A good example of this feature is Doniger's discussion of women as tricksters when she concludes that "thus, when women are not being blamed for being so stupid that they can be tricked, they are blamed for being too cunning to be tricked; heads she loses, tails she loses."[82] With her focus on myth, Doniger suggests that her approach to the study of religion emphasizes language, history, and culture instead of subjectivity (e.g., belief, cognition, inner states, and religious experience). The major exception would be her discussion of myths and dreams where her tool of choice is psychology.

Because of the nature of the web, a multidisciplinary approach to myth is necessary to unlock its messages. But is there an equality of methodologies within the toolbox approach? Even though Doniger asks this type of rhetorical question, she does not offer a substantial, exhaustive, or incisive answer to it. She merely hopes that she can be an eclectic scholar and still retain her intellectual respectability.[83] Although she does not directly answer her rhetorical question, she lucidly explains that eclecticism is forced on the comparative scholar by the many viewpoints within the myth, the many ways of telling a myth, the various ways that diverse "scholars will produce different micromyths and bring together different texts in their macromyths."[84] And there is always the issue of politics.

Both myth and the comparative project embody a political aspect. It is possible for the former to forge connections with political messages. Myths can also broaden our political vision.[85] In contrast to Roland Barthes's view of myth as nonpolitical or as depoliticized speech, Doniger grasps it as prepolitical.[86] When Doniger discusses, for instance, the horse, she finds "a contradictory symbol of human political power" and that the animal is "both victim and victimizer, a ready-made natural/cultural symbol of political inversion."[87] Moreover, myth is potentially revolutionary because it possesses the ability to subvert established hierarchies or the prevailing paradigm.[88] Nonetheless, the question about the politics of myth is complex with respect to the comparative project. On the one hand, the modern comparative study of myth is intended to teach us that other religions are like our own. This use of comparison reflects the hegemony of colonialism and its imperial enterprise.[89] On the other hand, the comparative project is perceived differently in the post-postcolonial era and its backlash where the sameness of religious phenomena from different cultures is viewed as demeaning by the other.[90]

Some have argued that the comparative method is socially and politically conservative.[91] But Doniger's use of the comparative method contradicts such a conclusion because there is little that is conservative about her use of it. Moreover, the attribution of social and political conservatism to the use of the comparative method by a scholar is indicative of the problematic nature of applying political labels to scholarship and methods.[92]

The political nature of myth and the comparative project raises the twin dangers of essentialism and universalism. The danger of essentialism occurs by overcontextualization of a myth in a single cultural group to the exclusion of other cultures. Doniger adds, "And by essentialism I mean hypotheses about the unity of a group that a scholar holds on to even when they have destructive results."[93] The great danger of universalism is that the other becomes identical to me.[94] Thereby, the other loses his or her uniqueness. By recognizing the dangers inherent in a universal approach to a subject like myth, Doniger does not imply that it might not have cross-cultural significance.[95] The dangers associated with either essentialism or universalism are connected to abuses associated with either an overemphasis on difference or similarity.

Difference tends to be threatening to stability and the status quo, which partly explains its attraction to the radical political proclivities of many postmodern thinkers, whereas similarity tends to be conservative and both a socially and politically stabilizing force. Doniger warns us that "either similarity or difference may lead to a form of paralyzing reduction and demeaning essentialism, and thence into an area where 'difference' itself can be politically harmful."[96] The important elements of a myth are not its similarities with other myths but rather its differences from the general pattern of other narratives. Thus it is important for the scholar to be aware of variations of a story because they hold "the key to the isolation of a motif, which in turn contributes to the final reconstruction of the total symbolism of the cycle."[97] The scholar must also be watchful for repetition within various versions of a narrative because it assists us to distinguish between the trivial and the essential themes of a myth.[98] In this way, Doniger gives priority to difference, but she acknowledges the importance of similarities. And she ultimately wants to hold them in tension with each other because both difference and similarities have contributions to make with respect to our understanding of a myth or cycle of myths within a web of meaning. If one does not hold them in tension with each other, there is the danger of falling into the trap of universalism.

Problems associated with universalism could be hypothetically over-come by "comparing the relations of texts to the contexts" in an approach that could represent a cultural morphology.[99] This type of approach could respond to such questions as the following: Do cultures with particular types of social structures have the same kind of myths? A cultural mor-phology could have interesting consequences for scholarship: "This project would take account of differences between men and women as storytellers, and also between rich and poor, dominant and oppressed, through the comparison of contexts."[100] Since Doniger also sees potential problems with this approach, she appears to be proposing this as a trial balloon to her readers as one possible way to combat universalism, to con-tinue comparative work, and to emphasize the importance of contextual-ism. Her awareness of these kinds of problems demonstrates a reflexivity, which is an ability "to become aware of the context of research and the presuppositions of the research programme."[101] By moving away from strict neutrality and objectivity, which Doniger thinks is an impossible goal,[102] she emphasizes context and a recognition that the scholar is a social being as are the others being studied.

Beside the importance of comparison and contextualization for the study of myth, the influence of Lévi-Strauss continues to shape Doniger's theory of myth, although this observation does not imply that she accepts his approach uncritically. After slowly moving away from the early struc-turalist approach of *Asceticism and Eroticism in the Mythology of Śiva*, pub-lished in 1973, a few years later with *The Origins of Evil in Hindu Mythology*, Doniger finds that the method of structuralism possesses limits with respect to the problem of evil "because so many of its jagged facets prove stubbornly irreducible, perhaps because it is almost always viewed in conceptual rather than symbolic terms."[103] Cognizant of some of the problems associated with structuralism, Doniger moves in a methodological direction in which a purely structuralist approach is less important than a more nuanced comparative method of more recent years, even though the influence of Lévi-Strauss is still evident in her recent work.

Besides citing Lévi-Strauss for support of her own position, Doniger is also critical of the structuralist's position where she deems it appropriate. Doniger criticizes the claim by structuralists to be able to isolate elementary structures within a myth:

> Structuralism isolates themes in a myth; it says, this *is*. But the myth is not a structure, it is a narrative; the myth adds to the structures speculations about the sequence of events, about causation; it says, this happens *because*. Structuralism does not arrange the pieces chronologically or sequentially or causally; the narrative does, and when it changes the arrangement it changes the point of the story, the point of the new answer to the old questions.[104]

Myth is more dynamic from Doniger's viewpoint because it alters or rejects elementary structures. Furthermore, Doniger criticizes the tendency to arrange mythemes in dyads, which results in the "dichotomization of thought."[105] Moreover, Doniger is critical of Lévi-Strauss's audacity when he claims that he achieved precision with his method, as well as the overly ambitious scope of his work.[106] Besides these types of criticisms, Doniger pays a debt of gratitude to Lévi-Strauss by defending him against his postmodern and other critics.

To those critics who assert that Lévi-Strauss reduces myths to logical oppositions, Doniger responds, "I see him as illuminating human ambivalences."[107] To those who assert that Lévi-Strauss is merely concerned with mental constructs, Doniger adds that he is also concerned about "emotional needs and conflicts."[108] In response to those who argue that Lévi-Strauss finds differences to be superficial in contrast to invariant elements, Doniger replies that his isolation of mythemes does "allow for difference as well as sameness."[109] Doniger admits that she wants to trace mythemes rather than graph them, and she wants to be able to make sense of inversion within a myth. Numerous critics charge that Lévi-Strauss's method is unhistorical, unconnected to the flow of time, and devoid of possible change. Because structural models allegedly exist in a Platonic realm of pure archetypes, according to some critics, Doniger defends the structural approach as embodying both synthesis and change, the synchronic aspect that transcends time and the diachronic feature that is subject to the changes of time. Even though structuralism possesses certain shortcomings and Lévi-Strauss should be interrupted just before he deconstructs himself, Doniger wants to save structuralism by enriching it with her eclectic, comparative, and multidisciplinary approach.

Since this is Doniger's program, it is a bit confusing why she refers to herself as a "postmodern Eliadean."[110] Although a scholar can call herself whatever she desires, it seems to be an oxymoronic allusion applied to herself because the method of Eliade possesses little in common with most postmodern thinkers. This is a topic that I have addressed at greater length in other contexts, which to pursue would lead us astray at this point.[111]

Reflections on Comparison and Difference

According to Jonathan Z. Smith's criticism of Eliade's and by implication Donger's use of the method, comparison reflects a recollection of similarity, explained as contiguity, constructed on contagion, a subjective experience, and it represents an invention and not a discovery because the latter implies finding something, whereas invention is an unintended realization of novelty. Smith concludes that comparison is an impressionistic matter of memory and not a sound method, although Smith does think that a controlled use of comparison is useful if it is limited to cultural items that are spatially and temporally contiguous.[112] Moreover, since comparison enables the scholar to bring differences together within his or her mind, it is the scholar who makes possible their sameness, which suggests that comparison does not inform us how things are but rather how they might be conceived.[113] From the perspective of Smith, a consequence of the use of comparison is that difference tends to be forgotten, which leads him to call for a discourse of difference.[114]

If one's method for the study of religion has been shaped in part by neo-Kantian philosophy and its representational type of thinking as is the case for Eliade and Doniger,[115] it is not easy to respond to such a call because there are hidden dangers. Depending on one's point of view, both the dangers and potential for liberating the mind from representational modes of thinking are reflected especially in the early philosophy of Gilles Deleuze, who attempts to develop a philosophy of difference. Without my going into great depth here, Deleuze wants to restore difference to thought just as Smith wants to restore the importance of difference in the comparative method, but it is first necessary to overcome the tendency to represent "difference through the identity of the concept and the thinking subject."[116] I have noted that within his philosophy, Deleuze rejects notions such as the one, universal being, or the multiple in general because such terms are too all encompassing or abstract. In place of these kinds of terms, Deleuze stresses the specific, particular, and singular. Difference is an aconceptual notion for Deleuze that undermines the certainties traditionally associated with rationality in the West. Since difference eludes reason, Deleuze finds himself at the limits of the Western philosophical tradition, whereas a more conservative scholar such as Eliade is more symbolically and ontologically comfortable at the center. At these limits of philosophy, the radical nature of difference becomes even more apparent when Deleuze asserts that difference inhabits the *Aion*, a past and future with no present, which means that difference is always past or about to be future. From Eliade's perspective, this type of approach makes it impossible to make comparisons and to ultimately understand religious actions, beliefs, and phenomena. This is also not the type of discourse about difference that Smith would appear to favor because he wants to preserve at least a limited role for comparison. If Deleuze's philosophy of difference undermines hermeneutics and the comparative method, is there another alternative that is sympathetic to Eliade, Doniger, and Smith and does not neglect difference?

There is another hermeneutical option, which involves altering and expanding one's understanding by remaking its forms and limits. Normally, we understand without articulating what or how we comprehend something, a pattern of behavior or unawareness that shapes our judgments. By means of past experiences, prior decisions, and previous modes of understanding, we develop an inarticulate and unaware mode of comprehension that is akin to a kind of preunderstanding, which shapes our mode of understanding without our being cognizant of its operation. This makes it very difficult, if not impossible, and even undesirable to enter into the viewpoint or worldview of another person. If it is extremely difficult or impossible to get into the mind of another, we should, then, not foolishly think that we can rise above or transcend our own point of view.[117] We must also recognize that our understanding can change over the course of time. Life experiences cause us to adopt, for instance, different modes of understanding our own behavior or that of another person, depending on our stage of life and experiences prior to the moment of

interpretation. An interpreter's state of mind during the process of interpretation can also unconsciously shape that interpretation. This alternative
hermeneutical option is more than a self-conscious examination or a
mode of becoming aware of our preunderstanding.

Concluding Remarks

If we are to interpret the religious actions and beliefs of another person or
community, it must be acknowledged that other understanding changes
our self-understanding. This implies that by attempting to understand the
religion of another culture we must also become aware that our understanding is a single possible mode of understanding among other possibilities. To a greater or lesser degree the scholars discussed in this chapter
exhibit some form of ethnocentrism. Although it is very difficult to completely eradicate one's ethnocentrism in practice, it is at least theoretically
possible to begin to overcome it by becoming aware that our individual
understanding possesses limits and aware of how it fits within a wider
context of attempts to understand the other. Furthermore, there is always
a comparative component to other understanding: "This is because we
make the other intelligible through our own human understanding."[118]
Within the context of this comparative process of recognizing, identifying,
and articulating differences, we liberate ourselves by increasing our
self-awareness, and we liberate the other by letting that person be who he
or she is. If we can recognize the differences between the other's understanding and our own, we are on our way to the termination of interpreting the other through our personal mode of understanding and allowing
the other to stand, undistorted by our understanding, in his or her own
authentic mode of being. Thus, by comparing, we can make progress
understanding the other, strive to escape our ethnocentrism, and transcend our previous understanding.

   This does not mean that our newly discovered or acquired understanding will be without limits. The philosopher Charles Taylor makes
this clear: "When we struggle to get beyond our limited home understanding, we struggle not toward liberation from this understanding as
such (the error of the natural science model) but toward a wider understanding which can englobe the other undistortively."[119] This implies that
our prior narrowness is overcome, while ethnocentrism is conquered by
inclusiveness, which suggests understanding the other within the context
of the other's own world. Therefore, the role of the comparative method in

understanding possesses an important value by elucidating cross-cultural misunderstandings and distortions, which represents a way to liberate not only oneself but also the other. It is thus not necessary to embrace the philosophy of difference espoused by Deleuze in order to emphasize the importance of difference, thus committing the error of neglecting or not recognizing similarities. Smith is justified in criticizing Eliade for neglecting difference and emphasizing sameness, but this does not mean that the method of comparison does not have a viable and useful role to play in cross-cultural hermeneutics. Although it is probably not totally possible to overcome one's ethnocentrism, the comparative method does have a useful hermeneutical role to play in understanding the religious beliefs, actions, and phenomena connected with the other when it is used in such a way that sameness and difference are kept in creative tension with each other within an overall historical context.

6

The Problematic Nature of Representational Thinking

IF WE USE Eliade as a distinguished representative of the field of religious studies for the sake of argument and illustration, his scholarly contributions are excellent examples of the use of the representational mode of thinking to interpret and understand various kinds of religious phenomena and behavior. The representational type of thinking is characteristic of Enlightenment philosophy, and Eliade is an inheritor of such philosophy; his scholarship indicates that he is quite comfortable using it and thinks that it can have positive results for grasping various aspects of religion. Various postmodern thinkers have attempted to break free of the heritage of representational thinking, and there are those in religious studies who have followed their lead by utilizing their philosophical proclivities.

This chapter examines the theme of representational thinking that many postmodern thinkers perceive as a form of intellectual bondage to the past intended to break free of the constraints of the Enlightenment. And since religious studies is a product of the Enlightenment, the postmodern quest holds implications for the discipline. I further propose to examine the problematic nature of representational thinking within the following areas: connections and problems of history, ontology, epistemology, and representational thinking itself.

As this chapter proceeds, I will compare aspects of Mircea Eliade's work with selected postmodern thinkers, such as Derrida, Foucault, Mark Taylor, and Julia Kristeva. I have selected the work of Eliade as a primary example of representational thinking because he is arguably the most prominent grand theorist of religion in the twentieth century, even though his encyclopedic style of scholarship is not really practiced by anyone today, having fallen out of fashion. This choice of Eliade as a product of the Enlightenment, which is also true for the field of religious studies, suggests that I do not think that he is a postmodern thinker or represents a precursor of postmodernism, even though there might be some superficial similarities with postmodern thinkers. Elide is not only a product of the Enlightenment; it is possible to find elements of romanticism, especially Goethe, and Eastern Orthodox Christianity, and he often speaks the language of existential philosophy. If we grant that Eliade uses the representational mode of thinking in his scholarship, this point by itself would exclude him from the intellectual camp of postmodernism, which is to a large extent a reaction against the philosophy of the Enlightenment and a search for new paradigms.

Problems with History

Thinkers of the postmodern era call into question criteria that take their orientation from the models supplied by another epoch, which suggests that they have reservations about the practice of imitating ancient models. If we look at the actual position of an acknowledged postmodern thinker, we find evidence of a distinctive philosophical perspective. Jean-François Lyotard, a major figure in postmodern philosophy, provides two perspectives on postmodernism, neither of which has much to do with traditional wisdom. Lyotard argues that the grammatical tense of postmodernism is the future perfect and not the present because the postmodern writer's work cannot be judged by established criteria. If the future perfect is a correct identifying mark for a postmodern work, such writers labor without established rules; instead, they create them. Thus, the product of the postmodern writer is an event.[1]

From another perspective, Lyotard sees the condition of postmodernism as a crisis of narratives, the quintessential form of knowledge: "Postmodern knowledge is not simply a tool of the authorities; it refines our sensitivity to differences and reinforces our ability to tolerate the incommensurable."[2] How did this crisis emerge? After societies entered the postindustrial age and cultures emerged in the postmodern period, the status of knowledge—which includes scientific and narrative knowledge and basic competence—was altered in such a way that it became a commodity to be produced in order to be sold to consumers.[3] If knowledge becomes the major focus of production, this involves major consequences because "knowledge ceases to be an end in itself, it loses its 'use-value.' "[4] Not all postmodern thinkers would, of course, define the period as does Lyotard, which simply suggests a variety of perspectives.

Although there might be some minor agreements between Eliade and Foucault, they are overshadowed by their disagreements on issues of method and the possibility of meaning. For example, Eliade's method of attempting to grasp occurrences within the flux of historical time and place is inadequate for Foucault, much as it was for Nietzsche before him, because it is impossible to reach a total picture of history. Furthermore, the history passed down to us is not a body of facts, as Eliade supposes; instead, it is a collection of interpretations of various kinds of data, interpretations that continue into the future. By means of scientific or research tools, it is impossible to reach primal, untainted material because even the most primary historical data is itself a product of interpretation.[5] The study of history is also difficult because the scholar, along with everyone else, stands within an interconnected web of power relations and cannot find a place outside this play of relations from where to make an accurate analysis. Because the scholar, or any other person for that matter, is a direct descendent of the web of power-knowledge, it is impossible for anyone to be a creator of history or a bearer of the continuity of history. Moreover, it is not possible for such a person to adequately account for the paradoxical nature of the discontinuity of history. Thus, it is essential, according to Foucault, for the historian to find a way of making sense of what is happening.

In his work *The Archaeology of Knowledge* (1972), Foucault turns to a purely descriptive approach that takes into consideration the discontinuity of history, its temporal ruptures, and its factual gaps. Focusing their attention on the discontinuities of history and integrating them into their discourse, historians no longer find those discontinuities problematic, and they refrain from themes of convergence, culmination, and the creation of totalities—themes that tend to be misleading because they neglect discontinuity and differences.[6] Foucault's emphasis on identifying differences, dividing, increasing diversity, and blurring lines of established communication by finding multiple layers of events within discourse in sum suggest eliminating meaning from the concerns of the historian. And since history represents a series of reinterpretations in narrative form, it is only possible, in the final analysis, for the historian to compose fiction. If the great man of Nietzsche's later writings is the skeptic, Foucault's skeptical historian is in the final analysis a creator of fictive history.

Although the general spirit of Foucault's approach to history remains the same, he turns again to Nietzsche and his notion of genealogy to complement his earlier archaeological method. He thereby develops a new theory of discourse in order to find a more adequate method for his purposes. For Foucault, the difference between archaeology and genealogy is that the latter broadens the approach of the former and focuses on the relations of power associated with discursive practices, whereas archaeology separates the rules for producing discourse and power relationships.[7]

Foucault agrees with Nietzsche, who, in *The Gay Science*, claims that a purely descriptive history is useless because of the limited perspective of so-called scientific history. Nietzsche argues that we need to explore patterns and trace developments, which can be accomplished by means of the method of genealogy, a historical sketch that elucidates values in transition. Foucault agrees with Nietzsche that history must serve the forces of life. In other words, history needs to be put to a practical use, which is the reason it can never become a pure science like mathematics.[8]

For Foucault, the descriptive role of the archaeologist is complemented by the diagnostic approach of the genealogist, which focuses on the inter-relations of power, knowledge, and the human body. The mutually creative relationship between power and knowledge is evident because "[i]t is not possible for power to be exercised with knowledge, it is impossible for knowledge not to engender power."[9] Although this statement does not mean that they are identical, there is an intimate connection between them, and they are joined together in discourse. Foucault is still concerned, however, with discontinuity, differentiation, dispersion, and mutations— the neglected and forgotten aspects of history. Foucault's book on madness, for instance, is not actually about mentally ill people as such, but is concerned with the madness of society and how it alienated certain people, classified them, isolated them, and designated them as unfit to be members of society.

Among the different phenomena to be discovered, Foucault wants to reconstruct the generative processes that are at work and to elucidate invisible relations among the various phenomena.[10] The genealogist there-fore concentrates on such sites as scientific statements, philosophy, moral propositions, architecture, institutions, laws, and administrative practices and decisions. This heterogeneous ensemble helps genealogists to discern the punctuating gaps of history in their attempt to compose a history of the present, which is a history of the basic duality of Western consciousness.[11] This can only be accomplished by being located within the web of power in the present moment.[12] This effective history (*wirkliche Historie*) is not connected with metaphysics, it acknowledges no absolutes, it does not claim to be objective, and it is without constants.[13] This radical type of history asserts no truth claims and recognizes that all knowledge is relative.[14] Thus, Foucault calls into question the foundations of thinking in order to undermine the solidity of its starting point. Since notions of method, starting point, and theory are anathema to Foucault, it does not take much imagination to understand that Eliade would agree with Richard Rorty and the dilemma that he isolates in Foucualt's work: "On the one hand, he wants to give up all the traditional notions which made up the 'system of possibilities' of a theory of knowledge. On the other hand, he is not content simply to give a genealogy of epistemology, to show us how this genre came into being."[15] The Nietzschean spirit in Foucault's work wants to abandon objectivity and any unitive vision of truth.

By acknowledging the limits of knowledge and attempting to write a history of the present, Foucault's genealogists find themselves in a non-place between conflicting forces, a location where new ideas and values can be discovered from within the dualities of Western consciousness. From one perspective, Foucault's nonlocation possesses certain advantages because it allows one to study the dispersions of descent, which reveals differences, discontinuities, and divisions, in contrast to the origins of accidental events, and it enables one to study the recurrence of events.[16] In contrast to this type of position, Eliade repeatedly emphasizes the importance of seeking the center.[17] He argues that there is a transhistorical content or significance for a concrete historical religious datum that is revealed through history,[18] and he asserts the nontemporality of religious forms: "the history of religions is concerned not only with the historical becoming of a religious form, but also with its structure. For religious forms are non-temporal; they are not necessarily bound to time."[19]

It should be clear that Foucault would not agree with Eliade's claim that religious reality transcends the plane of history, a claim the former would recognize as embodying a metaphysic of its own. Even more importantly, Eliade is convinced that when a religious object comes into being it also becomes real, significant, and knowable and not something opaque, incomprehensible, or meaningless.[20] According to Eliade, although one must be cautious, it is possible to make truth claims, to be confident of the objectivity of some data, to be able to find some constants within history, and to hold out the possibility of finding absolutes because all knowledge is not as relative as Foucault claims. Moreover, Eliade does not think that a modern human being can make history because it tends to be created by a shrinking number of beings who restrict either direct or indirect opportunities of others to intervene in the making of history,[21] whereas Foucault views his own work as revolutionary and an attempt to create history.[22]

If a thinker like Eliade believes that value, meaning, or some combination of them tends to motivate the actions and words of people, Foucault thinks in contrast that it is possible to demonstrate that what people do and say is not determined by mentally constructed rules. And since it is possible to prove this is the case, it is also possible to demonstrate that any belief in the efficacy of value, truth, or meaning is illusory.[23] Because of his conviction that truth is something that is discovered or revealed to a person and that meaning can be established by exegesis and comparison, Eliade can write, in sharp contrast to Foucault, that "it is impossible to imagine how consciousness could appear without conferring a meaning on man's impulses and experiences. Consciousness of a real and meaningful world is intimately linked with the discovery of the sacred."[24]

With respect to the nature of meaning, Derrida takes a different approach than Foucault or Eliade, although he arrives at a similar conclusion to that of Foucault. For Derrida, within a chain of signification meaning represents the space between terms—their relations and interrelations. By focusing on the terms as such, one stands to miss their relations to one another and their differences wherein their meanings—non-self-originating products—reside. If Eliade thinks that meaning can be discovered by the interpreter,[25] Derrida is not convinced that meaning can be found whatsoever; there is nothing that precedes it, and nothing ultimately controls it. This does not suggest that one cannot strive for meaning, but one must become aware that it involves a risk: "To risk meaning nothing is to start to play, and first to enter into the play of *différance* which prevents any word, any concept, any major enunciation from coming to summarize and to govern from the theological presence of a center the movement and textual spacing of differences."[26] Following Derrida, Mark C. Taylor calls attention to the contextual nature of meaning, which renders it relative due to its entanglement in a formative context that is radically relational. If meaning resides in the interconnections between things, it is liminal in nature and continually appears and disappears.[27]

With respect to issues of history and meaning, Eliade agrees with Derrida and Taylor concerning the relational and contextual nature of meaning and the risky nature of interpretation. But despite this agreement, Eliade does not share their conviction about the total relativity of meaning because he cannot imagine how it is possible for human beings to function without an assurance that there is something irreducibly real and meaningful in the world.[28]

Eliade is convinced that there is a depth to history that cannot always be discerned by the scholar. In contrast, there is a postmodern tendency to emphasize immanence, which is confirmed by the philosophy of Deleuze and Guattari. In their notion of the body without organs, an entity produced by desiring machines and emergent in the second moment of desiring production, Deleuze and Guattari argue that it represents a complex interplay of highly constructed social and symbolic forces, which is neither an essence nor a biological substance. The body without organs—a notion borrowed from Antonin Artaud—represents an immanent field of desire, and produces and distributes intensities that form a surface of intensities that is prior to organization and hierarchization, and devoid of depth or internal organization.[29] The surface of the body without organs, through which intensities flow and circulate, is marked by the binary chains of desiring machines, which can function like an eating, breathing, or speaking machine. By attaching themselves to the body without organs, desiring machines form points of disjunction that can serve as a network for a new synthesis, suggesting that the body without organs is a multiplicity of elements and an arbitrary relation of forces. Thus, the body without organs is a field of becomings, a surface of intensities, and a play of forces that is never simply subject or object or something that one can possess. Lacking depth or internal organization, the body without organs is similar to an egg with a smooth surface that represents its exterior prior to its being stratified, organized, regulated, and hierarchized by being inscribed by such items as race, culture, and deities.[30]

There is no affinity, then, between the notion of the body without organs and Eliade's use of morphological classification because the latter is produced as a whole, but the body without organs is not a whole that unifies or totalizes its constituent parts.[31] For Deleuze and Guattari, the whole is always peripheral because it is a sum of particular parts, even though it does not unify them. Thus, the whole is something added to the parts,[32] whereas Eliade thinks that morphological classification consists of the parts that make a cohesive whole.[33] In contrast to the partially subjective nature of Eliade's approach to his subject, the body without organs is a bulwark against a philosophy of subjectivity that is predisposed to seek a principle of individuation in a coherent, centered subject. Deleuze and Guattari also conceive of the body without parts as a pure simulacrum that lacks internal cohesion or latent significance, which is the exact opposite of Eliade's conception of morphological classification.

Behind Eliade's use of morphological classification, there are certain metaphysical presuppositions that Deleuze and Guattari think are examples of arborescent thinking, a model of thought much like an erect tree, because it has been shaped by arboreal metaphors from the moment of its origin. They explain: "Arborescent systems are hierarchical systems with centers of significance and subjectification, central automata like organized memories. In the corresponding models, an element only receives information from a higher unit, and only receives a subjective affection along preestablished paths."[34] Morphological classification is an excellent example of a hierarchical structure with centers of significance that necessarily stress identity and sameness, the very things that Deleuze and Guattari reject in order to emphasize difference, exteriority, and change. They accomplish their objectives by using rhizomatics, a root metaphor in sharp contrast to the tree metaphor of morphological classification and its presumption of linear movement and an ordered system. Even though it also presupposes a unity, rhizomatic unity is hidden or latent, much like the roots of a tree, but it represents an underground network of a multitude of roots and shoots that lack a central axis, direction of growth, or unified sphere or origin.

If morphological classification tends to emphasize similarities among its various elements—a criticism leveled by Jonathan Z. Smith against the method of Eliade[35]—rhizomatics is a decentered web of linkages that is based on heterogeneity, multiplicity, connections, breaks, discontinuities, and ruptures. By using this method, Deleuze and Guattari are able to enhance their chances to map surfaces, discern the interrelationship between things or events, measure speed and flows, and experiment generally. This method is therefore contrary to Eliade's hermeneutics, as well as semiotics, and especially psychoanalysis—each being an attempt to connect something objective with something hidden. In contrast to these rejected approaches, rhizomatics is pragmatic in the sense that it is concerned with what one can do, and represents an intertwining of unity and difference that concentrates on the surface and the connections between diverse fragments.

In contrast to Deleuze and Guattari and their type of stress on planes of immanence, Eliade tends to emphasize depths and not surfaces. Within the context of his discussion of the archaic ontology of *homo religiosus* and the sacred mode of Being, Eliade stresses its strength, power, efficaciousness, durability, reality, and depth.[36] Also, Eliade's sacred mode of Being is both horizontal and vertical, whereas Deleuze and Guattari stress horizontal layers of planes and tend to ignore or reject the possibility of vertical space, unless it is perceived as a series of horizontal layers. Therefore, unlike Deleuze and Guattari, Eliade perceives the cosmos as a place where onto- phany (manifestation of being) and hierophany (manifestation of the sacred) meet and where various modalities of being and the sacred are simultaneously revealed.[37] Although the archaic ontology of Eliade does share the dynamism found in the thought of Deleuze and Guattari, he also emphasizes the importance, for homo religiosus, of a static aspect of Being, something that is associated with eternal, static archetypes that must be continually repeated.

Ontological Issues

When Eliade writes about Being, he presupposes its presence,[38] whereas Derrida calls into question, for instance, the presence of Being, something he does from the standpoint of *différance*, a neologism that is not a being present; in fact, it does not exist within the category of being, and its movement represents the play of traces. Because of the movement of *dif- férance*, presence, which is usually a determination and an effect in a philosophical system, cannot have a privileged place in Derrida's thought. In fact, the Derridean movement of *différance* represents the play of traces that does not belong to the horizon of Being and effaces itself when pre- senting itself in a "simulacrum of a presence that dislocates, displaces, and refers beyond itself."[39] According to Eliade, Being locates us and refers to itself, although it can also refer beyond itself in certain situations. The radical relativity of Being, for Derrida, is anathema to Eliade's conception because manifestations of the sacred and concomitant Being represent both a structure and a prereflective language.[40] If the movement of *dif- férance* for Derrida represents something that is not a being present or never presents itself as present, this means that, from Derrida's perspec- tive, Eliade possesses nothing to unify, nothing to grasp, and nothing to interpret. Thus Being cannot accurately be presupposed to be present in anything (any more or less than it is present in everything else). The rec- ognition or ascription of Being to certain specific phenomena is a product of existential conditioning, a construction, and as such is liable to decon- struction. For Eliade, Being is not a human construct; it is equated with reality in his works, as is evident from previous discussion in this chapter. Nonetheless, it is possible to amplify the reality of Being for Eliade when we observe a lesson that he draws from archaic cosmogonic myths in his journal and stresses by emphasizing the key point: "It is a matter, naturally, of ontophany, for cosmogony means this: Being which comes into being."[41]

For postmodernists, the philosophical discussion about the presence or absence of being owes its origins to Martin Heidegger's reference to Being as presencing, although he does not mean this in the sense of becoming something permanent, because becoming present suggests emerging or opening up.[42] Heidegger also grasps presencing as a transition. He clarifies his position in *Holzwege* by affirming that Being "in being" does signify presence in the sense of an unconcealedness that lets beings happen. But what is truly present is presence itself.[43]

In contrast to Heidegger, Derrida gives a radical twist to the problem of presence by denying its privileged position in Western philosophy because presence, a determination and effect, only occurs within a system of difference.[44] Thus the self, for instance, cannot represent presence for Derrida because presence itself is problematic within a system of difference and the self cannot be present as itself and cannot render itself present to itself.[45] Within the system of difference, the self is nothing more than a trace, which represents an erasure of the self and its presence.[46] With the ability of the trace to inscribe itself as a difference into the gaps that it creates in space, it is impossible for a self, an unerasable trace, to attain presence.

The position on the presence of the self initiated by Derrida finds agreement among other postmodern thinkers like Mark Taylor, Jacques Lacan, Kristeva, and Deleuze, although I do not intend to suggest that they are in total agreement about all issues surrounding ontology and the self. Taylor thinks that we create a difference between ourselves and others when we assume a proper name that appears to give us presence. But this self-presence is only possible in the quickly passing present moment with its three related modalities of time.[47] Since the self, for Taylor, is radically temporal and an inseparable modality of each moment of time, it possesses a synthetic and not an enduring identity; difference is always associated with the identity of the self, representing a union of identity-difference and presence-absence. The interplay of identity-difference and presence-absence causes a disruption in the presence of the self and dislocation in its present modality of time, which suggests that the present is merely a trace and that time is forever a transition of moments.[48] Lacan and Kristeva agree that the self lacks presence and identity; is not an autonomous thinking and knowing unified subject, heterogenous, or decentered; and is fundamentally split and alienated without any hope of attaining whole-ness.[49] From the perspective of Deleuze, the power of Being within the flux of the eternal return and the genuine character of Being are associated with the simulacrum.[50] Within this earlier work, Deleuze probably says it best when he writes, "Ontology is the dice throw, the chaosmos from which the cosmos emerges."[51]

In contrast to Eliade, these postmodern thinkers stress in general that it is difference that sustains Being and represents its dynamic aspect, whereas Eliade tends to emphasize the steady, common features of Being. According to Eliade, Being is not a human construct because it is equated with reality and presence. How can we know this? Within the context of religion, Being reveals itself.

Epistemological Issues

According to Eliade's theory of religion, hierophanies, manifestations of the sacred or the real, are self-authenticating. Eliade thinks that hiero-phanies are thus reliable forms of knowledge from an epistemological stance by virtue of their ability to self-authenticate themselves to a person or group of people to whom they appear. Moreover, the self-authenticating nature of a hieropheny is also mysterious because it is wholly other (das ganz Andere), a reality not of this profane world, even though it is mani-fested within the profane realm and thus limits itself to it.[52] This is an excellent example of essentialism, a style of Western scholarly writing and thinking that is critiqued by postmodernists for its effort to build essences into its metaphors.[53] In part, Eliade claims to be a phenomenologist or to incorporate a phenomenological approach into his study of religion[54]—by the self-described nature of their philosophical discipline, phenomenolo-gists are looking for essences, whereas many postmodern thinkers warn us that essences cannot be discovered.

In contrast to Eliade's search for essences, Derrida's notion of decon-struction—which he denies is a method—suggests the disarranging of the construction of terms in a sentence and disassembling the parts of a whole.[55] The goal of deconstruction is to locate an instance of otherness within a text—an otherness that reflects a logocentric conceptuality—and then to deconstruct this conceptuality from the standpoint of alterity, a procedure that suggests obtaining a position of exteriority with respect to that which one is deconstructing. This position of alterity is a form of writing that is accomplished on the margin of the text. Without waiting for any conscious deliberation by a person, deconstruction does not occur as an event that enables it to deconstruct itself.[56] Derrida is suggesting that deconstruction is not a method because it is not reductive like an ordinary method, whether it is primary or derived, and it is not a nonmethod because it does not advocate uncontrollable free play. Moreover, deconstruction is not singular, homogenous, determinable, self-identical, and pure; its nature is identified by what "it does and what is done with it, there where it takes place."[57] We find it functioning in Derrida's works in a parasitic manner because it preys on other readings or interpretations in an endless process. In contrast to Eliade's method, deconstruction, according to Derrida, is antidialectical in the sense that it destroys any progress of the dialectic. And in sharp contrast to the archetypes of Eliade, deconstruction subverts preexisting structures from the inside, which is another way of overturning hierarchies.[58] Thus, the approaches of Eliade and Derrida to a text could not be more different. And the latter's philosophy undermines any confidence about the existence of an objective world, which leads to real confusion about what real events might be.

In contrast to various postmodernists, Eliade is not a skeptic; rather, he is convinced that valid knowledge can be obtained and that meaning can be discovered by historical research, exegesis, and comparison, even though the meaning of a religious phenomenon might not be obvious or it might be camouflaged in the banal. Eliade elucidates further: "Just as I believed in the unrecognizablity of miracle, so I also believed in the necessity (of a dialectical order) of the camouflage of the 'exceptional' in the banal, and of the trans-historic in historical events."[59] This is hardly the epistemological confession of a skeptic. The near certainty and hermeneutical plausibility that Eliade thinks that he can find when interpreting a religious phenomenon is partly based on his understanding of consciousness: "the sacred is not a stage in the history of consciousness, it is a structural element of that consciousness."[60]

Representational Thinking

When seen from a postmodern viewpoint, Eliade and other such thinkers are products of the Enlightenment and are therefore captive to a representational mode of thinking. As Walter H. Capps correctly observes, "religious studies is the product of a blending of Cartesian and Kantian instincts and talents."[61] Representational thinking assumes a correspondence between appearance and reality and is supported by a metaphysical edifice; it is this mode of thinking more than any other particular feature that disqualifies Eliade as a candidate for being a postmodernist or a precursor of postmodernism.[62] Evidence of representational thinking can be discerned within Eliade's use of phenomenology, intentionality, intuition, morphological classification, and rationality and his emphasis on the necessity of order.

The phenomenological aspect of Eliade's method presupposes a subject who perceives an object and is able to describe that perception in an attempt to discern its structure or essence, which in turn suggests a metaphysical position and a coherence theory of truth, an identity between thought and object. According to Deleuze's interpretation of his thought, Foucualt gives primacy to fields of statements over perceptual emphasis of phenomenology, and he breaks with phenomenology over the issue of intentionality because Foucault does not think that consciousness is directed toward things. Accordingly, Deleuze understands Foucault's major achievement to be "the conversion of phenomenology into epistemology."[63] Since there is nothing prior to or beneath it, according to Foucault, everything is knowledge.

Another notion central to the method of the phenomenologist is "intentionality." For Edmund Husserl, it explains how the objects of thinking are given structure. If consciousness is always conscious of something for Husserl, thinking necessarily entails an object that one thinks about and structures with which one thinks. This implies that the real is that which is intended. Being shaped by Husserl's notion of intentionality, Eliade's methodology stresses the danger of reductionism because of the danger of losing the original intentionality of the sacred as it is revealed in the world.[64] Thus, the initial task of the interpreter is to grasp the intentional structure of the sacred by imaginatively recreating the conditions of a sacred manifestation. Within the context of his methodology, there are times when imagination is used in the same or similar way as intuition. When examining the symbolism and powers of the moon, for instance, Eliade refers to the use of intuition to discern its significance.[65] Eliade uses the term *intuition* in a similar way to that of Husserl's term *Wesenschau* to refer to the intuition of essences. Even if Eliade's methodological approach might not be necessarily analytic at this point, his method never strays from the path of rationality.

The rationality of Eliade's method is especially evident with his use of morphological classification, which represents a rationalization that synchronically organizes material spread over vast expanses of time and space. By using morphological classification in the manner that he does, Eliade gives one the impression that he thinks that all diachrony can be eventually synchronized. Eliade's system of morphological classification is also a rational creation because it is a logical arrangement of particular items organized into a complex whole and assumes an a priori fitting economy, as Jonathan Z. Smith makes clear, that tends to neglect categories of time and place.[66] The apparent static nature of morphology is reminiscent of the static world envisioned by Kant, a major explicit or implicit criticism of his philosophy by many postmodern thinkers. From Eliade's perspective, his use of morphological classification also enables him to be rationally analytic and systematic in his treatment of religious phenomena. Moreover, the rationality of Eliade's approach is evident in his definition of the sacred, which is an a priori category of the mind, or as he claims an aspect of the structure of consciousness, possessing an independent status.[67] This type of grasp of the sacred is akin to Rudolf Otto's Kantian definition of the holy as an a priori category of the mind that also outwardly manifests itself in the world of appearances. Furthermore, Eliade's rational distinction between the sacred and the profane is reminiscent of the philosophical attempt by Enlightenment thinkers to establish first principles that are precise and certain in order to arrive at similar kinds of knowledge with the overall intention of making religion intelligible.

Postmodern thinkers tend to challenge the role of reason in Enlightenment philosophy. Lyotard, for instance, makes a distinction between a rationalist and a postrationalist path by drawing out their political consequences. Lyotard wants to save reason and to free it and knowledge, which is nothing more than a product to be sold, from the bondage of capitalist authorities. He wants reason to regain its practical use and to shift toward the plural, the indeterminate, the random, the irregular, and the formless in order to become more sensitive to differences and to assist us to cope with the incommensurable.[68] In sympathy with the thrust of Lyotard's leftist criticism of reason, Foucault attempts to show the power of reason to hide unreason (insanity) and to use it as a weapon in the construction of social normativity and the development of social conformity to the dominant social power.[69] In place of reason, Deleuze and Guattari advocate desire, which is an antirational force that can produce reality and is a life-affirming power. Kristeva undermines Kantian rationality by emphasizing abjection as a form of suffering that disturbs identity and order, which is not a suitable ground for the order of reason because it results in a marginal being outside the domain of rationality.[70] Motivated by what he perceives to be an opacity embodied within the system of rationality, Derrida wants to examine what is prior to reason or even thinking, and he finds that the actual possibility of reason cannot be grasped intellectually in accordance with patterns of rational necessity because of the supplemental nature of reason, which suggests that the origin of reason must be nonrational, a position that does not take the "non" as a logical negation.[71] Derrida thinks that the Enlightenment conception of reason tends to be self-legitimizing because it takes one historically and culturally specific notion of reason as its universal standard for all forms of reason, using this single standard in order to judge all competing examples of reason as unreasonable.[72] This type of exclusivistic rationalism, which tends to dominate and demand social conformity along with its concomitant metaphysical posture, is anathema to Derrida.

When thinkers like Eliade mention that the sacred is an element in the structure of consciousness, assume that there is a ground of Being, or attempt to establish a first principle by making a distinction between the sacred and the profane, these types of notions and procedures suggest a metaphysical position from the perspective of many postmodern thinkers. In part, the philosophical agenda for many postmodern thinkers is to move beyond the confines of traditional metaphysics associated with the rationalistic Enlightenment tradition. Deleuze and Guattari think, as I discussed earlier in the chapter, that metaphysics is an example of arborescent thinking that is shaped by arboreal metaphors.[73] By using their pragmatic method of rhizomatics, they are concerned with what one can do, representing an intertwining of unity and difference that concentrates on the surface and the connections between diverse fragments. Along somewhat similar lines of argument, Foucault emphasizes differences, discontinuities, and divisions within history and culture by adopting from Nietzsche his method of genealogy, a heterological approach that discovers the weak points of rationalism, separates history from metaphysics, and acknowledges no absolutes.[74] In contrast to Foucualt's thought, Lyotard criticizes metaphysics as a metanarratology,[75] whereas Derrida attempts to deconstruct Western metaphysics. With respect to the ground of being that is presupposed by Eliade, Deleuze is critical of such a position because grounding something is either an operation of logos or of sufficient reason that renders that which is grounded as similar to the ground, giving it a resemblance that is identical to the ground. Thereby, the identical assumes "the internal character of the representation itself, which resemblance has become its external relation with the thing."[76] From Deleuze's perspective, the danger of this kind of twofold possibility of the process of grounding something makes representation predominant. The process of grounding something, which always implies grounding representation, is ultimately underminded by that which it attempts to exclude, which Deleuze identifies with the simulacra.[77]

From another antimetaphysical position, Derrida denies that there is any such thing as a metaphysical concept or name: "The 'metaphysical' is a certain determination or direction taken by a sequence or 'chain.' "[78] Derrida also calls attention to the connection between visual metaphors and thought in Western philosophy—a connection that makes Western thought captive to heliocentric metaphysics. In fact, metaphysical concepts are worn-out metaphors, which themselves are metaphysical concepts.[79] Richard Rorty agrees with Derrida that visual metaphors play a major role in shaping our philosophical viewpoints. A basic presupposition from which Rorty argues his position is the role of the mirror in Western philosophy: "It is pictures rather than propositions, metaphors rather than statements, which determine most of our philosophical convictions. The picture which holds traditional philosophy captive is that of the mind as a great mirror. . . . Without the notion of the mind as mirror, the notion of knowledge as accuracy of representation would not have suggested itself."[80] Although metaphors do not have a precise meaning, they function as a new and useful way of speaking that can potentially produce an effect that steers a safe course between the hazards of realism, idealism, and skepticism.

In contrast to Rorty's philosophy, Derrida sees the Western metaphysical tradition as representing what he calls logocentrism, a perspective from which the Greek logos implicitly connects the faculty of speech with the notion of reason. He views logocentrism as supporting "the determination of the being of the entity as presence."[81] Since there is only a closed chain of signifiers that points only to itself for Derrida, it is not possible to have a direct encounter with an object of language, a position that is diametrically opposed to that of Eliade. Without anything external to the chain of signifiers for Derrida, presence is always deferred. Logocentrism can be overcome by means of grammatology, a new discipline of writing. Since it is impossible to step outside metaphysics, this new discipline uses the tools of metaphysics against it when deconstructing it. By pushing philosophy to its limits, Derrida writes about its problems on the margins of the Western philosophical tradition. Such a push of philosophy is evident in his treatment of meaning because he argues that it represents the space within terms within the context of a chain of signification. If one focuses on the terms as terms, one stands to miss their relations to one another and their differences wherein their meanings, non-self-originating products, reside. Following Derrida, Mark Taylor calls attention to the contextual nature of meaning, which renders it relative due to its entanglement in a formative context that is radically relational. If meaning resides in the interconnections between things, it is liminal in nature and continually appears and disappears.[82] In contrast to Derrida and Taylor, Eliade finds the lack of meaning antihuman because "to be human is to seek for meaning, for value—to invent it, project it, reinvent it."[83] Eliade's reaction to the postmodern position on meaning and other points makes perfect sense within the context of representational thinking.

Besides the critical postmodern attitudes toward metaphysics and meaning, another postmodern notion that stands in opposition to a representational mode of thinking is the simulacrum, which is discussed at length by Jean Baudrillard, a postmodern cultural critic, who finds himself within a simulacrum, an era of simulation. Because this is a period in which all referentials have been liquidated, this artificial and malleable time represents faking that which one does not possess, suggesting an absence rather than a presence and threatening the distinction between true and false, real and imaginary.[84] Although there is a logic operating with simulation, it does not have anything to do with logical facts or reason because its logic is characterized by a preceding of the model, which implies that simulation cannot be represented. The strange logic of simulation does not have anything to do with meaning or the real. In fact, it terminates meaning,[85] and renders the real and illusion impossible at the same time because the latter is no longer possible without the former.[86] Within such a confused context, the medium and the message also get confused because the former gets diffused and diffracted and becomes intangible.[87] We are left with just the phantom of simulation, a manifestation of the hyperreal, a more real than real, within a context in which the real never did truly exist.[88] Living within this hyperreality devoid of linear time and dominated by cyclical reversal means that history is lost to us as a mythical referential.[89] The image created by Baudrillard is one in which difference reigns supreme within a reversible realm in which metaphysics is lost, economic exchange is annulled, and accumulation of wealth and power are terminated.

The description of the simulacrum by Baudrillard is not all that different from that described by Deleuze, who tends to view it as difference in itself, which means for him that it possesses no identity and merely appears by disguising itself. Instead of the Platonic opposition of appearance and essence, Deleuze substitutes the simulacra, demonic images devoid of resemblance that function by themselves.[90] The functioning of the simulacrum, a Dionysian machine, is simulation, a phantasm itself that subverts the same or representative model and renders it false. By being constructed on a difference, the simulacrum internalizes a dissimilarity, but this does not mean that it is a degraded copy because "[i]t harbors a positive power which denies the original and the copy, the model and the reproduction."[91] Such a philosophical position manifests an anti-Kantian perspective that is aconceptual and nonrepresentational. The phantom of Nietzsche appears in Deleuze's notion of the simulacrum when the postmodernist equates it with the will to power and explicitly connects it with the eternal return. The simulacrum is the will to power as simulation.[92] But it cannot be understood apart from the eternal return, an expression of chaos itself. Representing the same and the similar in a simulated form, the cyclic return functions in an eccentric way in relationship to a decentered center.[93] In place of the coherence of representation, the eternal return substitutes its own errant chaos and causes only phantasms to return. Writing on behalf of all human beings, Deleuze concludes that "we have become simulacra."[94]

Derrida is probably not as radical as Deleuze with respect to the notion of the simulacrum, which he interprets as a force that continuously dislocates, displaces, and decenters. Within the context of his notion of effacing, Derrida asserts that the simulacrum possesses a strange essence: "For imitation affirms and sharpens its essence in effacing itself. Its essence is its nonessence."[95] Thus, there is no such thing as a perfect imitation because the tiniest difference renders the imitation absolutely distinct from the original.

The overall purpose behind the discussion of simulacra among such postmodernists as Derrida, Deleuze, and Baudrillard is to undermine the Kantian conviction that metaphysics is a natural disposition of the philosophical thinker because of the very nature of reason, which possesses the ability to unify the empirical cognitions of the understanding. From the perspective of the postmodern thinkers, it is not possible for metaphysics to extend our knowledge of reality as Kant thought possible if its propositions are synthetic and a priori. By adhering to the notion of the simulacra, the postmodernists make it clear that it is impossible to cling to the Cartesian ideal of precision and certitude in thinking. Unlike Kant, the postmodernists do not think that it is possible to identity fundamental principles that are implicit in valid knowledge. Kant wanted to find invariable and unalterable truths that could not be affected by time and change. If Kant wanted to secure fixed, uniform, permanent, absolute, universal truths in his static vision of the world, the notion of simulacra depicts an ever-changing, dynamic, pulsating, chaotic world that is always in a state of flux. Within the context of simulacra, metaphysics and its concomitant representational thinking are dead. This static realm of the same and similar is replaced by the dynamics of the simulacra, which represents a radical form of difference.

The nonplace of simulacra is devoid of the possibility of a center, groundless, and fragmented. This is not something within which Eliade would find himself comfortable because he views his own life and scholarly work as a search for a meaningful center;[96] he thinks that the method of comparison possesses the ability to introduce the universal element in what one is studying,[97] and he finds a continuity between archaic forms of religion and Christianity.[98] In contrast to the more pessimistic viewpoint of many postmodernists, Eliade is also hopeful about the fate of humankind: "I have a limitless confidence in the creative power of the mind. It seems to me that man will succeed—if he wishes—in remaining free and creative, in any circumstance, cosmic or historical."[99] This represents the optimism of the Enlightenment and not the often Dionysian project of many postmodern thinkers.

Another reason why Eliade cannot accept the postmodern notion of the simulacrum is because within such a context (and it is even doubtful that I can adequately use such a term due to the characteristics of simulacra), it is connected to the systematic nature of his process of thinking (and whether he is consistent and thorough in the application of his method is another matter). Although he does not specifically discuss his mode of thinking in any detailed way that I can recall, Eliade gives one the impression that his process of thinking always presupposes a unity for each individual act of analysis. Kant refers to such an achievement of unity as the synthetic unity of apperception. For Kant, thinking unifies itself at each stage because it represents a synthetic unity of various objects of thought that cannot appear unless they are thought. Moreover, Eliade's process of reflection also makes it impossible for him to embrace the simulacrum because it functions through a form of intuition. It is presupposed by Eliade that reflection is governed by certain organizing principles that help to shape conceptual categories used to understand religious phenomena and reality and help to form one's intuitive grasp of archetypes.

Concluding Remarks

Eliade's approach to the study of religion is shaped by fundamentals of Enlightenment philosophy and its representational mode of thinking, a mode of thinking that is evident in Eliade's use of the phenomenological method, intentionality, intuition, and morphological classification and his stress on order over the chaos represented by simulacra. The phenomenological aspects of Eliade's method presuppose a metaphysical stance and a coherence theory of truth, which are diametrically opposed to the overall postmodern position. The phenomenological search for structures or essences is an impossible quest from the viewpoint of some postmodern thinkers, who also reject the notions of intentionality and rationality. Many postmodernists also reject the static nature of Eliade's morphological classification, the a priori nature of the sacred, and his attempt to establish the distinction between the sacred and profane as a first principle. The postmodern lack of certainty and meaning is anathema to Eliade. And if the simulacrum manifests the postmodern emphasis on difference, Eliade's tendency to concentrate on sameness stands in sharp contrast to that position. Moreover, the presupposed unifying nature of Eliade's mode of thinking and the organizing principle of reflection are rejected by many postmodernists. In short, Eliade's embrace and use of a representational mode of thinking makes it impossible for him to be called a precursor to postmodernism or an actual postmodern figure.

7

Responding to the Postmodern Challenge

POSTMODERN THOUGHT CALLS into question prior methods used to study religion and its various aspects such as ritual action, devotional practices, myth, symbols, and texts. Many of these methods began as professional trends, reached a level of popularity, and eventually lost their novelty, although some approaches endured by changing and becoming institutionalized within subfields of religious studies. As the previous chapters make clear, postmodern thought challenged accepted concepts of religion; raised intriguing questions about issues such as eroticism, sacrifice, the gift, and myth; and subverted ways of understanding religion such as history, hermeneutics, and comparison. This chapter proposes to review these various challenges, to determine what is at stake when a scholar adopts a postmodern thinker's method, and to review one of the contested concepts, the possibility of a science of religion, and the notion of world religions previously used by scholars in the field of religious studies. Whether they are transformed by postmodern thought or not, I end by suggesting that all methods and concepts should be able to pass a pragmatic test. When a method or concept fails the test it should be discarded or revised until it passes the test.

Contested Concepts and Methods

Throughout this book, I have called attention to ways in which postmodern thinkers question, subvert, and reject traditionally acceptable concepts and methods in the study of religion. Methodological tools such as history, hermeneutics, and comparison have been questioned by postmodern thinkers because these approaches to religion are remnants of Enlightenment thinking, whereas postmodernists attempt to break out of the representational mode of thinking that is characteristic of Enlightenment thought.

The previous chapters have also focused on the postmodern transformation of certain concepts such as eroticism, sacrifice, and the gift. Since a conclusion is an appropriate time to recall previous discussions, it seems useful to critically reassess the postmodern positions on these methods and a specific concept in a summary fashion by concentrating on the methodological implications of the postmodern positions.

Chapter 3 involves a discussion of the possibility of a pure gift defined without exchange, return, or essence by Derrida and its excessive nature by Bataille, with both thinkers pushing the concept to its limit. If Mauss wants to strip the irrational from the gift and emphasize its harmonious reciprocity, Bataille stresses its excessive and disruptive nature in a way that attempts to undermine Mauss's theory. Rather than seeing it as a homogenous pattern of exchange, Bataille views the gift as a heterogeneous and irrational phenomenon. In order to support his conception of the gift, Bataille is selective in the sense that he uses the potlatch to prove his case, ignores other examples, and links his notion of the gift with eroticism.

By placing the gift within the flow of time, Derrida indicates that the gift is impossible because of the predominance of time, and because it lacks presence and cannot be intuitively identified. When using the three contradictions of the gift—donor, gift, and donee—Derrida attempts to demonstrate the impossibility of the gift because the identified elements of the gift produce annulment, annihilation, and destruction. Prior to any relationship to an object or multiple subjects, there is the event of the gift, a heterogeneous aspect that precedes any relationship between donor and donee. The gift is made possible by the khora, a location of no desire and the non-gift, and is destroyed by time, a holocaust. But the pure gift represents a giving without calculation or measure while the difference in the gift is marked by castration, creating an incompatibility between the gift and its exchange.

If Bataille renders the gift excessive, Derrida takes the event of the gift to the limit of thought while stressing the discontinuity of time in order to break free from the static view of Mauss. As a consequence, the gift for these postmodern thinkers is not a universal or timeless category. The empirical and rational nature of Mauss's thinking that presupposes unity is an excellent example of representational thinking that assures the thinker about his or her own presence. In contrast, Bataille and Derrida manifest an antifoundational position that is radically skeptical of any theory and distrusts any universal claims of reason. By disparaging reason, the postmodernists move in a dangerous direction that takes them toward an embrace of the irrational, leaving a scholar with mere rhetorical opinions.

The entire collection of postmodern thinkers who are covered in this book follow the lead of Bataille by devising some type of heterological approach. The method of heterology is excessive and transgresssive for Bataille because it is associated with violence, surpassing norms, and wastefulness, and its heterological object is the other, which cannot become an object of knowledge because it calls into question the identity of the subject.

In addition to deconstruction that preys on texts, the genealogy of Foucault is attractive to some scholars. Foucault's use of genealogy is intended to unmask what is a hidden, secret, neglected, or forgotten aspect of history. The result of this heterological method is a focus on discontinuity, differentiations, dispersions, mutations, and gaps of history. Because history is embedded in a web of power relations and genealogy, it is impossible to conduct accurate historical analysis, although the analysis of history can help one to grasp the interconnections of power. According to Foucualt, all historical data is a result of interpretation that lacks a foundation and merely represents a sign of another sign. Moreover, if all knowledge is relative, this suggests that history cannot make any truth claims. In conclusion, history becomes fiction, and Foucualt becomes an antihistorical historian, writing history in order to destroy it.[1]

Foucualt rejects the comparative method, typological method, causal explanation, and any explanation that appeals to the zeitgeist of an era. In following such a methodological path, what is his purpose? Hayden White explains, "By denying all of the conventional categories of historical description and explanation, Foucault hopes to find the 'threshold' of historical consciousness itself."[2] By attempting to achieve this goal, Foucault offers something that is the antithesis of the diachronic representation by celebrating disorder, fragmentation, and destruction.

If the method of genealogy exposes the fictive nature of history, this enables a borrower of this method such as Said to expose the evils of Orientalism. But by exposing a deeply flawed, derogatory, and illusory politically violent creation of the West, Said wraps himself and members of the Orient into a protective cocoon of victimhood. And if the genealogical method is intended to break away from the representational mode of thinking inherited from the Enlightenment, it fails when used by Foucault and Said because the former uses it for politically revolutionary purposes while the latter creates an inaccurate caricature of Western scholars and writers, which means that neither of them frees himself from the representational way of thinking. It is just that the representations fit their political agendas, which is easy to accomplish when one is writing fictive history. Another problem with genealogy is its danger of conflating the origin of a term or concept with its applicability. If this becomes the case, the genealogist commits the genetic fallacy.[3]

Said's conception of Orientalism helps to prove Martin Heidegger's argument that there is no presuppositionless philosophy because Said's fundamental presupposition is that there has not been any neutral, unbiased, objective scholarship on the subject of the Orient. Thus Western cultural prejudices, racism, and ethnocentrism have resulted in views of the non-Western world that are distortions, misconceptions, misunderstandings, and inaccurate stereotypes that have no existence in reality. The resulting books from such flawed scholarship allegedly function to serve political purposes that support the work of colonial hegemony. A reasonable question is the following: Is this genealogical scenario truth or fiction?

In contrast to genealogy, Derrida's deconstruction is a bit different because it exposes logocentrism, another term for metaphysics, and deconstructs it. From the perspective of altarity, Derrida uses a text against itself by revealing its inner contradictions. In the end, there is no place for the scholar to stand or be supported. The scholar is left alone to wander errantly and to return to repetitively deconstruct texts in a parasitic fashion.

From the perspective of postmodern thinkers, the history of religions is an impossible approach to its intended subject matter. Besides seeing a metaphysics embodied within history, a thinker such as Foucault envisions his own work as revolutionary and an attempt to make history, whereas someone such as Eliade thinks that history is made by selectively few people. If Eliade sees a depth to history, Deleuze and Guattari stress surface and immanence. Since it is impossible to achieve a total picture of history for Foucault because there is no body of facts or untainted material, history is merely a series of interpretations. Foucault envisions the historian standing in a web of power relations without an opportunity to stand outside of this web from which to conduct objective and unbiased analysis. If history is characterized by temporal ruptures, factual gaps, discontinuity, multiple layers of events, and a series of narrative reinterpretations, it is only possible to compose fiction, rendering descriptive history useless.

Devoid of a metaphysical foundation, absolutes, objectivity, constants, truth claims, and subverted by the relativity of all knowledge, history is lost and cannot be recaptured, and is not an adequate method for the study of religion or any other subject.

Postmodern methods, such as genealogy, deconstruction, and Deleuze's schizoanalysis, a dismantling or destruction that is associated with the liberation of desire, emphasize difference and altarity. Every one of these heterological methods possesses implications for scholars of religion because they reject presence and any scientific mode of measurement, which can only be applied to homogenous elements. Therefore, it is impossible for a systematic and all-encompassing method to exist. In order words, there can be no grand narratives such as the theory of evolution and no universal or timeless truths.

Postmodern thought stresses flux, contingency, relativity, chance, and difference. This means that human life is not rationally ordered and devoid of autonomous reason. As a consequence of the postmodern attitude toward reason, a scholar of religion must reject modes of classification and imitation of models of any kind because they are products of representational thinking that presupposes a correspondence between appearance and reality and is supported by a metaphysical edifice. From the postmodern perspective, the sacred cannot be an a priori category of the mind. Lyotard is, however, a postmodern thinker who wants to save reason from being transformed into a commodity, and to help it regain its practical use and become more sensitive to differences, whereas other postmodernists want to use reason as a political force or to completely undermine it with desire (an antirational force), as with Deleuze and Guattari.

The postmodern stress on difference undermines hermeneutics and the comparative method. If scholars of religion such as Eliade, Smith, and Doniger think that it is possible to find meaning in religious phenomena and actions within a world that is meaningful, real, valuable, and truthful, postmodernists tend to see the exact opposite. If representative scholars such as Eliade, Smith, and Doniger are convinced that an interpreter can discover meaning, even though it is a risky endeavor, postmodern thinkers such as Foucault view meaning as contextual, which renders it relative because of its entanglement in a formative context that is radically relational. For a thinker such as Foucault, meaning resides in the interconnections between things and events. Thus meaning is liminal in nature and continually appears and disappears, resulting in the total relativity of meaning. This suggests that a scholar of religion can say nothing definitive by means of the practice of interpretation or comparison, if we accept the postmodern position. At the same time, when a thinker begins with a heterological method the result is likely to be heterogeneous, irrational, and excessive. Doniger is right to insist that difference and sameness should be held in a dialectical tension instead of emphasizing that everything is difference. If everything is difference, such a position represents a new kind of universalism that is contrary to the spirit of postmodern thought.

Standing opposed to representational thinking and reason and calling all opposites into question, there is the postmodern simulacrum, a manifestation of the hyperreal, which is devoid of linear temporality and is dominated by cyclical reversal, rendering both the real and illusion impossible. Denying the validity of any model, copy, or reproduction, the simulacrum manifests a realm of difference for Baudrillard, whereas it is difference itself or the will to power for Deleuze.

The Promise of Postmodernism

In general, postmodern thought calls into question the entire enterprise of religious studies by undermining its methods and subverting its categories. Does this mean that religious studies is dead? Or is it simply on life support with its death a future possibility? Or are there inherent problems in the postmodern approach? Certainly, religious studies possesses its problems, but this is also true of postmodern thinking. The different types of understanding common to religious studies and postmodernism are akin to a *pharmakon*, a notion used by Derrida to suggest both a poison and a medicine that possesses the ability to destroy, to cure, to confuse, or to help us understand.

The choice by scholars of religious studies to adopt postmodern heterological approaches to the study of religion is fraught with danger. There are scholars in various areas of religious studies who have used postmodern thought selectively with good results, whereas someone such as Mark C. Taylor clones himself to Derrida when devising his "a/theology."[4] There are several other scholars who have raised the possibility of using postmodern thought to critique religious studies, such as McCutcheon, Jeffrey Kripal, the Buddhalogist James Taylor, and Tim Murphy, whose attraction to postmodernism is worth pausing to examine.

Even though postmodernism can be categorized as a recent academic tendency like so many others that have come, disappeared, endured, or been revived from previously forgotten or neglected methods, McCutcheon thinks that it can be used as a metacritique that can help scholars chart a course of study that takes them clear of any entanglement with metaphysics. McCutcheon thinks that it is important not to let theologians, who are among his favorite straw persons appropriate for critical whipping on occasion, to establish the agenda for a postmodern critique of the study of religion. From McCutcheon's perspective, postmodern theorists acknowledge the following useful guidelines: theoretical models are only advisable as tests that can withstand critical scrutiny over a period of time; predictions become an issue of probability; if theories are constructed ad hoc, the resulting models can never match reality; there are no final grand theories.[5]

On the surface, these guidelines seem reasonable enough to be used as a metacritique for the study of religion, but they embody some dangers and problems. The need to avoid metaphysics is overstressed by postmodernists as if the entire Western intellectual edifice would crumble if it is not avoided. Many postmodern thinkers are not seeking new models because they function to entangle and entrap the individual. If postmodernists think that everything is in a state of constant flux, how is it possible to make predictions that are probable? Theories may or may not be constructed in an ad hoc fashion, but scholars tend to create theories based on some type of presuppositions and evidence often assuming that valid knowledge and meaning can be achieved by their efforts. It is doubtful that many scholars would claim that their developed models exactly reflect reality because constructed models are more often intended to assist understanding and broaden our knowledge. I would, however, agree with McCutcheon that there are no longer any grand theories because essences cannot be discovered and historical evidence is either fragmentary or nonexistent, although this observation will not stop some from trying to develop an all-encompassing theory. If from the postmodern perspective everything is difference or simulation, is this not a different type of grand narrative?

But the danger for the metacritic is that the critic's own position is called into question because he or she possesses no foundation on which to critique anything. By adopting any of the heterological methods of postmodernists that are intended to subvert, undermine, or destroy other positions, metacritics subvert themselves as they undermine a theory about religion because ultimately everything is relative, including the metacritic's position. In the finally analysis, there are no secure philosophical positions from which to argue or critique another stance. Thus the best position is not to have any position in order to revel in the realm of the simulacrum. From within the simulacrum, the metacritic is absolutely free to critique all simulations of scholarship, but it is a meaningless exercise because the simulacrum is a realm of frivolity, merriment, and dizziness with pure play. Within this realm of play and carnival, it is possible to say and do anything without consequence because what you say does not mean anything. An important consequence is that no one, of course, needs to listen to your critical comments, take them seriously, or expect that you can solve any problems especially of an ethical nature. By adopting any of the heterological approaches, one is forced to admit that no constructed system or insightful observation provides certainty, stability, or security within a world of constant flux that is tenuously held together by a phalanx of multiple truths that often contradict each other but never rise to the level of a grand narrative.

In comparison to McCutcheon, Jeffrey Kripal is another scholar availing himself of postmodern thought by referring to himself as an unconverted postmodernist, a self- characterization that he uses because he admits to reservations concerning the death of the subject and the tendency toward relativism in postmodern thought. With the Western postmodern turn in thinking as a context, Kripal witnesses a potential for a genuine mystical or gnostic renewal, while his position is also modern in the sense that his comparative method intends to include both sameness and difference in a cross-cultural and historical manner.[6] Kripal views postmodernism not as a rejection of modernity but rather as an awakening and radicalization of knowing. Moreover, Kripal does not want to reject the reductive method and social-scientific scholarship, although he does want to combine Valentinian gnosis and the theosophical system of Jacob Boehme. This might suggest to some an esoteric approach to the study of religion. His genuine model is the postmodern gnostic intellectual, a person who privileges knowledge over belief, a knowledge that is beyond reason, and who is aware of the limits of this knowledge that cannot be reconciled with the historical claims of various religious traditions.

Kripal's position on reason is not contrary to it or antirational in spirit, but is recognition that reason cannot adequately grasp antirational experiences common, for example, to mystics. Thus it makes sense to Kripal to rely on the erotic body as a potential source of wisdom, an approach to the study of religion that eliminates attempting to explain it.[7] Kripal refers to his gnosis as a triple edged sword "implying at once a privileging of knowing over believing, an affirmation of altered states of consciousness and psychic functioning as valuable and legitimate modes of cognition, and a critical—but engaged—encounter with the faith traditions themselves."[8] Kripal's gnosis stands against orthodox traditions and exalts the individual over the collective with the intention of sparking a debate and dialogue about experiential issues.

Kripal's ambitious agenda is threatened by the very postmodern turn that he selectively embraces. Religious traditions that have endured over a long course of time become embedded in centuries of their own heritage. Postmodernists do not think that scholars can recover anything but elusive traces and fragments, which is not what Kripal intends to engage in a dialogue. Moreover, if one proposes to have a dialogue, where would one stand to find a secure location in which to engage the other in conversation, because everything is in a constant state of flux and all knowledge is relative from a postmodern perspective? Kripal's imaginative hissing, gnostic serpent would not be able to hiss loud enough to be heard by the cacophony of postmodern voices laughing and cavorting in the simulacrum. The radical skepticism of postmodern thought can only lead to further ambivalence, insecurity, and possibly nihilism. Postmodern thought is intended to subvert all types of subjective or objective gnosis, which makes it more of a poisonous pharmakon than a medicine that cures.

In comparison to Kripal, James Taylor demonstrates a different and more dangerous type of adoption of postmodern thought in his book on Buddhism in modern Thailand, in which he uses postmodern notions to interpret his subject.[9] Taylor paints a picture of a Buddhist society held captive by secularization and disenchanted by modernity. Thais also feel more insecure and dislocated because of globalization within a social context that intensifies personal insecurity because of political and economic instability. With increasing fragmentation and polarization within the Thai metropolis, people are not able to find refuge in their religious tradition, with Buddhism becoming more marginal to the lives of people or with people assuming a more private sphere of practice. Moreover, this bleak situation manifests a tension between rural locations (an outside area that is wild and dangerous) and city (an inside location that is urban and civilized) with urban residents becoming nostalgic for the former way of life.

Focusing his study of Thai society on the human body, location, and space, Taylor relies on the philosophy of Deleuze and Guattari to interpret the nomadic lives of forest monks as rhizomatic because this lifestyle ignores boundaries, hierarchical structures, established spaces, and pre-existing tracks. In his interpretation of contemporary Thailand extensively using postmodern thinkers, Taylor risks losing his reader in the post-modern jargon, and is guilty of imposing foreign Western notions on an Eastern culture. I think it is fair to ask: Would Thai readers recognize their own culture through the postmodern notions used by Taylor? It is highly doubtful that Thais would recognize themselves in this book, and might even become nomadic readers lost in postmodern jargon and discourse. If postmodernism is contextualized as a French intellectual movement with roots in art and architectural changes and political demonstrations of the later 1960s, it seems difficult to apply its methods and notions to an Eastern culture such as Thailand because the postmodern historical context is very distinct from those living in that southeast Asian country.

According to Tim Murphy, religious studies finds itself within a crisis of representation because the conception of religion has become reified, resulting in an identifiable essence, depicted as universal, and conceived as sui generis. This crisis of representation is an identity crisis for religious studies because its historicity is not recognized, and it is divorced from its discursive production. Murphy wants to remedy this situation, while acknowledging that solving the problem is difficult because "the discourses on 'religion' are many and are ensnarled in other discourses, each leading off in several directions at once."[10] Murphy thinks that there is a need for him to call into question the presuppositions, methods, categories, and norms of various disciplines because each of them has been guilty of establishing truth in situations where there are merely cultural fictions. If these different disciplines do not represent the truth or a quest for it, what do they represent? Murphy's answer is Eurocentrism, a project substituting nature for history, distorting the world, fostering heinous politics, corrupting knowledge, and constructing and imposing identity on the other.[11] In order to counter Eurocentrism and the crisis of representation, Murphy calls for a postmodern, poststructualist, and posthumanist reformulation of the science of religion.

Following the spirit of postmodern discourse, Murphy calls into question the viability of terms that imply a substantial identity, especially cross-culturally, categories promising mimetic equation to objects within the world, and representations grounded in mentalistic language because there is no secure foundation from which to refer to experience, intentions, ideas, or worldviews. Murphy optimistically argues that we can be more precise with our research.

This precision can be attained by turning to a semiotic theory of religion. Embracing Roland Barthes as his methodological hero, Murphy proposes to develop a semiotic theory of religion by combining the theory of Barthes with Jonathan Z. Smith's concept of the canon-hermeneute relationship, the structuralist concept of paradigm and syntagm, and Mikhail Bakhtin's concept of the structural addressivity of signification. Murphy envisions semiotics as analyzing the complete process of signification based on the axiom that there are only differences in language, an example of postmodern dogma about the primary importance of difference. Even though the use of the insights of Smith and Bakhtin hold promise for interpreting religion, Murphy adopts many of the shortcomings of postmodern baggage that I have previously reviewed.

Without intending to be repetitious, I should point out that the postmodern position on language emphasizes the instability of signs, which implies that a sign refers to other signs and not to nonlinguistic realities. This does not mean that "communication is impossible but that it is always incomplete, continually in flux."[12] There is neither enduring certainty nor meaning that can be discovered by a scholar because it is impossible to find that sign that refers only to itself and to no additional sign, or transcendental signified. By embracing this type of sign theory, Murphy will be a busy scholar because he is condemned to endless interpretation without any hope of achieving closure. It would also be interesting to learn from Murphy how his approach would work in a primarily oral culture.

Do these comments and others mean that postmodern thought is without value for the study of religion? Selective adoption of postmodern insights can prove useful, although a wholesale embrace of any of the heterological methods and perspectives should raise a cautionary flag, as is evident in the use of genealogy by Said, discussed in chapter 4, unless a scholar is comfortable writing fiction. Before jumping on the postmodern bandwagon, I think that a scholar should self-administer the following pragmatic test: Does the approach that I adopt enhance the understanding of the subject of religion or any other subject for me or my potential reader? If it can pass this pragmatic test, I argue that it can be used profitably but with caution because of all the baggage that accompanies postmodern thinking and its upside down metaphysical position that everything is difference.

The pragmatic test intended to be used as a guideline is grounded in ordinary experience, which is ever-present, regular, unified, comprehensive, spatiotemporal, and corporeal. Human beings are already immersed in ordinary experience, making actions of intending and attending possible, although it tends to be neglected by humans.[13] This ever-flowing continuity of experience in which we find ourselves is something to which we can appeal without even acknowledging it because it is what usually occurs. Therefore, it is something that we do not have to think about, and it provides comfort and security because we can count on it.[14] Ordinary experience manifests the complexity and richness of human existence, and does not represent an artificial construction of philosophical or scientific modes of thinking. It is ordinal because "it regulates the transformative disruptions because it continues to function as their matrix and womb."[15]

Ordinary experience is associated with common sense, of which the above appeal for a pragmatic test is an example. Within the context of everyday life, common sense decides what is most plausible in terms of actions or thoughts and thus what interpretations, for example, are most probable. Common sense operates this way not as a constructed body of doctrine, but as an ability to solve problems based on what we currently know that works successfully because it is grounded in prior experience also associated with common sense. Stanley Rosen clarifies the context of ordinary experience and common sense as a medium: "Ordinary experience is then not the solution any more than it is the problem: it is the medium within which problems and solutions arise, but it is also the standard against which we determine the plausibility of the interpretations put forward."[16] It is possible to see that common sense lacks a structure, but it does function as the horizon or cognitive context for every conceptual determination. In comparison to the extreme nature of postmodernism, common sense reaches judgments on the basis of local circumstances and protects us against thinking that is excessive or eccentric. This does not mean that common sense and ordinary experiences are connected with something static because "ordinary experience is saturated with the extraordinary."[17]

Being situated in ordinary experience and using commonsense judgments, a scholar of religion can exercise reflexivity, an ability to become aware of the contexts of what one is researching and the types of presuppositions that govern that research. It is reflexivity that enables one to understand the limits of method by means of creating critical distance from what one is studying and the creation of theories based on one's research, and becoming aware of the biases and presuppositions of a researcher's methodological approach. This pattern of scholarship renders the approach an object of critical inquiry and study. This type of scholarly approach is reminiscent of some features of the work of Pierre Bourdieu.

According to Bourdieu, there are three modes of theoretical knowledge for understanding the social world: phenomenological, objectivist, and dialectical. The experience of the social world and location of daily trans-actions and data are revealed by the first mode of knowledge, whereas the objectivist mode, possessing a self-evident nature, constructs objective relations (e.g., linguistic and economic), which affects scholarly practice. The objectivist mode shows us a rift between the experiences of the insider and the outsider's accounts of the insider's world of experience. The final mode of knowledge, dialectical, reveals relations between what one gains access to and the exposed dispositions, which creates a dialectical relation between the exposed dispositions, objective structures, and method employed by the researcher.[18] This involves stepping back from the object of study and the act of objectification itself, and calling into question hidden presuppositions of the researcher. In order to understand the intentionality of one's method one must grasp this process as dialogical, creating a dialogue between one's method and its object and extending such a dialogue to include methods used by the scholar. Bourdieu thus advocates a critical intersubjectivity and a dialogical reflexivity that repre-sents recognition of agency, which is not only constrained by context but can also influence context. This scenario has important consequences for the agent: "Each agent, wittingly or unwittingly, willy nilly, is a producer and reproducer of objective meaning."[19] Finally, reflexivity represents criti-cism of both the method and its object.

What Rosen calls ordinary knowledge is similar to what Bourdieu refers to as *habitus*, which he defines as "systems of durable, transposable dispositions, structures predisposed to function as structuring structures, that is, as principles of the generation and structuring of practices and representations which can be objectively 'regulated' and 'regular' without in any way being the product of obedience to rules, objectively adapted to their goals without presupposing a conscious aiming at ends or an express mastery of the operations necessary to attain them and, being all this, col-lectively orchestrated without being the product of the orchestrating action of a conductor."[20] Humans become socialized or conditioned by means of habitus that predisposes them to behave in certain ways, but they still remain free agents who can determine their own practice by virtue of practical, prereflective, and almost instinctual choices in accord with the process of conditioning. As a product of history, habitus conditions the future with its acts in the present and becomes internalized in the unconscious, making humans forget that habitus is a product of history. Habitus is not merely connected to time, change, and language but is also intimately associated with the body, working to generate commonsense and reasonable behavior.[21]

This type of reflexivity calls into question features of postmodern thought. From this commonsensible and reflexive perspective, it is possible to acknowledge that postmodern thought runs the danger of becoming a caricature of the simulation of an anti-Enlightenment way of thinking. From a more positive perspective, postmodernism can help us to recognize that old academic tendencies, such as the pursuit of the possibility of a science of religion and the evolution of the designation "world religions," have outgrowth their usefulness.

The Possibility of a Science of Religion

As part of its Enlightenment legacy, scholars of religious studies have long desired to develop a science of religion. Surely, no one boldly claims that one should study religion in a nonscientific manner. Why? From out of its Enlightenment context, the scientific method is the paradigm for truth and certainty and to have one's work accepted as serious, rigorous, and valid research a scholar's results must conform to the scientific model. There is even a scholarly chorus calling for the falsification of research results in order for one's findings to be declared valid. Sociology, psychology, and phenomenology are historical examples of efforts to establish a scientific method for the study of religion. The latest candidate holding promise as a truly scientific method for the study of religion is cognitive science, and many scholars have jumped on the cognitive bandwagon, a development that also embraces the more than century long search for the origins of religion and reflects the influence of evolutionary theory. The perpetuation of science and its method as the necessary paradigm for valid work by scholars of religious studies and other fields needs to be challenged as postmodernists fundamentally do because science is theoretically grounded in a representational mode of thinking from which postmodernists are attempting to escape. Before reviewing the postmodern challenge to science, a Western inheritance from the Enlightenment period, it might be wise to briefly examine what Western philosophers of science have to say about the subject.

Inductive reasoning, empirical testing, verification, and value-free research are all notions associated with the positivist model of science. According to some philosophers of science, this model of the discipline is a fallacy because of its own methodological problems, lack of authority, and a false impression created about its nature. In short, science is a false idol and people outside the discipline have been sold a false bill of goods. It is possible to witness this conclusion by briefly reviewing scientific testing and verification, its alleged value-free and objective nature, its selectivity and authoritative aspects, and the role of imagination and intuition native to science.

On the topics of scientific testing and verification, Karl R. Popper, the late British philosopher of science, writes that scientific theories can be tested by experience, but are not necessarily verifiable or justifiable.[22] By excluding metaphysics and anything related to alternative experience, one can test a particular scientific theory by means of what Popper calls "demarcation," which means falsifiability for him. The method of falsifiability operates by rejecting untenable theories and finding the fittest system "by exposing them all to the fiercest struggle for survival."[23] In other words, if a hypothesis or conclusion can be falsified, this means that the validity of the theory is called into question, assuming that one accepts the contradictory evidence that supports a contending view. What occurs in a case when any part of a theory cannot be falsified? Such a case provides a temporary respite for a theory because it is always possible for it to be found falsifiable and inadequate in the future. If all scientific claims can be tested by falsification and rejected when necessary, there can be no ultimate statements made in science.[24] In a process called "corroboration" by Popper, scientific theories can be provisionally accepted as long as they survive the process of falsification.[25] As a continual process of tests, trials, and fitness of survival, Popper establishes the following guideline: The degree of corroboration is greater to the extent that the hypothesis is falsifiable. Therefore, no scientific theory is ultimate and certain; its validity is merely provisional until it is successfully falsified and discarded.

Science is not as value free and as objective as alleged by a positivistic model of the discipline. Thomas S. Kuhn confirms this assertion when he shows that scientists accept given paradigms and reject others. Scientific paradigms unite theory, methods, and standards into a whole that provides scientists with a map and directions for further progress.[26] What Kuhn means is that paradigms represent beliefs, values, and techniques shared by a community of like-minded individuals.[27] The difficult choices that a particular scientist makes to solve a problem are tied to a given paradigm, which may manifest what Michael Polanyi calls "scientific passions" that function logically and are not merely something psychological. Polanyi is calling attention to something positive, exciting, precious, and intellectual.[28] These passions assist the scientist by determining what deserves greater attention. If science is not value free, it is also not objective. It is self-delusional to think that natural science is objective when personal judgments and guesswork play a role in science.[29] As does Polanyi, Popper alludes to scientific guesswork as subjective belief, meaning what appears to be promising.[30]

Philosophers of science also call into question the selectivity and authoritative nature of science because scientists are selective with their sources and even ignore evidence that is incompatible with their accepted theories. Polanyi asserts that scientists hope that contradictory evidence eventually proves to be false and irrelevant.[31] There are times when a problem is unsolvable and thus its solution is set aside until further evidence, new ideas, or procedures are able to assist with its resolution.[32] Anticipations, conjectures, and professional interests affect the alleged empirical method of a scientist and force him or her to be selective.[33] Since science represents a vast body of knowledge, which is impossible for one person to master the whole of, scientists must rely on the expertise of others, acknowledge the limited and fragmentary nature of their own knowledge, and recognize the impossibility of validating all results for themselves by accepting secondhand knowledge.

Imagination and intuition are not foreign to science, according to Popper and Kuhn, because they play a role in the discipline, even though they are unreliable and can mislead a researcher.[34] From Kuhn's perspective, scientists use imagination and intuition to provide sudden moments of insight and creativity that can lead to breakthroughs in knowledge and the formation of new paradigms, assuming that one gains an advantage by building on previous experience garnered from a past paradigm.[35] Any new intuitions become communal because they are tested by other scientists, transforming the intuitions into nonindividual and shared possessions. Because flights of imagination and flashes of intuition can be analyzed by a wider community of like-minded persons, this means that they are not simply rejected because they are not empirical.

Whether or not a reader accepts the insights of these philosophers of science or the radical skepticism of postmodern thinkers, the old and dated scientific ideal about achieving absolutely certain and demonstrable knowledge is a false idol, according to Popper, because knowledge gained by scientific means cannot claim the achievement of truth or even probability, a possible substitute for truth.[36] For Popper, it is possible to have something approaching absolute certainty only within our subjective faith. This does not mean that science should not strive for truth and knowledge in addition to adequate explanations or solutions to intractable problems. To expect final answers to problems is illusory, although advances, improvements, and new discoveries are always possible for the scientist. It is impossible to ascertain the final completion of science because additional change is always possible. Therefore, the body of scientific knowledge is an ideal construction, Nicolas Rescher argues, that needs a situational realism that acknowledges two fundamental things: any natural science is contextual and tied to the cognitive situation of its producers, and it can be successfully applied in practice and be theoretically informative.[37]

Assuming for the sake of argument that these philosophers are correct about how science actually operates, the possibility of developing a science of religion is a fool's errand, with the latest approach to hit religious studies—cognitive science—most probably being unable to meet the high hopes of its early promise, especially when one considers that the inherited Enlightenment ideal of science possesses no equivalency to the way that it is actually practiced in the laboratory. To randomly select someone from the area of cognitive science who is an advocate of a science of religion, Benson Saler is a good example because he clearly expresses four items that have been proposed by others as necessary for a science of religion: liberation of the study of religion from theology at secular universities, adoption of empirical methods used by scientists and philosophers of science, explanation of religious phenomena rather than just interpretation of them, and insistence that the scientific study of religion become a social science. Benson finds each of these features inadequate in religious studies because the social science model is defective, failing to connect findings in the social sciences with results from the natural sciences such as biology and cognitive sciences. Because of the problematic nature of a social science, Saler proposes his version of a science of religion: it must have clarity about the human subjects of its research instead of religions and cultures; it should focus on the essential questions pertaining to the meaning of religion, its organization, means of transmission, to what extent religions resemble each other, how they differ from one another, and the reasons for acceptance or rejection by some people; it should be associated explicitly with the cognitive and evolutionary sciences.[38] Benson and others advocating cognitive science think that by adopting religion within the context of the process of evolutionary brain development and genetic modifications, human beings have enhanced their chances for survival, and thus this development has been shaped by the choices of human beings. The choice of religion, in other words, gives individuals and social groups adaptive advantages as they struggle to survive in a hostile world. By understanding the development of the human brain, one can comprehend the nature of religion in a scientific way.

From one perspective, the science of religion is an attempt to construct a system of thought that can provide a secure foundation, stability, and certainty. Postmodern thinkers call into question these kinds of constructed mental edifices because they are convinced that all foundations and structures are instable and incomplete. The promise of neuroscience is as temporary as any made within the flux of temporality. From the standpoint of one postmodern thinker, the use of results from cognitive science to understand religion is merely the latest version of essentialism.[39] Postmodernists also insist that there is no science without assumptions, which implies that it is another philosophical narrative lacking a privileged status relative to other narratives. In fact, George Lakoff and Mark Johnson make clear that there is no science capable of being free of philosophical assumptions that determine the outcome of research. Lakoff and Johnson write, "Science is a social, cultural, and historical practice, knowledge is always situated, and what counts as knowledge may depend on matters of power and influence."[40] This position excludes the possibility that science is neutral, progresses linearly, can be trusted in all instances, and is the ultimate way to understand things. In contrast to postmodernists, Lakoff and Johnson assert that many scientific results are stable and withstand the test of time, although this is not true of all scientific findings.

If the possibility of a science of religion is problematic even with cognitive science serving as its latest model, why do religious studies scholars continue to call for the development of a science of religion or a rigorous social science approach to the study of religion? From almost its infancy, the academic discipline of religious studies manifests a search for a science of religion and an exploration for its origins—two interlinked quests—that represent nostalgic wishes by those within the discipline. The old German distinction between *Naturwissenschaft* and *Geisteswissenschaft* is helpful because religious studies is a humanistic discipline that fits into the latter form of science, even though this distinction never stops some scholars from using the former type of science, a natural science, as its paradigm. In fact, both forms of science have shortcomings, and they never truly achieve the level of an ideal science because such an achievement is impossible within an ever-changing temporal world inhabited by erring, finite, fallible, and delusional human beings. Pointing to fundamental problems associated with adopting models from the natural sciences, Gavin Flood argues, "General rules of inference or deduction cannot easily be applied to human behaviour that involves meanings and intentions."[41]

As mentioned previously, postmodern thinkers reinforce the attitudes expressed by the selected philosophers of science discussed. The emphasis on difference and an insistence that sameness is impossible subverts the empirical inductive method of science. The relativity of all knowledge, a lack of truth, and death of the subject are notions that inevitably lead to a radical skepticism that renders any method superfluous and any scientific researcher without hope because the representational mode of thinking common in scientific research is subverted. Various postmodern heterological methods call into question any constructed system of thought, including the scientific. Along with these philosophers of science, postmodern thought indicates the tenuous nature of any science of religion, which is more akin to a subjective mental projection of a wish that one hopes to be true.

The Problematic Nature of "World Religions"

The so-called world religions course is an educational staple of many college and university campuses, serving often as an introduction to the study of religion. Including surveys of numerous religions from the East and West, these courses tend to be rather superficial treatments of the covered religions. It would not be a bad idea for such courses to peacefully die within the field of religious studies because they embody questionable pedagogical usefulness and can be replaced with courses that go into depth on a single tradition, which would be complex enough by itself. Over the decades in higher education, world religions courses have attracted large numbers of students that in turn justify the need for a larger number of department members and mathematically compensate for lower enrollments in upper division courses. Moreover, the heavily enrolled world religions courses at universities with graduate programs often use graduate students to teach these courses because of the readily available supply of cheap labor necessary to keep higher education costs under control. Because such a scenario benefits departments and graduate students, the chances for a sudden change of curriculum is not great, even given the problematic nature of studying world religions.

Jonathan Z. Smith and Gavin Flood also find "world religions" a problematic designation for different reasons. According to Smith, the concept of world religions represents a creation of a basic dichotomy between "ours" and "theirs," or "true" and "false."[42] When looking at other religions we tend to see those like ours, but indigenous, tribal religious traditions are not like ours, and they tend to become invisible. Although the designation "world religion" recognizes the importance of history and geography with respect to religion, Flood agrees with Smith that it is abstracted from a wider cultural narrative, and discourse about religion cannot be divorced from discourse pertaining to culture, society, and politics. Flood asserts, "Religions take place within narratives that are constructed from particular perspectives, from particular positions of power, which a critical religious studies can decode."[43] In the final analysis, the study of religion needs to be aware of difference and the many layers of meaning embodied within a particular culture.

In addition to Smith's and Flood's arguments and the problematic possibility of a science of religion, postmodern thought can also help us to recognize the problematic nature of the concept of world religions. Tomoko Masuzawa provides one example with her appropriation of the postmodern insights of Deleuze and Guattari with respect to rhizomatics and its reliance on the metaphor of the root in contrast to a tree. Like a root, the rhizomatic approach is a hidden unity without a central axis, an order, a single point of origin, or linear direction of growth. Rhizomatics stresses difference, exteriority, decenteredness, and change in sharp contrast to any ordered system.

By adopting the rhizomatic approach, Masuzawa sets forth to seek the origins of the concept of world religions and to simultaneously subvert it. She argues that the notion of world religions demonstrates an underground growth before it emerges in a number of places within public discourse in Europe without a single identifiable source, but it does manifest a Eurocentric bias and a Eurohegemonic conception of the world. Beneath the apparent acknowledgment of other religions by the notion of world religions, this approach to the study of religion hides both a Christian and European universalism because both intertwined perspectives become the standard by which other religions are judged and deemed worthy of inclusion among other world religions.[44] Because of its religious, cultural, and political implications, which Masuzawa helps us to witness, the notion of world religions is no longer pedagogically useful for religious studies, and represents a remnant from the nineteenth century and early twentieth century that has endured well past its usefulness. Therefore, it should be retired to a museum sponsored and supported by the American Academy of Religion. Moreover, Masuzawa's work along with that of selected other scholars represents a positive and judicious use of postmodern thought, which can pass the pragmatic test previously suggested.

A positive side of the world religions type of approach to the study of religions is the need for comparison, because when we attempt to understand others, comparison is necessary. When we attempt to understand the other we do so by means of our self-understanding. Although we are limited by our own historical and cultural context, the use of the comparative method liberates the other and allows the other to stand apart. Any new understanding that we might achieve will necessarily have limits, but comparative understanding possess three potential benefits: the overcoming of ethnocentrism by the inclusive nature built into comparison; reaching a more comprehensive understanding because cultural horizons are fused, which allows the other to be noticed and stand out before the union; liberation of our self and the other.[45] This neither means that we must impose our viewpoint on the other nor that we must simply accept the other's perspective as the final word. Any interpretation of a religious phenomenon can be challenged by a better interpretation and not by any appeal to an ultimate body of truth. Again, any interpretation of the religion of the other can be subject to a simple pragmatic test: Does it make better sense? An interpreter or outsider must keep in mind that to arrive at absolute certainty when dealing with human affairs is impossible and a certain amount of ambiguity is unavoidable. And since religion is a multivalent phenomenon, it makes judicious sense to use a wide variety of interpretive tools in order to arrive at an understanding without forgetting the pragmatic test.

The Allure of Decadence

Based on previous statements, I can reiterate that postmodern approaches to the study of religion have limited utility. A postmodern approach might be able to pass the pragmatic test suggested as a guideline in some cases, but in the final analysis scholars using any of the heterological methods put forth by various postmodern thinkers arrives after research and writing with a product based on a radical skepticism embedded in relativism. Instead of enhancing comprehension of the subject, scholars embracing postmodern methods undermine their own findings and pass on more questions than answers. Nicholas Rescher agrees with this point when he writes, "The trouble with skepticism is that it aborts inquiry at the very start."[46] In addition, radical skeptics cannot defend their actions because there is no rational basis for action, communication with others is impossible, and withdrawal from community is a likely result.[47]

Although the time for grand theoretical narratives might have passed, this does not mean that we cannot undertake more modest scholarly journeys. We can agree with the postmodernists that there is no certain knowledge for all time, that there are gaps in history, or that essences are difficult or impossible to isolate, but it is still possible to know something, however inexact our knowledge might prove to be. We are not condemned to write fictive history, and we do not have to write history for some political purposes. We do not have to buy into the banality of postmodernism or its impetus toward nihilism as suggested by deconstruction or other heterological methods that proceed potentially from relativism to nihilism.[48]

We also do not have to embrace the subverting of objectivity by postmodernists because socially dependent facts are epistemically objective despite their being ontologically subjective. Because they require human subjectivity, the way different socially dependent facts are ontologically subjective is similar. In order for socially dependent facts to exist, for instance, they are dependent for their initial and continued existence on collective agreement. In addition to this type of dependence, socially dependent facts are epistemically objective because they remain independent of individual thought. Thus, whatever true value they have stands separate from any single person and what that person might think about them.[49]

In addition to postmodernism's relativism, postmodern thinkers embrace decadence in the form of the carnivalesque, which is a transgressive game and an erring wandering without goals, rewards, or results. This form of play lacks usefulness, seriousness, purposefulness, and meaning. It upsets traditional hierarchies by inverting established values and meanings, and does not conform to common sense or logic. In short, it is a perverse and subversive type of play.[50] This perverse and subversive type of play is depicted by Derrida as writing, a form of play that risks meaning nothing and represents the play of *différance* taking place within the simulacrum. Derrida portrays writing as a process of disseminating or scattering seeds (words) that can never be recovered and that can never inseminate anything, like a sperm without a tail.[51] Bataille's notion of eroticism, an excessive emotion that responds to one's desire to merge with the universe, is another form of decadence, representing a realm of chaos with a violent and dreamlike quality that dissolves separate beings and manifests their basic continuity. The postmodern emphasis on the carnivalesque, eroticism, and simulacra is an embrace of the Dionysian aspect of life to which Stanley Rosen reacts in the following way: "Postmodernism is the Enlightenment gone mad."[52] Rosen more specifically means that the theoretical extremism of postmodernism is a consequence of this madness. In historical hindsight, a lack of order leads to a chaotic situation like that proposed by some postmodernists that serves as a basis for potential evil to fill the vacuum created by the embrace of the Dionysian. As Charles Taylor observes about the flux of postmodernism, there is nothing worth affirming that emerges.[53]

What postmodernists do affirm is a revolutionary political stance. For Deleuze and Guattari, desire threatens society because it is revolutionary.[54] Kristeva follows and advocates a Marxist ideology, especially that of Mao Tse-tung.[55] Bataille envisions and intends his writings to be revolutionary, whereas Foucualt views historical analysis as an essential aspect of the political struggle.[56] The revolutionary and decadent features of postmodern philosophy are examples of its excessive nature that places its thinkers on the periphery of thought.

Postmodern decadence includes an antirational attitude that is certainly contrary to the spirit of the Enlightenment. Among other thinkers, Robert Nozick makes a strong case for rationality because it gives us the power to study, discover, control, and direct our behavior. It also enables us to make correct judgments and decisions, and controls factors that might lead us astray.[57] Along similar lines of argument, Hilary Putnam thinks that in playing their skeptical games, postmodernists refuse to recognize the common world that we all share in order to construct a better world.[58] Not only does their antirationalism subvert or blind them to what we share in common, but their exaggerated attention to metaphysics and the false assumption that it forms the basis of Western culture is misplaced, and its destruction will not result in the total collapse of the Western edifice.[59]

Integrating pragmatism and idealism in his philosophy, Rescher argues that "rationality consists in the appropriate use of reason to resolve choices in the best possible way."[60] Rationality is not merely a matter of thought, but is also related to action by calling for the intelligent quest of proper ends. Rationality is realistic in the sense that it does not require what is not possible with respect to our beliefs, actions, and evaluations. Rescher argues further that "rationality is thus a two-sided, Janus-faced conception. On the side of means, it reflects a pragmatic concern for efficient process, while on the side of the appropriateness of ends it reflects a value-geared concern for product."[61] Rescher views rationality as an ideal in part that can only be partly realized by humans.

Following Nietzsche, several postmodernists can be identified as antihumanistic thinkers because they revolt against the primacy of life. This antihumanism is especially evident in their fascination with death that they appear at times to deify by equating God with death. Edmond Jabès connects, for instance, the immortality of God with the equally immortal nature of death, which actually preceded God in the sense that it existed before God.[62] Maurice Blanchot unequivocally equates God with death: "From the death of God, it follows that death is God."[63] From Derrida's perspective, the term "God" is a mere trace that names nothing permanent, whereas the death of God is liberating in the sense that it can reawaken us to the divine. If God is dead, does this mean that humans have nothing to fear? Derrida expresses his negative answer in the following way: "It is not the living God, but the Death-God that we should fear, God is Death."[64] Charles Taylor makes an astute observation when he writes that death achieves the status of a paradigm that offers a privileged perspective: "Modern life-affirming humanism breeds pusillanimity."[65] This is a recurring accusation made by those reacting counter to the Enlightenment.

With the emphasis on reversal and eternal return in postmodern thought, the end simply signifies a new beginning, which means that there can be no real conclusion to this book. In retrospect, this book possesses a final chapter—this one—but it does not really have a definitive conclusion or offer a final solution. In the spirit of postmodernism, I offer an inconclusive conclusion. If there is no definitive conclusion with what are we left? We are left with an interlude, a pause that signals danger to those who might consider adopting a heterological method. In a sense, the interlude characterizes the current state of religious studies. This is a time between the grand narratives of earlier contributors to the development of religious studies, such a Tylor, Frazier, Freud, Eliade, and others, and the current grand narratives with the possible emergence of cognitive science or something else to this status. During the interlude, we can be assured that we are free to play and experiment with new possibilities. Following the lead of Jean-Luc Marion, Hent de Vries is correct when he observes that religion is a saturated phenomenon "that manifests itself to the point of rendering itself nearly invisible."[66] This seems to partially imply that religion is difficult to exhaust with any single interpretation or grand narrative.

Notes

CHAPTER I

1. See Daniel Dubuisson, *The Western Construction of Religion*, trans. William Sayers (Baltimore: Johns Hopkins University Press, 2003); Timothy Fitzgerald, *The Ideology of Religious Studies* (New York: Oxford University Press, 2000); Russell McCutcheon, *Manufacturing Religion: The Discourse on Sui Generis Religion and the Politics of Nostalgia* (New York: Oxford University Press, 1997).

2. See Jonathan Z. Smith, *Relating Religion: Essays in the Study of Religion* (Chicago: University of Chicago Press, 2004); Bruce Lincoln, *Authority: Construction and Corrosion* (Chicago: University of Chicago Press, 1994).

3. Herbert Spencer, *The Principles of Sociology*, 3 vols. (New York: Appleton, 1898), I: 304–305.

4. Tomoko Masuzawa, *In Search of Dreamtime: The Quest for the Origin of Religion* (Chicago: University of Chicago Press, 1993).

5. Some worthwhile contributions to this emerging field are the following: Justin Barrett, "Exploring the Natural Foundations of Religion," *Trends in Cognitive Sciences* 4/1 (2000): 29–34; Pascal Boyer, "Religious Thought and Behavior as By-products of Brain Function," *Trends in Cognitive Sciences* 7/3 (2003): 119–124; Stewart Guthrie, *Faces in the Clouds* (New York: Oxford University Press, 1993); Harvey Whitehouse, *Modes of Religiosity: A Cognitive Theory of Religious Transmission* (Walnut Creek, CA: AltaMira Press, 2004); Armin W. Geertz, "Brain, Body and Culture: A Biocultural Theory of Religion," *Method and Theory in the Study of Religion* 22/4 (2010): 304–321.

6. See Ann Taves for a positive embrace of cognitive science in *Religious Experience Reconsidered: A Building-Block Approach to the Study of Religion and Other Special Things* (Princeton, NJ: Princeton University Press, 2009), and "No Field Is an Island: Fostering Collaboration between the Academic Study of Religion and the Sciences," *Method and Theory in the Study of Religion* 22 (2010): 170–188. In contrast to Taves, the anthropologist Maurice Bloch thinks that an evolutionary or cognitive science of religion rests on the dubious premise that religion is something distinct and set apart from the rest of human society in "Why Religion Is Nothing Special but Is Central," *Philosophical Transactions of the Royal Society B* 363 (2008): 2055–2061, esp. 2060.

7. Xinzhong Yao and Yanxia Zhao, *Chinese Religion: A Contextual Approach* (London: Continuum, 2010), pp. 27–40.

8. For a more complete examination of dharma, see Ariel Glucklich, *Religious Jurisprudence in the Dharma±āstras* (New York: Macmillan, 1982), and *The Sense of Adharma* (New York: Oxford University Press, 1994); Patrick Olivelle, *The Ā±rama System: The History and Hermeneutic of a Religious Institution* (New York: Oxford University Press, 1993); Alf Hiltebeitel, *Dharma: Its Early History in Law, Religion, and Narrative* (New York: Oxford University Press, 2011); and a more condensed discussion by Carl Olson, *The Many Colors of Hinduism: A Thematic-Historical Introduction* (New Brunswick, NJ: Rutgers University Press, 2007).

9. Jeremy Carrette, "Post-Structuralism and the Study of Religion," in *The Routledge Companion to the Study of Religion*, 2nd ed., ed. John Hinnells (London: Routledge, 2010), p. 277.

10. Louis Dupré, *The Enlightenment and the Intellectual Foundations of Modern Culture* (New Haven, CT: Yale University Press, 2004), p. 9.

11. Ibid., p. 76.

12. Ibid., p. 187.

13. Peter Gay, *The Rise of Modern Paganism*, vol. 1, *The Enlightenment: An Interpretation* (New York: Knopf, 1966), p. 3.

14. John Pocock, "Historiography and Enlightenment: A View of Their History," *Modern Intellectual History* 5/1 (2008): 83–96.

15. Dan Edelstein, *The Enlightenment: A Genealogy* (Chicago: University of Chicago Press, 2010), p. 13.

16. Ibid., p. 13.

17. Ibid., p. 2.

18. Ibid., p. 117.

19. Isaiah Berlin, *The Roots of Romanticism* (Princeton, NJ: Princeton University Press, 1999), pp. 8–9, 138.

20. Martin Riesebrodt, *The Promise of Salvation: A Theory of Religion*, trans. Steven Rendall (Chicago: University of Chicago Press, 2010), p. 3.

21. Hans G. Kippenberg, *Discovering Religious History in the Modern Age*, trans. Barbara Harshaw (Princeton, NJ: Princeton University Press, 2002).

22. Gilles Deleuze, *What Is Philosophy?*, trans. Hugh Tomlinson and Graham Bouchell (New York: Columbia University Press, 1994), p. 5.

23. Gilles Deleuze, *Difference and Repetition*, trans. Paul Patton (New York: Columbia University Press, 1994), pp. 127–128.

24. Gilles Deleuze, *Logic of Sense*, trans. Mark Lester and ed. Constantin V. Boundas (New York: Columbia University Press, 1990), p. 262.

25. Jean Baudrillard, *Simulacra and Simulation*, trans. Sheila Faria Glaser (Ann Arbor: University of Michigan Press, 1994), p. 82.

26. Jean Baudrillard, *Fatal Strategies*, trans. Philip Beitchman and W. G. J. Niesluchowski (New York: Semiotext(e), 1990), p. 108.

27. Didier Eribon, *Michel Foucault*, trans. Betsy Wing (Cambridge, MA: Harvard University Press, 1991), p. 325.

28. Fredric Jameson, *Postmodernism or, the Cultural Logic of Late Capitalism* (Durham, NC: Duke University Press, 1991), p. 382.

29. Friedrich Nietzsche, *The Will to Power*, trans. Walter Kaufmann and R. J. Hollingdale (New York: Random House, 1967), pp. 26–27.

30. Robert B. Pippin, *Modernism as a Philosophical Problem: On the Dissatisfactions of European High Culture* (Cambridge, MA: Basil Blackwell, 1991), p. 156. See Arnold Toynbee, *A Study of History*, 3 vols. (London: Oxford University Press, 1939–1961).

31. Martin Heidegger, *Nietzsche*, vol. 4, *Nihilism*, trans. Frank A. Capuzzi (San Francisco: Harper and Row, 1982), p. 28.

32. Mark C. Taylor, *Nots* (Chicago: University of Chicago Press, 1993), p. 61.

33. Jean-François Lyotard, *The Inhuman: Reflections on Time*, trans. Geoffrey Bennington and Rachel Bowlby (Cambridge: Polity Press, 1977), p. 25.

34. Jeremy R. Carrette, *Foucault and Religion: Spiritual Corporality and Political Spirituality* (London: Routledge, 2000).

35. Jacques Derrida, "Faith and Knowledge: The Two Sources of Religion at the Limits of Reason Alone," in *Religion*, ed. Jacques Derrida and Gianni Vatttimo (Stanford, CA: Stanford University Press, 1998), p. 27.

36. Hent de Vries, "Introduction: Why Still 'Religion'?," in *Religion: Beyond a Concept*, ed. Hent de Vries (New York: Fordham University Press, 2008), p. 8.

37. Ibid., p. 13.

38. Ibid., p. 36.

39. Ibid., p. 37.

40. Mark C. Taylor, *After God* (Chicago: University of Chicago Press, 2007), p. 12.

41. Michael Lambek, ed., *A Reader in the Anthropology of Religion*, 2nd ed. (Malden, MA: Blackwell, 2008), p. 40.

42. Kevin Schillbrack, "Religions: Are There Any?," *Journal of the American Academy of Religion* 78/4 (2010): 1112–1138.

43. Riesebrodt, *The Promise of Salvation*, pp. 5–6.

44. Ibid., p. 169.

CHAPTER 2

1. Jacques Derrida, *Positions*, trans. Alan Bass (Chicago: University of Chicago Press, 1981), p. 64.

2. Michel Foucault, "Presentation de Michel Foucault," in Georges Bataille, *Oeuvres completes*, 12 vols. (Paris: Gallimard, 1970–1988), 1: i.

3. Alan Megill, *Prophets of Extremity: Nietzsche, Heidegger, Foucault, Derrida* (Berkeley: University of California Press, 1985), p. 189.

4. Bataille, *Oeuvres completes*, 11: 94, 103.

5. Julia Kristeva, *Revolution in Poetic Literature*, trans. Margaret Waller (New York: Columbia University Press, 1984), p. 82.

6. Alan Stoekl, "Truman's Apotheosis: Bataille, 'Planisme,' and Headlessness," *Yale French Studies* 78 (1990): 181–205, esp. 181. A couple of good biographies have been published: Michel Surya, *Georges Bataille: La Mort à l'oeuvre* (Paris: Sèguier, 1987), trans. into English by Krzysztof Fijalkowski and Michael Richardson as *Georges Bataille: An Intellectual Biography* (London: Verso, 2002); and Stuart Kendall, *Georges Bataille* (London: Reaktion Books, 2007). The following are useful single-author studies of Bataille's work: Michele Richman, *Reading Georges Bataille: Beyond the Gift* (Baltimore: Johns Hopkins University Press, 1982); Mario Perniola, *L'instant eternal: Bataille et la pensée de la marginalité* (Paris: Medidiens Anthropos, 1982); Denis Hollier, *La prise de la Concorde: Essais sur Georges Bataille* (Paris: Gallimard, 1974); Francis Marmande, *Georges Bataille politique* (Lyon: Presses universitaires de Lyon, 1985); Rodolphe Gasché, *System und Metaphorik in der Philosophie von Georges Bataille*, Europäische Hochschultschriftrin, Reihe 20, Philosophie, vol. 39 (Bern: Peter Lang, 1978). A few worthwhile anthologies devoted to Bataille are: *Stanford French Review* 12/2 (1988); Alan Stoekl, ed., "On Bataille," *Yale French Studies* 78 (1990); Dominique Lecog and Jean-Luc Lory, eds., *Ecrits d'ailleurs: Georges Bataille et les ethnologues* (Paris: Maison des sciences de l' Home, 1987).

7. Jean Baudrillard views pornography as equivocal because it terminates all seduction (a term of his similar in meaning to Bataille's notion of the erotic) and simultaneously ends the accumulation of the signs of sex. Pornography is also a simulacrum, which means that it is not an ideology that hides the truth; it rather hides the truth's nonexistence. See *Fatal Strategies*, trans. Philip Beitchman and W. G. J. Niesluchowski (New York: Semiotext(e), 1990), p. 35.

8. Jürgen Habermas, *Der philosophische Diskurs der Moderne: Zwölf Vorlesungen* (Frankfurt am Main: Suhrkamp, 1985), pp. 251–252.

9. Georges Bataille, "Hegel, la mort et le sacrifice," *Deucalion* 5 (1955): 21–43, esp. pp. 22, 24.

10. Ibid., pp. 31–32.

11. Georges Bataille, *Visions of Excess: Selected Writings, 1927–1939*, trans. Alan Stoekl, Theory and History of Literature, vol. 14 (Minneapolis: University of Minnesota Press, 1985), p. 8.

12. Ibid., pp. 24–30.

13. Georges Bataille, *Theory of Religion*, trans. Robert Hurley (New York: Zone Books, 1989), p. 18.

14. Ibid., p. 39.

15. Ibid., p. 41.

16. Ibid., pp. 13, 42.

17. Bataille, *Oeuvres completes*, 6: 313.

18. Bataille, *Visions of Excess*, p. 92. Charles Larmore places a discussion of Bataille's heterology within the context of Hegel's philosophical program and refers to heterology as the science of encountering the other in "Bataille's Heterology," *Semiotexte* 2/2 (1976): 87–104. Jean Helmont thinks that Bataille's method of heterology prefigures and is continued by Jacque Derrida's notion of *différance* in "From Bataille to Derrida: Différance and Heterology," trans. A. Engstrom, *Stanford French Review* 22/1 (1988): 129–147.

19. Bataille, *Visions of Excess*, p. 97.

20. Allen S. Weiss, *The Aesthetics of Excess* (Albany: State University of New York Press, 1989), p. 90. Mark C. Taylor elaborates further that " 'heterology' is actually an oxymoron. *Heteros* is, for Bataille, precisely what eludes the *logos*. Consequently, heterology is an impossible science" (*Altarity* [Chicago: University of Chicago Press, 1987], p. 133).

21. Bataille, *Visions of Excess*, p. 95.

22. Bataille, *Theory of Religion*, pp. 27–33.

23. Ibid., p. 53.

24. Ibid., p. 53.

25. Mircea Eliade, *Traité d'histoire des religions* (Paris: Payoit, 1970), pp. 15–45, trans. Willard R. Trask as *The Sacred and the Profane: The Nature of Religion* (New York: Harcourt, Brace, 1959). For a look at Eliade's distinction between the sacred and the profane within the context of a discussion of Jacques Derrida's notion of *différance*, see Carl Olson, *The Theology and Philosophy of Eliade: A Search for the Centre* (London: Macmillan, 1992), pp. 102–109.

26. Emile Durkheim, *The Elementary Forms of Religious Life*, trans. Joseph Ward Swain (London: George Allen & Unwin, 1954), pp. 37–38.

27. Henri Hubert and Marcel Mauss, *Sacrifice: Its Nature and Function*, trans. W. D. Halls (Chicago: University of Chicago Press, 1968).

28. Bataille, *Theory of Religion*, p. 52.

29. Ibid., pp. 69–70.

30. Ibid., p. 72.

31. Georges Bataille, *The Tears of Eros*, trans. Peter Connor (San Francisco: City Lights Books, 1989), p. 66.

32. Ibid., pp. 31–32, 23. For a more complete discussion of Bataille's understanding of death, see Denis Hollier, "Baitaille's Tomb: A Halloween Story," trans. Richard Miller, *October* 33 (1985): 73–91. For a wider discussion of death within the philosophies of various postmodern thinkers, see Carl Olson, "The Deification of Death in Postmodern Thought: A Critical Examination," *International Journal of Humanistic Ideology* 1/1 (Summer 2008): 25–42.

33. Bataille, *The Tears of Eros*, p. 44.

34. Ibid., p. 48. For Baudrillard, seduction is a game, it is a passion, and it implies a reversible indeterminate order that is also false and abusive. Baudrillard prefers a form of seduction that is similar to a duel and not a response because he

wants it to be a challenge that allows for the playing out of a rule. He writes, "Seduction is dual: I cannot seduce if I am not already seduced, no one can seduce me if he is not already seduced" (*Seductions*, trans. Brian Singer [New York: St. Martin's Press, 1990], p. 105).

35. Georges Bataille, *Death and Sensuality: A Study of Eroticism and the Taboo* (New York: Walker, 1962; reprint, Salem, NH: Ayer, 1984), p. 17.

36. Ibid., p. 17.

37. Ibid., p. 18. Jeremy R. Carrette criticizes Bataille for the following reason: "Bataille seems to be unaware of the fact that in eroticism the so-called 'violation of self-possession' can be a mutually agreed adventure and an 'affirmation' (not violation) of the other; whereas in an act of violence the action is usually based on a conflict of interest" (*Foucault and Religion: Spiritual Corporality and Political Spirituality* [London: Routledge, 2000], p. 72).

38. Bataille, *Death and Sensuality*, p. 282.

39. Ibid., pp. 29, 31. Bataille's notion of eroticism is similar to what Michel Foucault refers to as sexuality, which is an individual matter that concerns private pleasures and gives rise to the notion of sex (*Death and Sensuality*, p. 157). Foucualt's primary interest is how sexuality functions as a transfer for regions of power. See *The History of Sexuality*, vol. 1, *An Introduction*, trans. Robert Hurley (New York: Vintage Books, 1980).

40. Bataille, *Death and Sensuality*, p. 134.

41. Ibid., p. 130.

42. Ibid., p. 258. Baudrillard places a different emphasis on desire: "For seduction, desire is a myth. If desire is a will to power and possession, seduction places before it an equal will to power by the simulacrum" (*Seductions*, p. 87).

43. Bataille, *Death and Sensuality*, p. 24. Again, Baudrillard stresses a different angle: "*To seduce is to die as reality and reconstitute oneself as illusion. It is to be taken in by one's own illusion and move in an enchanted world*" (*Seductions*, p. 69).

44. Bataille, *Death and Sensuality*, p. 83.

45. Ibid., p. 129.

46. Surya, *Georges Bataille*, p. 450.

47. Ibid., p. 69.

48. René Girard, *Violence and the Sacred*, trans. Patrick Gregory (Baltimore: Johns Hopkins University Press, 1989), pp. 8–24; Bataille, *Death and Sensuality*, p. 48.

49. Bataille, *Death and Sensuality*, p. 16.

50. Bataille, *Theory of Religion*, p. 43.

51. Ibid., p. 44.

52. Ibid., pp. 65–66.

53. Ibid., pp. 56–58.

54. Georges Bataille, *The Accursed Share: An Essay on General Economy*, vol. 1, trans. Robert Hurley (New York: Zone Books, 1988), p. 59.

55. Bataille, *Death and Sensuality*, p. 92.

56. Ibid., p. 90.

57. Ibid., p. 23.

58. Bataille, *Theory of Religion*, p. 47.

59. Bataille, *The Tears of Eros*, p. 74. In contrast to Bataille, Stanley Tambiah does not think that ritual can directly evoke feelings or express the mental orientation of participants. He stresses the formalism of ritual as a performative communication in "A Performative Approach to Ritual," *Proceedings of the British Academy* 65 (1979): 113–169, and "The Magical Power of Words," *Man*, n.s., 3/2 (1968): 175–208. For criticism of the performative approach to interpreting ritual, see Catherine Bell, *Ritual Theory, Ritual Practice* (New York: Oxford University Press, 1992), pp. 41–42.

60. Jonathan Z. Smith argues, "Ritual is, above all, an assertion of difference" (*To Take Place: Toward Theory in Ritual* [Chicago: University of Chicago Press, 1987], p. 109).

61. Georges Bataille, *Inner Experience*, trans. Leslie Anne Boldt (Albany: State University of New York Press, 1988), pp. 136–137.

62. This approach is suggested by the theoretical work of Clifford Geertz, "Religion as a Cultural System," in *Anthropological Approaches to the Study of Religion*, ed. Michael Banton (London: Tavistock Publications, 1971), pp. 1–46; and the work of Victor Turner, who refers to a symbol as the smallest unit of ritual or as storage units of dynamic entities in *The Forest of Symbols: Aspects of Ndembu Ritual* (Ithaca, NY: Cornell University Press, 1967), *The Drums of Affliction: A Study of Religious Processes among the Ndembu of Zambia* (Oxford: Clarendon Press, 1968), and *Dramas, Fields and Metaphors: Symbolic Action in Human Society* (Ithaca, NY: Cornell University Press, 1975).

63. James R. Walker, *Lakota Belief and Ritual*, ed. Raymond J. de Mallie and Elaine A. Jahner (Lincoln: University of Nebraska Press, 1980).

64. Joseph G. Jorgensen, *The Sun Dance Religion* (Chicago: University of Chicago Press, 1972), pp. 206, 236.

65. Michael E. Melody, "The Lakota Sun Dancer: A Composite View and Analysis," *South Dakota History* 6 (1976): 452–454.

66. Ake Hultkrantz, *Belief and Worship in Native North America*, ed. Christopher Vecsey (Syracuse, NY: Syracuse University Press, 1981), p. 238.

67. Royal B. Hassrick, *The Sioux: Life and Customs of a Warrior Society* (Norman: University of Oklahoma Press, 1967), pp. 238, 248.

68. Thomas S. Lewis, "The Oglala (Teton Dakota) Sun Dance: Vicissitudes of Its Structure and Functions," *Plains Anthropologist* 17 (1972): 44–49, on 47.

69. Walker, *Lakota Belief and Ritual*, pp. 107–108.

70. Joseph Epes Brown, ed., *The Sacred Pipe* (New York: Penguin Books, 1979), p. 79.

71. Ibid., p. 69.

72. Ibid., pp. 69, 75–76.

73. Ibid., pp. 71–72.

74. Ibid., p. 89.

75. Walker, *Lakota Belief and Ritual*, p. 114.

76. Bataille, *Oeuvres completes*, 2: 56.

77. Brown, *The Sacred Pipe*, pp. 72, 78.

78. J. Owen Dorsey, *A Study of Siouan Cults*, Eleventh Annual Report (Washington, DC: Bureau of American Ethnology, 1894), p. 452.

79. William E. Powers, *Oglala Religion* (Lincoln: University of Nebraska Press, 1977), p. 100.

80. Ibid., p. 98.

81. Ibid., pp. 98–99.

82. T. O. Beidelman finds that pain is an essential feature within the context of ritual that transforms a person and enables that person to verify an invisible reality, which suggests that it is equated with certainty among the Kaguru people. See *The Cool Knife: Imagery of Gender, Sexuality, and Moral Education in Kaguru Initiation Ritual* (Washington, D C: Smithsonian Institution Press, 1997). Ariel Glucklich agrees with Beidelman in *Sacred Pain: Hurting the Body for the Sake of the Soul* (Oxford: Oxford University Press, 2001), p. 6.

83. Bataille, *The Accursed Share*, 1: 59.

84. Brown, *The Sacred Pipe*, p. 85.

85. Ibid., p. 74.

86. Ibid., p. 95.

87. Walker, *Lakota Belief and Ritual*, p. 182.

88. Brown, *The Sacred Pipe*, p. 72.

89. Georges Bataille, *L'Expérience intérieure* (Paris: Gallimard, 1954), p. 216.

90. Julian Pefanis, *Heterology and the Postmodern: Bataille, Baudrillard, and Lyotard* (Durham, NC: Duke University Press, 1991), p. 41.

91. Fredric Jameson, *Postmodernism, or, The Cultural Logic of Late Capitalism* (Durham, NC: Duke University Press, 1991), p. 382.

92. Stanley Rosen, *Hermeneutics as Politics* (New York: Oxford University Press, 1987), p. 142.

93. The religious significance of the human body is made evident by the work of Mary Douglas, *Natural Symbols: Explorations in Cosmology* (New York: Pantheon Books, 1970). In this work she examines how symbolic behavior works through the human body. In another study she explores the relationship between ritual and the body and how ritual works on society through the symbolic medium of the physical body. See *Purity and Danger: An Analysis of Concepts of Pollution and Taboo* (New York: Praeger, 1970). Ronald L. Grimes also emphasizes the body's significance: "The body is a specially marked off preserve, a repository of ultimate value. The human body does not merely front for or point to the sacred; it is sacred, a locus of revelation and hierophany" (*Ritual Criticism: Case Studies in*

Its Practice, Essays on Its Theory [Columbia, SC: University of South Carolina Press, 1990], p. 148).

CHAPTER 3

1. Jacques Derrida, *Spurs*, trans. Barbara Harlow (Chicago: University of Chicago Press, 1979), p. 121.
2. Jacques Derrida, *Glas*, trans. John P. Leavey Jr. and Richard Rand (Lincoln: University of Nebraska Press, 1986), 243.
3. John D. Caputo and Michael J. Scanlon, "Introduction: Apology for the Impossible: Religion and Postmodernism," in *God, the Gift, and Postmodernism*, ed. John D. Caputo and Michael J. Scanlon (Bloomington: Indiana University Press, 1999), p. 4.
4. Jonathan P. Parry, "The Gift, the Indian Gift, and the 'Indian Gift,'" *Man*, n.s., 24 (1986): 433–473, on p. 455.
5. James Carrier, "Gifts, Commodities, and Social Relations: A Maussian View of Exchange," *Sociological Forum* 6 (1991): 19–136, quotation on p. 127.
6. Ibid., p. 132.
7. Marcel Mauss, *The Gift: The Form and Reason for Exchange in Archaic Societies*, trans. W. D. Halls (New York: W. W. Norton, 1990), p. 5, and "Rapports réels et pratiques de la psychologie et de la sociologie," in *Sociologie et anthropologie* (Paris: Presses Universitaires de France, 1966), p. 150.
8. Carrier, "Gifts, Commodities, and Social Relations," p. 124.
9. N. J. Allen, "The Category of the Person: A Reading of Mauss' Last Essay," in *The Category of the Person: Anthropology, Philosophy, History*, ed. Michael Carrithers, Steven Collins, and Steven Lukes (Cambridge: Cambridge University Press, 1985), p. 28.
10. Mauss, *The Gift*, p. 12, and *Essai sur le don: Forms et reason de l' èchange dons les sociétés archaiques*. In *Sociologie et anthropology*, 3rd ed. (Paris: Presses Universitaires de France. 1966), p. 161.
11. Mauss, *The Gift*, p. 13, and *Essai*, pp. 162–63.
12. Mauss, *The Gift*, pp. 22–23, and *Essai*, p. 189.
13. Mauss, *The Gift*, p. 35, and *Essai*, p. 199.
14. Carrier, "Gifts, Commodities, and Social Relations," pp. 86–87.
15. Mauss, *The Gift*, p. 37, and *Essai*, p. 200.
16. Mauss, *The Gift*, p. 41, and *Essai*, p. 208.
17. Mauss, *The Gift*, p. 44, and *Essai*, pp. 220–21.
18. Georges Bataille, *Oeuvres completes*, 12 vols. (Paris: Gallimard, 1970–1988), 7: 16.
19. Georges Bataille, *The Accursed Share: An Essay on General Economy*, vol. 2, *The History of Eroticism*, and vol. 3, *Sovereignty* (New York: Zone Books, 1991), p. 56.
20. Georges Bataille, *The Accursed Share: An Essay on General Economy*, vol. 1, trans. Robert Hurley (New York: Zone Books, 1988), p. 69. Instead of power, Jean

Starobinski views the gift as a two-sided drama with dark and light sides that is distributed on the bases of equality and disparity. In addition to belonging to the language of the body, there is also a poison in the gift. See *Largesse*, trans. Jane Marie Todd (Chicago: University of Chicago Press, 1997), p. 7.

21. Bataille, *The Accursed Share*, 1: 70. In contrast to Bataille, Rodney Stark, a sociologist of religion, views exchange relations as events, and he explores the nature of exchanges between humans and divine beings in "Micro-Foundations of Religion: A Revised Theory," *Sociological Theory* 17/3 (1999): 264–289. Philip E. Tetlock, a psychologist of religion, stresses the objects of exchange instead of the parties to an exchange and what groups would not exchange in certain circumstances in "Thinking the Unthinkable: Sacred Values and Taboos Cognitions," *Trends in Cognitive Science* 7/17 (2003): 320–324.

22. Michele Richman, *Reading Georges Bataille: Beyond the Gift* (Baltimore: Johns Hopkins University Press, 1982), p. 23.

23. Bataille, *Accursed Share*, 1: 72.

24. Ibid., pp. 73–74.

25. Ibid., p. 76.

26. Henri Hubert and Marcel Mauss, *Sacrifice: Its Nature and Function*, trans. W. D. Halls (Chicago: University of Chicago Press, 1968), p. 4.

27. M. E. Combs-Schilling, *Sacred Performance: Islam, Sexuality, and Sacrifice* (New York: Columbia University Press, 1989), p. 242.

28. Georges Bataille, *Death and Sensuality: A Study of Eroticism and the Taboo* (New York: Walker, 1962; reprint, Salem, NH: Ayer, 1984), p. 211.

29. Bataille, *Accursed Share*, 2–3: 48.

30. Ibid., p. 57.

31. Richman, *Reading Georges Bataille*, p. 75.

32. Jacques Derrida, *Given Time: 1, Counterfeit Money*, trans. Peggy Kamuf (Chicago: University of Chicago Press, 1992), p. 7.

33. Richard Kearney, moderator, "On the Gift: A Discussion between Jacques Derrida and Jean-Luc Marion," in Caputo and Scanlon, *God, the Gift, and Postmodernism* (Bloomington: Indiana University Press, 1999), p. 59.

34. Ibid., p. 9.

35. Jacques Derrida, *Psyché: Inventions de l'autre* (Paris: Galilée, 1987), p. 164.

36. Derrida, *Given Time*, p. 12.

37. Ibid., p. 16.

38. Ibid., p. 18.

39. Jacques Derrida, *Cinders*, trans. Ned Lukacker (Lincoln: University of Nebraska Press, 1991).

40. Derrida, *Given Time*, p. 19.

41. Kearney, "On the Gift," p. 76.

42. Derrida, *Given Time*, p. 35.

43. Ibid., p. 38.
44. Derrida, *Glas*, p. 59.
45. Derrida, *Given Time*, p. 41.
46. Derrida, *Glas*, p. 244.
47. Derrida, *Given Time*, p. 147.
48. Ibid., p. 148.
49. Derrida, *Glas*, p. 243.
50. Louis Renou and Jean Filliozat, *L'Inde classique: Manuel des etudes indienne*, 2 vols. (Paris: Imprimerie national, 1953, 1957), 1: 273.
51. Jan Gonda, "Gifts and Giving in the Rig-Veda," *Vishveshvaranda Indological Journal* 2/1 (1964): 9–30, quotation on 25.
52. Pandurang Vaman Kane, *History of Dharmaśāstra*, 5 vols. (Poona: Bhandarkar Research Institute, 1953–1973), 2: 847, 849.
53. Jan Gonda, *Die Religionen Indiens*, vol. 1, *Veda und alterer Hinduismus* (Stuttgart: Kohlhammer, 1960), p. 42.
54. Gonda, "Gifts," p. 16, and *Change and Continuity in Indian Religion* (The Hague: Mouton, 1965), p. 209.
55. Gonda, *Change and Continuity*, p. 214.
56. Kane, *History of Dharmaśāstra*, 2: 886.
57. Kane, *History of Dharmaśāstra*, 3: 474.
58. J. C. Heesterman, "Brahmin, Ritual, and Renouncer," *Wiener Zeitschrift für die Kunde Südasiens und Archiv für indische Philosophie* 8 (1964): 1–31, on 3.
59. Madeleine Biardeau and Charles Malamoud, *Le Sacrifice dans l'Inde ancienne*, Bibliothéque de l'Études, Scieneces religieuses, 79 (Paris: Presses Universitaires de France, 1976), p. 27.
60. Romila Thapar, "Sacrifice, Surplus, and the Soul," *History of Religions* 33 (1994): 305–324, on 315–316.
61. J. C. Heesterman, *The Broken World of Sacrifice: An Essay in Ancient Indian Ritual* (Chicago: University of Chicago Press, 1993), p. 14.
62. Ibid., 18.
63. Derrida, *Glas*, p. 244.
64. Heesterman, *Broken World of Sacrifice*, pp. 206–207.
65. Gloria Raheja, *The Poison in the Gift: Ritual, Possession, and the Dominant Caste in a North Indian Village* (Chicago: University of Chicago Press, 1988), p. 32.
66. Jonathan P. Parry, *Death in Banares* (Cambridge: Cambridge University Press, 1994), p. 136.
67. Ibid., p. 121.
68. Ibid., p. 123.
69. Ibid., p. 128.
70. Ibid., p. 137.
71. Jacques Derrida, *The Gift of Death*, trans. David Wills (Chicago: University of Chicago Press, 1995), p. 44.

72. Pierre Bourdieu, *Outline of a Theory of Practice*, trans. Richard Nice (Cambridge: Cambridge University Press, 1986), p. 8.

73. Ibid., pp. 5–6.

74. Catherine Bell, *Ritual Theory, Ritual Practice* (New York: Oxford University Press, 1992), p. 83.

75. Derrida, *Gift of Death*, p. 96.

76. Ibid., p. 97.

77. Steven Collins, "Categories, Concepts or Predicaments? Remarks on Mauss' Use of Philosophical Terminology," in Carrithers, Collins, and Lukes, *The Category of Person*, p. 54.

78. Mauss, "Rapports," p. 151.

79. James Carrier, "Maussian Occidenalism: Gift and Commodity Systems," in *Occidentalism: Images of the West*, ed. James G. Carrier (Oxford: Clarendon Press, 1995), p. 86.

80. Jacques Derrida, "The Principle of Reason: The University in the Eyes of its Pupils," *Diacritics* 13 (1983): 3–20, quotation on 9.

81. Ibid., p. 16.

82. Calvin O. Schrag, *The Resources of Reason: A Response to the Postmodern Challenge* (Bloomington: Indiana University Press, 1992), pp. 167–168.

83. Robert C. Neville, *Reconstruction of Thinking* (Albany: State University of New York Press, 1981), p. 170.

84. Emile Durkheim and Marcel Mauss, *Primitive Classification*, trans. Rodney Needham (Chicago: University of Chicago Press, 1963), pp. 82–83.

85. Ibid., p. 84.

86. Jacques Derrida, *Of Grammatology*, trans. Gayatri Chakravorty Spivak (Baltimore: Johns Hopkins University Press, 1976) p. 24, and *Positions*, trans. Alan Bass (Chicago: University of Chicago Press), p. 41.

87. Hilary Putnam, *Renewing Philosophy* (Cambridge, MA: Harvard University Press, 1992), p. 124.

CHAPTER 4

1. Salman Rushdie, *Midnight's Children* (New York: Alfred A. Knopf, 1980), p. 7.

2. Homi K. Bhabha, *The Location of Culture* (1994; London: Routledge, 2002), p. 171.

3. Ibid., p. 6.

4. Gayatri Chakravorty Spivak, *A Critique of Postcolonial Reason: Toward a History of the Vanishing Present* (Cambridge, MA: Harvard University Press, 1999), p. 172.

5. Ashis Nandy, *Intimate Enemy: Loss and Recovery of Self under Colonialism* (Delhi: Oxford University Press, 1983), and *Traditions, Tryanny and Utopias: Essays in the Politics of Awareness* (Delhi: Oxford University Press, 1987).

6. Robert J. C. Young, *Postcolonialism: An Historical Introduction* (Oxford: Blackwell, 2001), p. 65.

7. Bernard Lewis, *Islam and the West* (New York: Oxford University Press, 1993), pp. 100–101, 104.

8. Edward W. Said, *Orientalism* (New York: Vintage Books, 1979), p. 5.

9. Ibid., p. 93.

10. Edward W. Said, *The World, the Text, and the Critic* (Cambridge, MA: Harvard University Press, 1983), p. 39.

11. Gauri Viswanathan, ed., *Power, Politics, and Culture: Interviews with Edward W. Said* (New York: Pantheon Books, 2001), p. 18.

12. Ibid., p. 47.

13. Michel Foucault, *The Archaeology of Knowledge and the Discourse on Language*. trans. A. M. Sheridan Smith (New York: Pantheon Books, 1972), pp. 21–39.

14. Michel Foucault, *Essential Works of Foucault, 1954–1984*, 3 vols., ed. Paul Rabinow (New York: New Press, 1994). Charles Taylor argues for an individual form of agency by distinguishing between disengaged and engaged agency. The former type distinguishes the agent from the rational and social worlds, which suggests that the subject's identity is no longer defined by what is external to the subject in the world. The engaged agent is an embodied subject who is engaged in and open to the world, which means that the subject acts in the world and on the world. See *Philosophical Papers I: Human Agency and Language* (Cambridge: Cambridge University Press, 1985).

15. Said, *Orientalism*, p. 95.

16. Ibid., p. 322.

17. Viswanathan, *Power, Politics, and Culture*, p. 40.

18. Michel Foucault, *Power/Knowledge: Selected Interviews and Other Writings, 1972–1977*, ed. Colin Gordon and trans. Colin Gordon, Leo Marshall, John Mepham, and Kate Soper (New York: Pantheon Books, 1980), p. 142.

19. John McGowan, *Postmodernism and Its Critics* (Ithaca, NY: Cornell University Press, 1991), p. 172.

20. Lisa Lowe, *Critical Terrains: French and British Orientalism* (Ithaca, NY: Cornell University Press, 1991), pp. ix–x.

21. David Smith, "Orientalism and Hinduism," in *The Blackwell Companion to Hinduism*, ed. Gavin Flood (Oxford: Blackwell, 2003), p. 49.

22. Rosane Rocher, "British Orientalism in the Eighteenth Century: The Dialectics of Knowledge and Government," in *Orientialism and the Postcolonial Predicament*, ed. Carol A. Breckenridge and Peter van der Veer (Philadelphia: University of Pennsylvania Press, 1993), pp. 215–249. Siauddin Sardar thinks that Said's notion of the Orient is too limited and too general because his Orient is explicitly limited to the Middle East and is so abstract that it transcends time and history. See *Orientalism* (Buckingham: Open University Press, 1999).

23. Bhabha, *Location of Culture*, p. 72.

24. Robert J. C. Young, *White Mythologies: Writing History and the West* (London: Routledge, 1990), pp. 127–129.

25. Lewis, *Islam and the West*, p. 108. Said ignores complex motivations for Orientalism and fails to recognize the agency of Oriental subjects, according to Ronald B. Inden, *Imagining India* (Cambridge: Blackwell, 1990), p. 217; and Robert Eric Frykenberg, "Constructions of Hinduism at the Nexus of History and Religion," *Journal of Interdisciplinary History* 23/2 (1993): 523–550, on p. 534.

26. Sardar, *Orientalism*, p. 76.

27. Bhabha, *Location of Culture*, p. 86.

28. Young, *Postcolonialism*, pp. 39–91.

29. Wilhelm Halbfass, *Tradition and Reflection: Explorations in Indian Thought* (Albany: State University of New York Press, 1991), p. 12.

30. Ibid., p. 13.

31. Catherine Gallagher, "Politics, the Profession, and the Critic," *Diacritics* 15 (1985): 37–43, quotation on p. 37.

32. J. J. Clarke, *Oriental Enlightenment: The Encounter between Asian and Western Thought*. London: Routledge, 1997), p. 9.

33. Ibid., p. 27.

34. Ibid., p. 27.

35. Hugh B. Urban, *Tantra, Sex, Secrecy, Politics, and Power in the Study of Religion* (Berkeley: University of California Press, 2003), p. 88.

36. Edward W. Said, *Culture and Imperialism* (New York: Vintage Books, 1993), pp. 31–43.

37. Daniel Martin Varisco, *Reading Orientalism: Said and the Unsaid* (Seattle: University of Washington Press, 2007).

38. Foucault, *Power/Knowledge*, p. 52. Said also calls attention to the anti-Foucault-ian elements in his work. Responding in an interview about his book *Orientalism*, Said replies that "the notion of a kind of non-coercive knowledge, which I come to at the end of the book, was deliberately anti-Foucault" (Viswanathan, *Power, Politics, and Culture*, p. 80) in.

39. Said, *The World*, p. 11.

40. Ibid., p. 14.

41. Foucault, *Power/Knowledge*, p. 142.

42. McGowan, *Postmodernism and Its Critics*, p. 175.

43. Bhabha, *Location of Culture*, p. 1.

44. Homi K. Bhabha, "Unsatisfied Notes on Vernacular Cosmopolitianism," in *Postcolonial Discourse: An Anthology*, ed. Gregory Castle (Oxford: Blackwell, 2001), p. 51.

45. Ibid., p. 51.

46. Gayatri Chakravorty Spivak, "Can the Subaltern Speak? Speculations on Widow Sacrifice," *Wedge* 7/8 (1985): 120–130, on p. 120.

47. Young, *White Mythologies*, p. 170.

48. Gayatri Chakravorty Spivak, "The Rani of Sirmur," in *Europe and Its Others*, 2 vols., ed. Francis Barker et al. (Colchester: University of Essex, 1985), 1: 130.

49. Leela Gandhi, *Postcolonial Theory: A Critical Introduction* (New York: Columbia University Press, 1998), p. 8.

50. Young, *Postcolonialism*, p. 7.

51. See Friedrich Nietzsche, *On the Genealogy of Morals*, trans. Carol Diethe (Cambridge: Cambridge University Press, 1994), and *The Gay Science*, trans. Josefine Nauckhoff (Cambridge: Cambridge University Press, 2001).

52. Robert Soloman, "Nietzsche's *ad hominem*: Perspectivism, Personality, and *Ressentiment* Revisited," in *The Cambridge Companion to Nietzsche*, ed. Bernd Magnus and Kathleen M. Higgins (Cambridge: Cambridge University Press, 1996), p. 204.

53. Michel Foucault, "Nietzsche, Freud, Marx," in *Nietzsche*, Proceedings of the Seventh International Philosophical Colloquium of the Cahiers de Royaumont, July 4–8 (Paris: Editions de Minuit, 1967), p. 189. Constantin Fasolt criticizes Foucault because he leaves history unscathed in the sense that he uses traditional periodizations of European history in ancient, medieval, and modern periods See Fasolt, *The Limits of History* (Chicago: University of Chicago Press, 2004), p. 37.

54. Foucault, "Nietzsche, Freud, Marx," p. 189.

55. Arnold I. Davidson, "Archaeology, Genealogy, Ethics," in *Foucault: A Critical Reader*, ed. David Couzens Hoy (London: Basil Blackwell, 1986), p. 227.

56. Michel Foucault, "Nietzsche, Genealogy, History," in *Language, Counter-Memory, Practice: Selected Essays and Interviews*, ed. Donald F. Bouchard and trans. Donald F. Bouchard and Sherry Simon (Ithaca, NY: Cornell University Press, 1977), pp. 137–138.

57. Ibid., pp. 152–157.

58. Garrett Green, "Hermeneutics," in *The Routledge Companion to the Study of Religion*, 2nd ed., ed. John Hinnells (London: Routledge, 2010), p. 422.

59. For a more complete discussion of the representational mode of thinking and postmodern philosophy, see Carl Olson, *Zen and the Art of Postmodern Philosophy: Two Paths of Liberation from the Representational Mode of Thinking* (Albany: State University of New York Press, 2000). See also Philip A. Mellor, "Orientalism, Representation, and Religion: The Reality behind the Myth," *Religion* 14/1 (2004): 99–112. According to Gauri Viswanathan, what Said wants to accomplish is the elimination of representations that are essentially authoritative and repressive. See *Power, Politics, and Culture*, pp. 41–42. Richard King calls attention to ambiguities and limitations of following Foucault because Said at times endorses an antirepresentational mode of thinking that means there is no authentic Orient to be discovered while also claiming that there is an authentic

Orient. See King, *Orientalism and Religion: Postcolonial Theory, India, and "The Mystic East"* (London: Routledge, 1999), p. 83.

60. Alistair C. MacIntyre, *Three Rival Versions of Moral Enquiry: Encyclopedia, Genealogy, and Tradition* (Notre Dame: University of Notre Dame Press, 1990), p. 205.

61. Hans G. Kippenberg, *Discovering Religious History in the Modern Age*, trans. Barbara Harshaw (Princeton, NJ: Princeton University Press, 2002), p. 188.

62. Jacques Derrida, *Psyché: Inventions de l'autre* (Paris: Galilée, 1987), pp. 387–388.

63. Ibid., p. 391.

64. Ibid., p. 392.

65. Hilary Putnam, *Renewing Philosophy* (Cambridge, MA: Harvard University Press, 1992), p. 140.

66. Ibid., p. 124.

67. Charles Taylor, *Sources of the Self: The Making of Modern Identity* (Cambridge: Cambridge University Press, 1989), p. 489.

68. Said, *Culture and Imperialism*, p. 60.

69. Ibid., p. xxii.

70. Gandhi, *Postcolonial Theory*, p. 167.

71. Bhabha, *Location of Culture*, p. 175.

72. See Clarke, *Oriental Enlightenment*.

73. Rushdie, *Midnight's Children*, p. 585.

CHAPTER 5

1. Mircea Eliade, *Patterns in Comparative Religion*, trans. Rosemary Sheed (Cleveland: World, 1968), p. 5.

2. Mircea Eliade, *Journal II, 1957–1969*, trans. Fred H. Johnson, Jr. (Chicago: University of Chicago Press, 1977), p. 45.

3. Mircea Eliade, *Ordeal by Labyrinth: Conversations with Claude-Henri Rocquet*, trans. Derek Coltman (Chicago: University of Chicago Press, 1982), p. 144, and "Autobiographical Fragment," in *Imagination and Meaning: The Scholarly and Literary Worlds of Mircea Eliade*, ed. Norman J. Girardot and Mac Linscott Ricketts (New York: Seabury Press, 1982), 114–15.

4. Mircea Eliade, *Shamanism: Archaic Techniques of Ecstasy*, trans. Willard R. Trask, Bollingen Series 76 (New York: Pantheon Books, 1964), p. xv.

5. Some of these criticisms can be discovered among the following scholars: John A. Saliba, *Homo Religiosus in Mircea Eliade: Anthropological Evaluation* (Leiden: E. J. Brill, 1976); Ioan Culianu, *Mircea Eliade* (Assisi: Cittadella Editrice, 1977); Ninian Smart, "Beyond Eliade: The Future of Theory in Religion," *Numen* 25/2 (1978): 171–183; Robert D. Baird, *Category Formation and the History of Religions* (The Hague: Mouton, 1971); Guilford Dudley III, *Religion on Trial: Mircea Eliade and His Critics* (Philadelphia: Temple University Press, 1977; Ivan Strenski,

Religion in Relation: Method, Application, and Moral Location (Columbia, SC: University of South Carolina Press, 1993).

6. Gilles Deleuze, *Difference and Repetition*, trans. Paul Patton (New York: Columbia University Press, 1994), p. 182.

7. Gilles Deleuze, *What is Philosophy?*, trans. Hugh Tomlinson and Graham Bouchell (New York: Columbia University Press, 1994), p. 36.

8. Mircea Eliade, *The Quest: History and Meaning in Religion* (Chicago: University of Chicago Press, 1969), p. 58.

9. Ibid., p. 62.

10. Mircea Eliade, "Methodological Remarks on the Study of Religious Symbolism," in *The History of Religions: Essays in Methodology*, ed. Mircea Eliade and Joseph M. Kitagawa (Chicago: University of Chicago Press, 1959), p. 100.

11. Eliade, *Shamanism*, p. xvii.

12. Eliade, *Journal II*, p. 162f.

13. Ibid., p. 298.

14. Eliade, *Shamanism*, p. xv.

15. Eliade, *Quest*, p. 25.

16. Ibid., p. 19.

17. Ibid., pp. 60–61.

18. Mircea Eliade, *Symbolism, the Sacred, and the Arts*, ed. Diane Apostolos-Cappadona (New York: Crossroad, 1986), p. 155.

19. Mircea Eliade, *Autobiography*, vol. 1, 1907–1937: *Journey East Journey West*, trans. Mac Linscott Ricketts (San Francisco: Harper and Row, 1981), p. 274.

20. Mircea Eliade, *Myth and Reality*, trans. Willard R. Trask (New York: Harper and Row, 1963), p. 181.

21. Roger Corless, "After Eliade, What?" *Religion* 23 (1993): 373–377.

22. Eliade, *Ordeal*, p. 153.

23. Charles Tilly, *Big Structure, Large Processes, Huge Comparisons* (New York: Russell Sage Foundation, 1984), p. 82.

24. Ibid., p. 82.

25. Ibid.

26. Ibid., p. 83.

27. Jonathan Z. Smith views Eliade's encompassing morphology as a metaphysical hierarchy in *Relating Religion: Essays in the Study of Religion* (Chicago: University of Chicago Press, 2004), p. 94. Smith cannot imagine thought without comparison because it is fundamental to our way of thinking (p. 30).

28. Jonathan Z. Smith, *Map Is Not Territory: Studies in the History of Religions* (Leiden: E. J. Brill 1978), p. 291.

29. Ibid., p. 134.

30. Jonathan Z. Smith, *To Take Place: Toward Theory in Ritual* (Chicago: University of Chicago Press, 1987), pp. 102–103.

31. Smith, *Map*, p. 141.

32. Deleuze, *What Is Philosophy?*, p. 36.
33. Deleuze, *Difference and Repetition*, p. 86.
34. Ibid., pp. 76, 103.
35. Jonathan Z. Smith, *Imagining Religion: From Babylon to Jonestown* (Chicago: University of Chicago Press, 1982), pp. 22–26. See also his essay "Prologue: In Comparison a Magic Dwells," in *A Magic Still Dwells: Comparative Religion in the Postmodern Age*, ed. Kimberley C. Patton and Benjamin C. Ray (Berkeley: University of California Press, 2000), pp. 23–44.
36. Smith, *Imagining Religion*, 35.
37. Smith, *Relating Religion*, pp. 197–198.
38. Ibid., p. 29.
39. Jonathan Z. Smith, *Drudgery Divine: On the Comparison of Early Christianities and the Religions of Late Antiquity* (Chicago: University of Chicago Press, 1990), p. 42.
40. Ibid., p. 52.
41. Smith, *Relating Religion*, p. 241.
42. Ibid.
43. Ibid., p. 271.
44. Gilles Deleuze, *Logic of Sense*, trans. Mark Lester and ed. Constantin V. Boundas (New York: Columbia University Press, 1994), p. 310, and *Difference and Repetition*, p. 281.
45. Deleuze, *Difference and Repetition*, p. 5.
46. See Sam Gill, "No Place to Stand: Jonathan Z. Smith as *Homo Ludens*, the Academic Study of Religion *Sub Specie Ludi*," *Journal of the American Academy of Religion* 66/2 (1998): 283–312.
47. Ibid., p. 303.
48. See for instance, Alf Hiltebeitel, *The Cult of Draupadī*, vol. 1, *Mythologies: From Gingee to Kuruksetra* (Chicago: University of Chicago Press, 1988), and *The Cult of Draupadī*, vol. 2, *On Hindu Ritual and the Goddess* (Chicago: University of Chicago Press, 1991); Gregory Schopen, *Bones, Stones, and Buddhist Monks: Collected Papers on the Archaeology, Epigraphy, and Texts in India* (Honolulu: University of Hawaii Press, 1997), *Figments and Fragments of Mahāyāna Buddhism in India: More Collected Papers* (Honolulu: University of Hawaii Press, 2005), and *Buddhist Monks and Business Matters: Still More Papers on Monastic Buddhism in India* (Honolulu: University of Hawaii Press, 2004).
49. Wendy Doniger, *The Implied Spider: Politics and Theology in Myth* (New York: Columbia University Press, 1998), p. 28.
50. Wendy Doniger, *Dreams, Illusion, and Other Realities* (Chicago: University of Chicago Press, 1984), p. 260. Sam Gill agrees that comparison is at the root of all learning, but there is no development of knowledge without discerning differences (p. 969). Gill warns that comparison must not be used to make phenomena conform to an already preexisting paradigm (p. 965). See "The

Academic Study of Religion," *Journal of the American Academy of Religion* 62/4 (1994): 965–975.

51. Doniger, *Implied Spider*, p. 34.
52. Ibid., p. 34.
53. Wendy Doniger, *Other Peoples' Myths: The Cave of Echoes* (New York: Macmillan, 1988), p. 136.
54. Doniger, *Implied Spider*, p. 34.
55. Wendy Doniger, *Splitting the Difference: Gender and Myth in Ancient Greece and India* (Chicago: University of Chicago Press, 1999), p. 4.
56. Doniger, *Implied Spider*, p. 35.
57. Ibid., p. 36.
58. See my comparative philosophical treatments of these questions in *Zen and the Art of Postmodern Philosophy: Two Paths of Liberation from the Representational Mode of Thinking* (Albany: State University of New York Press, 2000), and *Indian Philosophers and Postmodern Thinkers: Dialogues on the Margins of Culture* (Delhi: Oxford University Press, 2002).
59. Gilles Deleuze and Féix Guattari, *Anti-Oedipus: Capitalism and Schizophrenia*, trans. Robert Hurley, Mark Seem, and Helen R. Lane (Minneapolis: University of Minnesota Press, 1983), p. 16.
60. Doniger, *Implied Spider*, p. 65.
61. Ibid., p. 60.
62. Strenski, *Religion in Relation*, pp. 57–74. Russell T. McCutcheon, *Manufacturing Religion: The Discourse on Sui Generis Religion and the Politics of Nostalgia* (New York: Oxford University Press, 1997), pp. 193–194.
63. Doniger, *Implied Spider*, p. 65.
64. Ibid.
65. Brian A. Hatcher, *Eclecticism and Modern Hindu Discourse* (New York: Oxford University Press, 1999), p. 91.
66. See Wendy Doniger, *The Bedtrick: Tales of Sex and Masquerade* (Chicago: University of Chicago Press, 2000), chapters 3–10.
67. Wendy Doniger, *Women, Androgynes, and Other Mythical Beasts* (Chicago: University of Chicago Press, 1980), p. 8.
68. Ibid., pp. 149–237.
69. Doniger, *Other Peoples' Myths*, p. 112.
70. Doniger, *Implied Spider*, p. 9.
71. Doniger, *Dreams, Illusions and Other Realities*, p. 5.
72. Ibid., p. 79. See also "When a Lingam Is Just a Good Cigar: Psychoanalysis and Hindu Sexual Fantasies," in *Vishnu on Freud's Desk: A Reader in Psychoanalysis and Hinduism*, ed. T. G. Vaidyanathan and Jeffrey J. Kripal (Delhi: Oxford University Press, 1999), p. 284.
73. Doniger, *Women, Androgynes, and Other Mythical Beasts*, p. 10.
74. Deleuze, *What Is Philosophy?*, p. 274.

75. Deleuze, *The Logic of Sense*, p. 262.

76. See, for example, the following writers: Donald Wiebe, "Is the New Comparativism Really New?" *Method and Theory in the Study of Religion* 8/1 (1996): 21–29; E. Thomas Lawson, "Theory and the Comparativism, Old and New," *Method and Theory in the Study of Religion* 8/1 (1996): 31–35; Jacques Waardenburg, "*Religionswissenschaft* New Style: Some Thoughts and Afterthoughts," *Annual Review of the Science of Religion* 2 (1978): 116–125, on p. 119; Thomas A. Idinopulos, "The Difficulties of Understanding Religion," in *What is Religion? Origins, Definitions, and Explanations*, ed. Thomas A. Idinopulos and Brian C. Wilson (Leiden: E. J. Brill, 1998), pp. 28–29.

77. Smith, *Map Is Not Territory*, p. 259, *Imagining Religion*, pp. 22–23, and *To Take Place*, p. 14.

78. Doniger, *Implied Spider*, p. 37.

79. See Doniger, *Splitting the Difference*.

80. Idem, *Implied Spider*, p. 61.

81. Ibid.

82. Doniger, *Splitting the Difference*, p. 130.

83. Doniger, *Implied Spider*, p. 153.

84. Ibid., p. 153.

85. Ibid., p. 19.

86. Ibid., p. 101. From another perspective, Bruce Lincoln views myth as "ideology in narrative form" (147) in *Theorizing Myth: Narrative, Ideology, and Scholarship* (Chicago: University of Chicago Press, 1999).

87. Wendy Doniger, "Presidential Address: 'I Have Scinde': Flogging a Dead (White Male Orientalist) Horse," *Journal of Asian Studies* 58/4 (1999): 940–960.

88. Doniger, *Implied Spider*, p. 107.

89. Ibid., p. 70.

90. Ibid., p. 66.

91. For examples of this type of tendency, see Donald Wiebe, *The Politics of Religious Studies: The Continuing Conflict with Theology in the Academy* (New York: St. Martin's Press, 1991), p. 289; Ivan Strenski, *Four Theories of Myth in Twentieth-Century History: Cassirer, Eliade, Lévi-Strauss and Malinowski* (London: Macmillan; Iowa City: University of Iowa Press, 1987), pp. 78–102.

92. See Catherine Albanese, "The Problem of Bias: Interpretive Strategies in Religious Studies," *Soundings* 71/2–3 (1988): 279–293, on p. 248.

93. Doniger, *Implied Spider*, p. 67.

94. Ibid., p. 68.

95. Doniger, *The Bedtrick*, p. xxi.

96. Doniger, *Implied Spider*, p. 68.

97. Doniger, *Asceticism and Eroticism in the Mythology of Śiva* (London: Oxford University Press, 1973), p. 18.

98. Ibid.

99. Doniger, *Implied Spider*, p. 46.

100. Ibid.

101. Gavin Flood, *Beyond Phenomenology: Rethinking the Study of Religion* (London: Cassell, 1999), p. 35.

102. Wendy Doniger, "The Uses and Misuses of Other Peoples' Myths," 1985 presidential address, *Journal of the American Academy of Religion* 54/2 (1986): 219–239.

103. Wendy Doniger, *The Origins of Evil in Hindu Mythology* (Berkeley: University of California Press, 1976), p. 9.

104. Doniger, *Implied Spider*, pp. 148–149.

105. Ibid., p. 148.

106. Ibid., p. 147.

107. Ibid.

108. Ibid.

109. Ibid., p. 150.

110. Wendy Doniger, "Minimyths and Maximyths and Political Points of View," in *Myth and Method*, ed. Laurie L. Patton and Wendy Doniger (Charlottesville: University Press of Virginia, 1996), p. 110.

111. See my comparison of Mircea Eliade and various postmodern thinkers in *The Theology and Philosophy of Eliade: A Search for the Centre* (London: Macmillan, 1992), and my response to Bryan S. Rennie and his book *Reconsidering Eliade: Making Sense of Religion* (Albany: State University of New York Press, 1996), pp. 232–238, in which he attempts to argue that Eliade was a precursor of postmodernism, in my essay "Mircea Eliade, Postmodernism, and the Problematic Nature of Representational Thinking," *Method and Theory in the Study of Religion* 11 (1999): 357–385.

112. Smith, *Imagining Religion*, pp. 21–24.

113. Smith, *Drudgery Divine*, pp. 51–52.

114. Ibid., p. 42.

115. Eliade and Doniger, although to a lesser extent, share with the neo-Kantian and Enlightenment philosophical traditions a number of convictions such as that the universe is intelligible; truths are fixed, uniform, permanent, absolute, and universal; and religion is a sui generis reality that is unique and irreducible.

116. Deleuze, *Difference and Repetition*, p. 66.

117. Hans-Georg Gadamer, *Truth and Method*, trans. Garrett Barden and John Cumming (New York: Crossroad, 1982), p. 238.

118. Charles Taylor, *Philosophical Arguments* (Cambridge, MA: Harvard University Press, 1985), p. 150.

119. Ibid., pp. 150–151.

CHAPTER 6

1. Jean-François Lyotard, "Réponse à la question: Qu'est-ce la postmoderne?" *Critique* 419 (1982): 356–367, on p. 367.
2. Jean-François Lyotard, *The Postmodern Condition: A Report on Knowledge*, trans. Geoff Bennington and Brian Massumi, Theory and History of Literature, vol. 10 (Minneapolis: University of Minnesota Press, 1984), p. xxv.
3. Ibid., p. 3.
4. Ibid., p. 5.
5. Michel Foucault, "Nietzsche, Freud, Marx," in *Nietzsche*, Proceedings of the Seventh International Philosophical Colloquium of the Cahiers de Royaumont, July 4–8 (Paris: Editions de Minuit, 1967), p. 189.
6. Michel Foucault, *The Archaeology of Knowledge and the Discourse on Language*, trans. A. M. Sheridan Smith (New York: Pantheon Books, 1972), p. 9.
7. Arnold I. Davidson, "Archaeology, Genealogy, Ethics," in *Foucualt: A Critical Reader*, ed. David Couzens Hoy (Oxford: Basil Blackwell, 1986), p. 227.
8. Friedrich Nietzsche, *The Use and Abuse of History*, trans. Adrian Collins (New York: Macmillan, 1957), p. 12.
9. Michel Foucault, *The History of Sexuality*, vol. 1, *An Introduction*, trans. Robert Hurley (New York: Vintage/Books, 1980), p. 52.
10. v, *Power/Knowledge: Selected Interviews and Other Writings 1972–1977*, ed. and trans. Colin Gordon, Leo Marshall, John Mepham, and Kate Soper (New York: Pantheon Books, 1980), p. 50.
11. Michel Foucault, *Language, Counter-Memory, Practice: Selected Essays and Interviews*, ed. Donald F. Bouchard and trans. Donald F. Bouchard and Sherry Simon (Oxford: Blackwell, 1977), p. 230.
12. Foucault, *History of Sexuality*, 1: 5–6.
13. Michel Foucault, "Nietzsche, Genealogy, History," in *Language, Counter-Memory, Practice: Selected Essays and Interviews*, ed. Donald F. Bouchard and trans. Donald F. Bouchard and Sherry Simon (Ithaca, NY: Cornell University Press, 1977), p.153.
14. Ibid., pp. 152–157.
15. Richard Rorty, "Foucault and Epistemology," in *Foucault: A Critical Reader*, ed. David Couzens Hoy (London: Basil Blackwell, 1986), p. 43.
16. Foucault, "Nietzsche, Freud, Marx," p. 190.
17. Mircea Eliade, *Ordeal by Labyrinth: Conversations with Claude-Henri Racquet.*, trans. Derek Coltman (Chicago: University of Chicago Press, 1982), p. 100, *Autobiography*, vol. 1, *1907–1937: Journey East Journey West*, tran. Mac Linscott Ricketts (San Francisco: Harper & Row, 1981), p. 189, *Myth of the Eternal Return*, trans. Willard R. Trask (New York: Pantheon Books, 1954), p. 17, and *Patterns in Comparative Religion*, trans. Rosemary Sheed (Cleveland: World Publishing, 1968), pp. 373–382.

18. Mircea Eliade, *Shamanism: Archaic Techniques of Ecstasy*, trans. Willard R. Trask, Bollingen Series 76 (New York: Pantheon Books, 1964), p. xv.

19. Mircea Eliade, *Myths, Dreams and Mysteries: The Encounter between Archaic Realities*, trans. Philip Mairet (New York: Harper & Row, 1967), p. 178.

20. Mircea Eliade, *Myth and Reality*, trans. Willard R. Trask (New York: Harper & Row, 1963), p. 142.

21. Eliade, *Myth of the Eternal Return*, p. 156.

22. Foucault, *Power/Knowledge*, pp. 132–133.

23. Foucault, *Archeology of Knowledge*, p. 120.

24. Eliade, *Ordeal by Labyrinth*, p. 153.

25. Mircea Eliade, *The Quest: History and Meaning in Religion* (Chicago: University of Chicago Press, 1969), p. 2.

26. Jacques Derrida, *Dissemination*, trans. Barbara Johnson (Chicago: University of Chicago Press, 1981), p. 14.

27. Mark C. Taylor, *Erring: A Postmodern A/theology* (Chicago: University of Chicago Press, 1984), p. 173.

28. Eliade, *Ordeal by Labyrinth*, p. 153.

29. Gilles Deleuze and Felix Guttari, *Anti-Oedipus: Capitalism and Schizophrenia*, trans. Robert Hurley, Mark Seem, and Helen R. Lane (Minneapolis: University of Minnesota Press, 1983), pp. 8–9.

30. Ibid., p. 85.

31. Ibid., p. 326.

32. Ibid., p. 42.

33. Eliade, *Patterns in Comparative Religion*, p. 42.

34. Gilles Deleuze and Félix Guttari, *A Thousand Plateaus: Capitalism and Schizophrenia*, trans. Brian Massumi (Minneapolis: University of Minnesota Press, 1988), p. 16.

35. Jonathan Z. Smith, *To Take Place: Toward Theory in Ritual* (Chicago: University of Chicago Press, 1987), p. 14.

36. Eliade, *Myths, Dreams and Mysteries*, p. 130.

37. Mircea Eliade, *The Sacred and the Profane*, trans. Willard R. Trask (New York: Harcourt, Brace, 1959), p. 117.

38. Carl Olson, *The Theology and Philosophy of Eliade: A Search for the Centre* (London: Macmillan, 1992), p. 107.

39. Jacques Derrida, *Of Grammatology*, trans. Gayatri Chakravorty Spivak (Baltimore: Johns Hopkins University Press, 1976), pp. 156, 154.

40. Eliade, The Quest, p. ii.

41. Mircea Eliade, *No Souvenirs, Journal: 1957–1969*, trans. Fred H. Johnson, Jr. (New York: Harper & Row, 1977), p. 290.

42. Martin Heidegger, *Basic Concepts*, trans. Gary E. Aylesworth (Bloomington: Indiana University Press, 1993), p. 97.

43. Martin Heidegger, *Holzwege* (Frankfurt: Victtorio Klostermann, 1963), p. 277.

44. Jacques Derrida, *Writing and Difference*, trans. Alan Bass (Chicago: University of Chicago Press, 1978), p. 147.

45. Jacques Derrida, *Psyché: Inventions de l' autre* (Paris: Galilée, 1987), p. 168.

46. Derrida, *Writing and Difference*, p. 230.

47. Taylor, *Erring*, p. 42.

48. Ibid., pp. 49–50.

49. Jacques Lacan, *The Seminar of Jacques Lacan, Book II: The Ego in Freud's Theory and in the Technique of Psychoanalysis* 1954–1955, trans. Sylvan Tomaselli (New York: W. W. Norton, 1988), p.178, and *Écrits: A Selection*, trans. Alan Sheridan (New York: W. W. Norton, 1977), p. 99; Julia Kristeva, *Polylogue* (Paris: Éditions du Seuil, 1977), pp. 78, 96, and *Revolution in Poetic Language*, trans. Margaret Waller (New York: Columbia University, 1984), pp. 46–47.

50. Gilles Deleuze, *Difference and Repetition*, trans. Paul Patton (New York: Columbia University Press, 1994), p. 67.

51. Ibid., p. 199.

52. Eliade, *Myths, Dreams and Mysteries*, p. 125.

53. Roland Inden, *Imagining India* (Oxford: Basil Blackwell, 1990), p. 2.

54. Eliade, *The Quest*, p. iii.

55. Derrida, *Psyché*, pp. 387–388, 390.

56. Ibid., p. 391.

57. Jacques Derrida, *Limited Inc.*, trans. Samuel Weber (Evanston, IL: Northwestern University Press, 1988), p. 141.

58. Derrida, *Of Grammatology*, p. 24, and *Dissemination*, p. 41.

59. Eliade, *Autobiography*, 1: 274.

60. Eliade, *Ordeal by Labyrinth*, pp. 153–154.

61. Walter Capps, *Religious Studies: The Making of a Discipline* (Minneapolis: Fortress Press, 1995), p. 6.

62. Bryan Rennie uses secondary sources on postmodern thinkers to make his argument, which is akin to using "Cliff's Notes" instead of reading the primary sources. This choice does not enable him to see that postmodernists are opposed to representational thinking and those who practice it such as Eliade. Like Kant, Eliade thinks that it is possible to identity fundamental epistemological principles associated with valid knowledge. See Rennie's book *Reconstructing Eliade: Making Sense of Religion* (Albany, N. Y: State University of New York Press, 1996), pp. 232–241.

63. Gilles Deleuze, *Foucault*, trans. Sean Hand (Minneapolis: University of Minnesota Press, 1988), p. 109.

64. Eliade, *The Quest*, p. 19.

65. Eliade, *Patterns in Comparative Religion*, p. 157.

66. Jonathan Z. Smith, *Map Is Not Territory: Studies in the History of Religions* (Leiden: E. J. Brill, 1978), p. 259, and *Imagining Religion: From Babylon to Jonestown* (Chicago: University of Chicago Press, 1982), p. 23.

67. Eliade, *No Souvenirs*, p. 313.

68. Lyotard, *Postmodern Condition*, p. 7; Jean-François Lyotard and Jean-Loup Thébaud, *Just Gaming*, trans. Wlad Goodrich, Theory and History of Literature, vol. 20 (Minneapolis: University of Minnesota Press, 1985), p. 86.

69. Michel Foucault, *Madness and Civilization: A History of Insanity to the Age of Reason*, trans. Richard Howard (New York: Random House, 1973), p. 70.

70. Julia Kristeva, *Powers of Horror: An Essay on Abjection*, trans. Leon S. Roudiez (New York: Columbia University Press, 1982).

71. Derrida, *Of Grammatology*, p. 259.

72. Jacques Derrida, *Glas*, trans. John P. Leavey, Jr and Richard Rand (Lincoln: University of Nebraska Press, 1986), p. 213.

73. Deleuze and Guttari, *Anti-Oedipus*, p. 16.

74. Foucault, *Language, Counter Memory, Practice*, p. 153.

75. Lyotard, *Postmodern Condition*, p. xxv.

76. Deleuze, *Difference and Repetition*, pp. 272–273.

77. Ibid., p. 274.

78. Derrida, *Dissemination*, p. 6.

79. Derrida, *Glas*, pp. 258, 261.

80. Richard Rorty, *Philosophy and the Mirror of Nature* (Princeton, NJ: Princeton University Press, 1979), p. 12.

81. Derrida, *Of Grammatology*, p. 12.

82. Taylor, *Erring*, p. 173.

83. Eliae, *Ordeal by Labyrinth*, p. 167.

84. Jean Baudrillard, *Simulacra and Simulation*, trans. Shelia Faria Glaser (Ann Arbor: University of Michigan Press, 1994), p. 3.

85. Jean Baudrillard, *Forget Foucault* (New York: Semiotex(e), 1987), p. 82.

86. Baudrillard, *Simulacra and Simulation*, p.19.

87. Ibid., p. 30.

88. Jean Baudrillard, *Fatal Strategies*, trans. Philip Beitchman and W. G. J. Niesluchowski (New York: Semiotext(e), 1990), p. 108.

89. Baudrillard, *Simulacra and Simulation*, p. 43, and *Symbolic Exchange and Death*, trans. Hamilton Grant (London: Sage Publications, 1993), p. 2.

90. Deleuze, *Difference and Repetition*, p. 301.

91. Gilles Deleuze, *Logic of Sense*, and trans. Mark Lester ed. Constantin V. Bounds (New York: Columbia University Press, 1990), p. 262.

92. Ibid., p. 301.

93. Ibid., pp. 264–265.

94. Ibid., p. 257.

95. Derrida, *Dissemination*, p. 139.

96. See Olson, *The Theology and Philosophy of Eliade*.

97. Eliade, *No Souvenirs*, p. 298.

98. Eliade, *Patterns in Comparative Religion*, p. 463.

99. Eliade, *No Souvenirs*, p. 80.

CHAPTER 7

1. Hayden V. White, *Topics of Discourse: Essays in Cultural Criticism* (Baltimore: Johns Hopkins University Press, 1978), pp. 233–234.
2. Ibid., p. 239.
3. Robert Segal, "Classification and Comparison in the Study of Religion: The Work of Jonathan Z. Smith," *Journal of the American Academy of Religion* 73/4 (2005): 1175–1188.
4. A couple of the following scholars and their works have had good results using some postmodern material: Amy Hollywood, *Sensible Ecstasy: Mysticism, Sexual Difference, and the Demands of History* (Chicago: University of Chicago Press, 2002); Hugh Urban, "The Remnants of Desire: Sacrificial Violence and Sexual Transgression in the Cult of the Kāpālikas and in the Writings of George Bataille," *Religion* 25 (1995): 67–90, and *The Power of Tantra: Religion, Sexuality and the Politics of South Asian Studies* (London: I. B. Tauris, 2010).
5. Russell T. McCutcheon, *Critics Not Caretakers: Redescribing the Public Study of Religion* (Albany: State University of New York Press, 2001), pp. 61, 112–114.
6. Jeffrey J. Kripal, *The Serpent's Gift: Gnostic Reflections on the Study of Religion* (Chicago: University of Chicago Press, 2007), p. 9.
7. Ibid., p. 12.
8. Ibid., p. 13.
9. James Taylor, *Buddhism and Postmodern Imaginings in Thailand: The Religiosity of Urban Space* (Farnham, England: Ashgate, 2008).
10. Tim Murphy, *Representing Religion: Essays in History, Theory and Crisis* (London: Equinox, 2007), p. 8.
11. Ibid., pp. 11–12.
12. Garrett Green, "Hermenuetics," in *The Routledge Companion to the Study of Religion*, 2nd ed., ed. John R. Hinnells (London: Routledge), p. 421.
13. Stanley Rosen, *The Elusiveness of the Ordinary: Studies in the Possibility of Philosophy* (New Haven, CT: Yale University Press, 2002), p. 272.
14. Ibid., p. 267.
15. Ibid., p. 295.
16. Ibid., p. 297.
17. Ibid., p. 10.
18. Pierre Bourdieu, *Outline of a Theory of Practice*, trans. Richard Nice (Cambridge: Cambridge University Press, 1986), p. 3.
19. Ibid., p. 79.
20. Ibid., p. 72.
21. Pierre Bourdieu, *The Logic of Practice*, trans. Richard Nice (Stanford, CA: Stanford University Press, 1990), pp. 55, 72.
22. Karl R. Popper, *The Logic of Scientific Discovery* (1959; London: Hutchinson, 1986), pp. 40, 44.

23. Ibid., p. 42.

24. Ibid., p. 47.

25. Ibid., p. 251.

26. Thomas S. Kuhn, *The Structure of Scientific Revolutions*, International Encyclopedia of United States, 2nd ed., vol. 2, no. 2 (Chicago: University of Chicago Press, 1979), p. 109.

27. Ibid., p. 175.

28. Michael Polanyi, *Personal Knowledge: Towards a Post-Critical Philosophy* (1958; London: Routledge & Kegan Paul, 1983), p. 134.

29. Ibid., pp. 18, 143.

30. Karl R. Popper, *Objective Knowledge: An Evolutionary Approach* (1972; Oxford: Clarendon Press, 1986), pp. 9, 111.

31. Polanyi, *Personal Knowledge*, p. 138.

32. Kuhn, *The Structure of Scientific Revolutions*, p. 84.

33. Karl R. Popper, *Conjectures and Refutations: The Growth of Scientific Knowledge* 4th ed. (1963; London: Routledge & Kegan Paul, 1985), p. 47.

34. Ibid., p. 28.

35. Kuhn, *The Structure of Scientific Revolutions*, p. 123.

36. Popper, *Logic*, p. 278.

37. Nicholas Rescher, *A System of Pragmatic Idealism*, vol. 1, *Human Knowledge in Idealistic Perspective* (Princeton, NJ: Princeton University Press, 1992), p. 125.

38. Benson Saler, "Towards a Realistic and Relevant 'Science of Religion,'" *Method and Theory in the Study of Religion* 16/3 (2004): 205–233, on pp. 208, 212, 215. Contrary to Saler, Gavin Flood argues, "cognitive theory cannot give an adequate account of the historical and linguistic specificity of cultural formations" (*Beyond Phenomenology: Rethinking the Study of Religion* [London: Cassell, 1999], p. 59). Flood goes on to say that culture and language "exist independently of cognition" (p. 62).

39. Mark C. Taylor, *After God* (Chicago: University of Chicago Press, 2007), p. 10.

40. George Lakoff and Mark Johnson, *Philosophy in the Flesh: The Embodied Mind and Its Challenge to Western Thought* (New York: Basic Books, 1999), p. 89.

41. Flood, *Beyond Phenomenology*, p. 75.

42. Jonathan Z. Smith, *Relating Religion: Essays in the Study of Religion* (Chicago: University of Chicago Press, 2004), p. 167.

43. Flood, *Beyond Phenomenology*, p. 235.

44. Tomoko Masuzawa, *The Invention of World Religions, or How European Universalism Was Preserved in the Languages of Pluralism* (Chicago: University of Chicago Press, 2005), p. 11.

45. Charles Taylor, *Philosophical Arguments* (Cambridge, MA: Harvard University Press, 1985), pp. 150–164.

46. Rescher, *A System of Pragmatic Idealism*, p. 25.

47. Ibid., pp. 27, 33.

48. Hilary Putnam, *Renewing Philosophy* (Cambridge, MA: Harvard University Press, 1992), p. 72.

49. See John R. Searle, *The Construction of Social Reality* (New York: Free Press, 1995).

50. Mark C. Taylor, *Erring: A Postmodern A/theology* (Chicago: University ofChicago Press, 1984), pp. 160–161. See also Julia Kristeva, *Powers of Horror: An Essay on Abjection*, trans. Leon S. Roudiez (New York: Columbia University Press, 1982), *Revolution in Poetic Language*, trans. Margaret Waller (New York: Columbia University Press, 1984), and *Desire in Literature: A Semiotic Approach to Literature and Art*, trans. Thomas Gora, Alice Jardine, and Leon S. Roudiez (New York: Columbia University Press, 1980).

51. Jacques Derrida, *Dissemination*, trans. Barbara Johnson (Chicago: University of Chicago Press, 1981).

52. Stanley Rosen, *The Ancients and the Moderns: Rethinking Modernity* (New Haven, CT: Yale University Press, 1989), p. 20.

53. Charles Taylor, *Sources of the Self: The Meaning of Modern Identity* (Cambridge: Cambridge University Press, 1989), p. 489.

54. Gilles Deleuze and Félix Guattari, *Anti-Oedipus: Capitalism and Schizophrenia*, trans. Robert Hurley, Mark Seem, and Helen R. Lane (Minneapolis: University of Minnesota Press, 1983), p. 341.

55. Kristeva, *Revolution*, pp. 200–201.

56. Allen S. Weiss, *The Aesthetics of Excess* (Albany: State University of New York Press, 1989), p. 90; Allan Megill, *Prophets of Extremity: Nietzsche, Heidegger, Foucault, Derrida* (Berkeley: University of California Press, 1985), p. 243.

57. Robert Nozick, *The Nature of Rationality* (Princeton, NJ: Princeton University Press, 1993), p. xi.

58. Putnam, *Renewing Philosophy*, p. 140.

59. Ibid., p. 124.

60. Rescher, *A System of Pragmatic Idealism*, p. 3.

61. Ibid., p. 8.

62. Edmond Jabès, *The Books Questions*, vol. 2, trans. Rosemarie Waldrop (Middletown, CT: Wesleyan University Press, 1991), pp. 312, 293.

63. Maurice Blanchot, *The Writing of Disaster*, trans. Ann Smock (Lincoln: University of Nebraska Press, 1986), p. 91.

64. Jacques Derrida, *Writing and Difference*, trans. Alan Bass (Chicago: University of Chicago Press, 1978), p. 246.

65. Charles Taylor, *A Secular Age* (Cambridge, MA: Belknap Press of Harvard University Press, 2007), p. 373.

66. Hent De Vries, "Introduction: Why Still 'Religion'?," in *Religion: Beyond a Concept*, ed. Hent de Vries (New York: Fordham University Press, 2008), p. 15.

Bibliography

Albanese, Catherine. "The Problem of Bias: Interpretive Strategies in Religious Studies." *Soundings* 71/2–3 (1988): 279–293.

Allen, N. J. "The Category of the Person: A Reading of Mauss' Last Essay." In *The Category of the Person: Anthropology, Philosophy, History*. Edited by Michael Carrithers, Steven Collins, and Steven Lukes. Cambridge: Cambridge University Press, 1985, pp. 23–35.

Baird, Robert D. *Category Formation and the History of Religions*. The Hague: Mouton, 1971.

Barrett, Justin. "Exploring the Natural Foundations of Religion." *Trends in Cognitive Sciences* 4/1 (2000): 29–34.

Bataille, Georges. *The Accursed Share: An Essay on General Economy*. Volume 1. Translated by Robert Hurley. New York: Zone Books, 1988.

———. *The Accursed Share: An Essay on General Economy*. Volume 2 *The History of Eroticism*, and volume 3, *Sovereignty*. New York: Zone Books, 1991.

———. *Death and Sensuality: A Study of Eroticism and the Taboo*. New York: Walker, 1962; reprint, Salem, NH: Ayer, 1984.

———. "Hegel, la mort et le sacrifice," *Deucalion* 5 (1955): 21–43.

———. *Inner Experience*. Translated by Leslie Anne Bolt. Albany: NY: State University of New York Press, 1988.

———. *L' Expérience intérieure*. Paris: Gallimard, 1954.

———. *Oeuvres completes*. 12 volumes. Paris: Gallimard, 1970–1988.

———. *The Tears of Eros*. Translated by Peter Connor. San Francisco: City Lights Books, 1989.

———. *Theory of Religion*. Traslated by Robert Hurley. New York: Zone Books, 1989.

———. *Visions of Excess: Selected Writings, 1927–1939*. Translated by Alan Stoekl. Theory and History of Literature, volume 14. Minneapolis: University of Minnesota Press, 1985.

Baudrillard, Jean. *Fatal Strategies*. Translated by Philip Beitchman and W. G. J. Niesluchowski. New York: Semiotext(e), 1990.

———. *Forget Foucault*. New York: Semiotex(e), 1987.

————. *Seductions*. Translated by Brian Singer. New York: St. Martin's Press, 1990.

————. *Simulacra and Simulation*. Translated by Sheila Faria Glaser. Ann Arbor: University of Michigan Press, 1994.

————. *Symbolic Exchange and Death*. Translated by Hamilton Grant. London: Sage Publications, 1993.

Beidelman, T. O. *The Cool Knife: Imagery of Gender, Sexuality, and Moral Education in Kagaru Initiation Ritual*. Washington, D C: Smithsonian Institution Press, 1997.

Bell, Catherine. *Ritual Theory, Ritual Practice*. New York: Oxford University Press, 1992.

Benjamin, Walter. *Selected Writings*, volume 4, 1938–1994. Translated by Edmund Jephcott et al. and edited by Howard Eiland and Michael W. Jennings. Cambridge, MA: Harvard University Press, 2003.

Berlin, Isaiah. *The Roots of Romanticism*. Princeton, NJ: Princeton University Press, 1999.

Bhabha, Homi K. *The Location of Culture*. 1994; London: Routledge, 2002.

————. "Unsatisfied Notes on Vernacular Cosmopolitianism." in *Postcolonial Discourse: An Anthology*. Edited by Gregory Castle. Oxford: Blackwell, 2001, pp. 38–52.

Biardeau, Madeleine, and Charles Malamoud. *Le Sacrifice dans l'Inde ancienne*. Bibliothéque de l' Études, Scieneces religieuses, 79. Paris: Presses universitaires de France, 1976.

Blanchot, Maurice. *The Writing of Disaster*. Translated by Ann Smock. Lincoln: University of Nebraska Press, 1986.

Bloch, Maurice. "Why Religion Is Nothing Special but Is Central." *Philosophical Transactions of the Royal Society* B 363 (2008): 2055–2061.

Bourdieu, Pierre. *The Logic of Practice*. Translated by Richard Nice. Stanford, CA: Stanford University Press, 1990.

————. *Outline of a Theory of Practice*. Translated by Richard Nice. Cambridge: Cambridge University Press, 1986.

Boyer, Pascal. "Out of Africa: Lessons from a By-Product of Evolution." In *Religion as Human Capacity: A Festschrift in Honor of E. Thomas Lawson*. Ed. Timothy Light and Brian C. Wilson. Leiden: E. J. Brill, 2004, pp. 27–43.

————. *Religion Explained: The Evolutionary Origins of Religious Thought*. New York: Basic Books, 2001.

————. "Religious Thought and Behavior as By-products of Brain Function." *Trends in Cognitive Sciences* 7/3 (2003): 119–124.

Brown, Joseph Epes, ed. *The Sacred Pipe*. New York: Penguin Books, 1979.

Calinescu, Matei, "Eliade and Ionesco in the Post-World War II Years: Questions of Identity in Exile." In *Hermeneutics, Politics, and the History of Religions: The Contested Legacies of Joachim Wach and Mircea Eliade*. Edited by Christian K. Wedemeyer and Wendy Doniger. Chicago: University of Chicago Press, 2010, pp. 103–131.

Capps, Walter H. *Religious Studies: The Making of a Discipline*. Minneapolis: Fortress Press, 1995.

Caputo, John D., and Michael J. Scanlon. "Introduction: Apology for the Impossible: Religion and Postmodernism." In *God, the Gift, and Postmodernism*. Edited by John D. Caputo and Michael J. Scanlon. Bloomington: Indiana University Press, 1999, pp. 1–19.

Carrette, Jeremy R. *Foucault and Religion: Spiritual Corporality and Political Spirituality*. London: Routledge, 2000.

———. "Post-Structuralism and the Study of Religion." In *The Routledge Companion to the Study of Religion*. 2nd ed. Edited by John Hinnells. London: Routledge, 2010, pp. 274–290.

Carrier, James. "Gifts, Commodities, and Social Relations: A Maussian View of Exchange." *Sociological Forum* 6 (1991): 19–136.

———. "Maussian Occidentalism: Gift and Commodity Systems." In *Occidentalism: Images of the West*. Edited by James G. Carrier. Oxford: Clarendon Press, 1995, pp. 85–108.

Chantepie de la Saussaye, P. D. *Manuel of the Science of Religion*, Translated by Beatrice C. Colyer-Fergusson. London: Longman, Green, 1891.

Clarke, J. J. *Oriental Enlightenment: The Encounter between Asian and Western Thought*. London: Routledge, 1997.

Collins, Steven. "Categories, Concepts or Predicaments? Remarks on Mauss' Use of Philosophical Terminology." In *The Category of Person: Anthropology, Philosophy, History*. Edited by Michael Carrithers, Steven Collins, and Steven Lukes. Cambridge: Cambridge University Press, 1985, pp. 46–58.

Combs-Schilling, M. E. *Sacred Performance: Islam, Sexuality, and Sacrifice*. New York: Columbia University Press, 1989.

Corless, Roger. "After Eliade, What?" *Religion* 23 (1993): 373–377.

Culianu, Ioan. *Mircea Eliade*. Assisi: Cittadella Editrice, 1977.

Davidson, Arnold I. "Archaeology, Genealogy, Ethics." In *Foucault: A Critical Reader*. Edited by David Couzens Hoy. London: Basil Blackwell, 1986, pp. 221–233.

Deleuze, Gilles. *Difference and Repetition*. Translated by Paul Patton. New York: Columbia University Press, 1994.

———. *Foucault*. Translated by Sean Hand. Minneapolis: University of Minnesota Press, 1988.

———. *Logic of Sense*. Translated by Mark Lester and edited by Constantin V. Boundas. New York: Columbia University Press, 1990.

———. *What Is Philosophy?* Translated by Hugh Tomlinson and Graham Bouchell. New York: Columbia University Press, 1994.

Deleuze, Gilles, and Félix Guattari. *Anti-Oedipus: Capitalism and Schizophrenia*. Translated by Robert Hurley, Mark Seem, and Helen R. Lane. Minneapolis: University of Minnesota Press, 1983.

———. *A Thousand Plateaus: Capitalism and Schizophrenia*. Translated by Brian Massumi. Minneapolis: University of Minnesota Press, 1988.

Derrida, Jacques. *Cinders*. Translated by Ned Lukacker. Lincoln: University of Nebraska Press, 1991.

——. *Dissemination*. Translated by Barbara Johnson. Chicago: University of Chicago Press, 1981.

——. "Faith and Knowledge: The Two Sources of 'Religion' at the Limits of Reason Alone." In *Religion*. Edited by Jacques Derrida and Gianni Vattimo. Stanford, CA: Stanford University Press, 1998, pp. 1–78.

——. *The Gift of Death*. Translated by David Wills. Chicago: University of Chicago Press, 1995.

——. *Given Time 1: Counterfeit Money*. Translated by Peggy Kamuf. Chicago: University of Chicago Press, 1992.

——. *Glas*. Translated by John P. Leavey Jr. and Richard Rand. Lincoln: University of Nebraska Press, 1986.

——. *Limited Inc*. Translated by Samuel Weber. Evanston, IL: Northwestern University Press, 1988.

——. *Margins of Philosophy*. Translated by Alan Bass. Chicago: University of Chicago Press, 1986.

——. *Of Grammatology*. Translated by Gayatri Chakravorty Spivak. Baltimore: Johns Hopkins University Press, 1976.

——. *Positions*. Translated by Alan Bass. Chicago: University of Chicago Press, 1981.

——. *The Postcard: From Socrates to Freud and Beyond*. Translated by Alan Bass. Chicago: University of Chicago Press, 1987.

——. "The Principle of Reason: The University in the Eyes of its Pupils." *Diacritics* 13 (1983): 3–20.

——. *Psyché: Inventions de l'autre*. Paris: Galilée, 1987.

——. *Speech and Phenomena and Other Essays on Husserl's Theory of Signs*. Translated by David B. Allison. Evanston: Northwestern University Press, 1973.

——. *Spurs*. Translated by Barbara Harlow. Chicago: University of Chicago Press, 1979.

——. *Writing and Difference*. Translated by Alan Bass. Chicago: University of Chicago Press, 1978.

Doniger, Wendy. *Asceticism and Eroticism in the Mythology of Śiva*. London: Oxford University Press, 1973.

——. *The Bedtrick: Tales of Sex and Masquerade*. Chicago: University of Chicago Press, 2000.

——. *Dreams, Illusion, and Other Realities*. Chicago: University of Chicago Press, 1984.

——. *The Implied Spider: Politics and Theology in Myth*. New York: Columbia University Press, 1998.

——. "Minimyths and Maximyths and Political Points of View." In *Myth and Method*. Edited by Laurie L. Patton and Wendy Doniger. Charlottesville: University Press of Virginia, 1996, pp. 109–127.

———. *The Origins of Evil in Hindu Mythology*. Berkeley: University of California Press, 1976.

———. *Other Peoples' Myths: The Cave of Echoes*. New York: Macmillan, 1988.

———. "Presidential Address: 'I Have Scinde': Flogging a Dead (White Male Orientalist) Horse." *Journal of Asian Studies* 58/4 (1999): 940–960.

———. *Splitting the Difference: Gender and Myth in Ancient Greece and India*. Chicago: University of Chicago Press, 1999.

———. "The Uses and Misuses of Other Peoples Myths." 1985 presidential address. *Journal of the American Academy of Religion* 54/2 (1986): 219–239.

———. "When a Lingam is Just a Good Cigar: Psychoanalysis and Hindu Sexual Fantasies." In *Vishnu on Freud's Desk: A Reader in Psychoanalysis and Hinduism*. Edited by T. G. Vaidyanathan and Jeffrey J. Kripal. Delhi: Oxford University Press, 1999, pp. 279–303.

———. *Women, Androgynes, and Other Mythical Beasts*. Chicago: University of Chicago Press, 1980.

Dorsey, J. Owen. *A Study of Siouan Cults*. Eleventh Annual Report. Washington, DC: Bureau of American Ethnology. 1894.

Douglas, Mary. *Natural Symbols: Explorations in Cosmology*. New York: Pantheon Books, 1970.

———. *Purity and Danger: An Analysis of Concepts of Pollution and Taboo*. New York: Praeger, 1970.

Dubuisson, Daniel. *The Western Construction of Religion*. Translated by William Sayers. Baltimore: Johns Hopkins University Press, 2003.

Dudley, Guilford, III. *Religion on Trial: Mircea Eliade and His Critics*. Philadelphia: Temple University Press, 1977.

Durkheim, Emile. *The Elementary Forms of Religious Life*. Trans. Joseph Ward Swain. London: George Allen & Unwin, 1954.

Durkheim, Emile, and Marcel Mauss. *Primitive Classification*. Translated by Rodney Needham. Chicago: University of Chicago Press, 1963.

Dupré, Louis. *The Enlightenment and the Intellectual Foundations of Modern Culture*. New Haven, CT: Yale University Press, 2004.

Edelstein, Dan. *The Enlightenment: A Geneaology*. Chicago: University of Chicago Press, 2010.

Eliade, Mircea."Autobiographical Fragment." In *Imagination and Meaning: The Scholarly and Literary Worlds of Mircea Eliade*. Edited by Norman J.Girardot and Mac Linscott Ricketts. New York: Seabury Press, 1982, pp. 113–127.

———. *Autobiography*. Volume 1, 1907–1937: *Journey East Journey West*. Translated by Mac Linscott Ricketts. San Francisco: Harper & Row, 1981.

———. *Autobiography*. Volume 2, 1937–1960: *Exile's Odyssey*. Translated by Mac Linscott Ricketts. Chicago: University of Chicago Press, 1988.

———. *The Forbidden Forest*. Translated by Mac Linscott Ricketts and Mary Park Stevenson. Notre Dame, Ind.: University of Notre Dame Press, 1978.

———. *Images and Symbols: Studies in Religious Symbols.* Translated by Philip Mairet. New York: Sheed & Ward, 1961.

———. *Journal II, 1957–1969.* Translated by Fred H. Johnson Jr. Chicago: University of Chicago Press, 1977.

———. *Journal III: 1970–1978.* Translated by Teresa Lavender Fagan. Chicago: University of Chicago Press, 1989.

———. *Journal IV: 1979–1985.* Translated by Mac Linscott Ricketts. Chicago: University of Chicago Press, 1990.

———. *Mephistopheles and the Androgyne: Studies in Religious Myth and Symbol.* Translated by J. M. Cohen. New York: Sheed and Ward, 1965.

———. "Methodological Remarks on the Study of Religious Symbolism." In *The History of Religions: Essays in Methodology.* Edited by Mircea Eliade and Joseph M. Kitagawa. Chicago: University of Chicago Press, 1959, pp. 86–107.

———. *Myth and Reality.* Translated by Willard R. Trask. New York: Harper & Row, 1963.

———. *The Myth of the Eternal Return.* Translated by Willard R. Trask. New York: Pantheon Books, 1954.

———. *Myths, Dreams and Mysteries: The Encounter between Archaic Realities.* Translated by Philip Mairet. New York: Harper & Row 1967.

———. *No Souvenirs, Journal: 1957–1969.* Translated by Fred H. Johnson Jr. New York. Harper & Row, 1977.

———. *Ordeal by Labyrinth: Conversations with Claude-Henri Racquet.* Translated by Derek Coltman. Chicago: University of Chicago Press, 1982.

———. *Patterns in Comparative Religion.* Translated by Rosemary Sheed. Cleveland: World, 1968.

———. *The Quest: History and Meaning in Religion.* Chicago: University of Chicago Press, 1969.

———. *Rites and Symbols of Initiation: The Mysteries of Birth and Rebirth.* Translated by Willard R. Trask. New York: Harper & Row, 1958.

———. *The Sacred and the Profane.* Translated by Willard R. Trask. New York: Harcourt, Brace, 1959.

———. *Shamanism: Archaic Techniques of Ecstasy.* Translated by Willard R. Trask. Bollingen Series 76. New York: Pantheon Books, 1964.

———. *Symbolism, the Sacred and the Arts.* Edited by Diane Apostolos-Cappadona. New York: Crossroad, 1986.

———. *Traité d'histoire des religions.* Paris: Payoit, 1970.

———. *Yoga: Immortality and Freedom.* 2nd ed. Translated by Willard R. Trask, Bollingen Series 56. Princeton, NJ: Princeton University Press, 1969.

Ellwood, Robert. *The Politics of Myth: A Study of C. G. Jung, Mircea Eliade, and Joseph Campbell.* Albany: State University of New York Press, 1999.

Eribon, Didier. *Michel Fouault.* Translated by Betsy Wing. Cambridge, MA: Harvard University Press, 1991.

Fasolt, Constanin. *The Limits of History*. Chicago: University of Chicago Press, 2004.

Fisher, Elaine. "Fascist Scholars, Fascist Scholarship: The Quest for Ur-Fascism and the Study of Religion." In *Hermenuetics, Politics, and the History of Religions: The Contested Legacies of Joachim Wach and Mircea Eliade.* Edited by Christian K. Wedemeyer and Wendy Doniger. Chicago: University of Chicago Press, 2010, pp. 261–284.

Fitzgerald, Timothy. *The Ideology of Religious Studies*. New York: Oxford University Press, 2000.

Flood, Gavin. *Beyond Phenomenology: Rethinking the Study of Religion*. London: Cassell, 1999.

Foucault, Michel. *The Archaeology of Knowledge and The Discourse on Language.* Translated by A. M. Sheridan Smith. New York: Pantheon Books, 1972.

———. *Essential Works of Foucault, 1954–1984*. 3 volumes. Edited by Paul Rabinow. New York: New Press, 1994.

———. *The History of Sexuality*. Volume 1, *An Introduction*. Translated by Robert Hurley. New York: Vintage Books, 1980.

———. *Language, Counter-Memory, Practice: Selected Essays and Interviews*. Edited by Donald F. Bouchard and translated by Donald F. Bouchard and Sherry Simon. Oxford: Blackwell, 1977.

———. *Madness and Civilization: A History of Insanity in the Age of Reason.* Translated by Richard Howard. New York: Random House, 1973.

———. "Nietzsche, Freud, Marx." In *Nietzsche,* Proceedings of the Seventh International Philosophical Colloquium of the Cahiers de Royaumont, July 4–8. Paris: Editions de Minuit, 1967, pp. 183–200.

———. "Nietzsche, Genealogy, History." In *Language, Counter-Memory, Practice: Selected Essays and Interviews*. Edited by Donald F. Bouchard and trans. Donald F. Bouchard and Sherry Simon. Ithaca, NY: Cornell University Press, 1977, pp. 137–164.

———. *The Order of Things: An Archaeology of the Human Sciences*. Translated by Alan Sheridan Smith. New York: Random House, 1973.

———. *Power/Knowledge: Selected Interviews and Other Writings, 1972–1977*. Edited by Colin Gordon and translated by Colin Gordon, Leo Marshall, John Mepham, and Kate Soper. New York: Pantheon Books, 1980.

———. "Presentation de Michel Foucualt." in Georges Bataille, *Oeuvres completes.* 12 vols. Paris: Gallimard, 1970–1988.

Frazer, James George. *The Golden Bough: A Study in Magic and Religion*. 3 Volumes. Third Edition. London: Macmillan, 1951.

Frykenberg, Robert Eric. "Construction of Hinduism at the Nexus of History and Religion." *Journal of Interdisciplinary History* 23/2 (1993): 523–550.

Gadamer, Hans-Georg. *Philosophical Hermeneutics*. Translated and edited by David E. Linge. Berkeley University of California Press, 1977.

———. *Truth and Method.* Translated by Garrett Barden and John Cumming. New York: Crossroad, 1982.

Gallagher, Catherine. "Politics, the Profession, and the Critic." *Diacritics* 15 (1985): 37–43.

Gandhi, Leela. *Postcolonial Theory: A Critical Introduction.* New York: Columbia University Press, 1998.

Gasché, Rodolphe. *System und Metaphorik in der Philosophie von Georges Bataille.* Europäische Hochschultschriftrin, Reihe 20, Philosophie, vol. 39. Bern: Peter Lang, 1978.

Gay, Peter. *The Rise of Modern Paganism.* Volume 1, *The Enlightenment: An Interpretation.* New York: Knopf, 1966.

Geertz, Armin W. "Brain, Body and Culture: A Biocultural Theory of Religion." *Method and Theory in the Study of Religion* 22/4 (2010): 304–321.

Geertz, Clifford. "Religion as a Cultural System." In *Anthropological Approaches to the Study of Religion.* Edited by Michael Banton. London: Tavistock Publications, 1971, pp. 1–46.

Gennap, Arnold van. *The Rites of Passage.* Translated by Monika B Vizedom and Gabrielle C. Caffee. Chicago: University of Chicago Press, 1969.

Gill, Sam D. "The Academic Study of Religion." *Journal of the American Academy of Religion* 62/4 (1994): 965–975.

———. "No Place to Stand: Jonathan Z. Smith as *Homo Ludens*: The Academic Study of Religion *Sub Specie Ludi.*" *Journal of the American Academy of Religion* 66/2 (1998): 283–312.

Ginzburg, Carlo. "Mircea Eliade's Ambivalent Legacy." In *Hermeneutics, Politics and the History of Religions: The Contested Legacies of Joachim Wach and Mircea Eliade.* Edited by Christian K. Wedemeyer and Wendy Doniger. Chicago: University of Chicago Press, 2010, pp. 307–323.

Girard, René. *Violence and the Sacred.* Translated by Patrick Gregory. Baltimore: Johns Hopkins University Press, 1989.

Glucklich, Ariel. *Religious Jurisprudence in the Dharmaśāstras.* New York: Macmillan, 1982.

———. *Sacred Pain: Hurting the Body for the Sake of the Soul.* Oxford: Oxford University Press, 2001.

———. *The Sense of Adharma.* New York: Oxford University Press, 1994.

Gonda, Jan. *Change and Continuity in Indian Religion.* The Hague: Mouton, 1965.

———. "Gifts and Giving in the Rig-Veda." *Vishveshvaranda Indological Journal* 2/1 (1964): 9–30.

———. *Die Religionen Indiens.* Volume1, *Veda und alterer Hinduismus.* Stuttgart: W. Kohlhammer, 1960.

Green, Garrett. "Hermeneutics." In *The Routledge Companion to the Study of Religion.* 2nd ed. Edited by John Hinnells. London: Routledge, 2010, pp. 411–425.

Grimes, Ronald L. *Ritual Criticism: Case Studies in Its Practice, Essays on Its Theory*. Columbia, SC: University of South Carolina Press, 1990.

Guthrie, Stewart. *Faces in the Clouds*. New York: Oxford University Press, 1993.

Habermas, Jürgens. *Der philosophische Diskurs der Moderne: Zwölf Vorlesungen*. Frankfurt am Main: Suhrkamp, 1985.

Halbfass, Wilhelm. *Tradition and Reflection: Explorations in Indian Thought*. Albany: State University of New York Press, 1991.

Harris, Marvin. *The Rise of Anthropological Theory: A History of Theories of Culture*. New York: Columbia University Press, 1969.

Hassrick, Royal B. *The Sioux: Life and Customs of a Warrior Society*. Norman: University of Oklahoma Press, 1967.

Hatcher, Brian A. *Eclecticism and Modern Hindu Discourse*. New York: Oxford University Press, 1999.

Heesterman, J. C. "Brahmin, Ritual, and Renouncer." *Wiener Zeitschrift für die Kunde Südasiens und Archiv für indische Philosophie* 8 (1964): 1–31.

———. *The Broken World of Sacrifice: An Essay in Ancient Indian Ritual*. Chicago: University of Chicago Press, 1993.

Heidegger, Martin. *Basic Concepts*. Translated by Gary E. Aylesworth. Bloomington: Indian University Press, 1993.

———. *Being and Time*. Translated by John Robinson and John Macquarrie. New York: Harper & Row, 1962.

———. *Holzwege*. Frankfurt: Vittorio Klostermann, 1963.

———. *Nietzsche*. Volume 4, *Nihilism*. Translated by Frank A. Capuzzi. San Francisco: Harper and Row, 1982.

Helmont, Jean. "From Bataille to Derrida: Différance and Heterology." Translated by A. Engstrom. *Stanford French Review* 22/1 (1988): 129–147.

Hiltebeitel, Alf. *The Cult of Draupadī*. Volume 1, *Mythologies: From Gingee to Kuruksetra*. Chicago: University of Chicago Press, 1988.

———. *The Cult of Draupadī*. Volume 2, *On Hindu Ritual and the Goddess*. Chicago: University of Chicago Press, 1991.

———. *Dharma: Its Early History in Law, Religion, and Narrative*. New York: Oxford University Press, 2011.

Hollier, Denis. "Bataille's Tomb: A Halloween Story." Translated by Richard Miller. *October* 33 (1985): 73–91.

———. *La prise de la Concorde: Essais sur Georges Bataille*. Paris: Gallimard, 1974.

Hollywood, Amy. *Sensible Ecstasy: Mysticism, Sexual Difference, and the Demands of History*. Chicago: University of Chicago Press, 2002.

Hubert, Henri, and Marcel Mauss. *Sacrifice: Its Nature and Function*. Translated by W. D. Halls. Chicago: University of Chicago Press, 1968.

Hultkrantz, Ake. *Belief and Worship in Native North America*. Edited by Christopher Vecsey. Syracuse, NY: Syracuse University Press, 1981.

———. "Ecology of Religion: Its Scope and Methodology." In *Science of Religion Studies in Methodology*. Edited by Lauri Honko. Berlin: Mouton, 1979, pp. 221–236.

Idinopulos, Thomas A. "The Difficulties of Understanding Religion." In *What Is Religion? Origins, Definitions, and Explanations*. Edited by Thomas A. Indinopulos and Brian C. Wilson. Leiden: E. J. Brill, 1998, pp. 27–42.

Inden, Ronald B. *Imagining India*. Cambridge: Basil Blackwell, 1990.

Jabès, Edmond. *The Books Questions*. Volume 2. Translated by Rosemarie Waldrop. Middletown, CT: Wesleyan University Press, 1991.

Jameson, Fredric. *Postmodernism or, The Cultural Logic of Late Capitalism*. Durham, NC: Duke University Press, 1991.

Jorgensen, Joseph G. *The Sun Dance Religion*. Chicago: University of Chicago Press, 1972.

Kane, Pandurang Vaman. *History of Dharmaśastra*. 5 volumes. Poona: Bhandarkar Research Institute, 1953–1973.

Kearney, Richard, moderator. "On the Gift: A Discussion between Jacques Derrida and Jean-Luc Marion." In *God, the Gift, and Postmodernism*. Edited by John D. Caputo and Michael J. Scanlon. Bloomington: Indiana University Press, 1999, pp. 54–78.

Kendall, Stuart. *Georges Bataille*. London: Reaktion Books, 2007.

King, Richard. *Orientalism and Religion: Postcolonial Theory, India, and "The Mystic East."* London: Routledge, 1999.

Kippenberg, Hans G. *Discovering Religious History in the Modern Age*. Translated by Barbara Harshaw. Princeton, NJ: Princeton University Press, 2002.

Kripal, Jeffrey J. *The Serpent's Gift: Gnostic Reflections on the Study of Religion*. Chicago: University of Chicago Press, 2007.

Kristeva, Julia. *Desire in Literature: A Semiotic Approach to Literature and Art*. Translated by Thomas Gora, Alice Jardine, and Leon S. Roudiez. New York: Columbia University Press, 1980.

———. *Polylogue*. Paris: Éditions du Seuil, 1977.

———. *Powers of Horror: An Essay on Abjection*. Translated by Leon S. Roudiez. New York: Columbia University Press, 1982.

———. *Revolution in Poetic Literature*. Translated by Margaret Waller. New York: Columbia University Press, 1984.

Kuhn, Thomas S. *The Structure of Scientific Revolutions*. International Encyclopedia of United States, 2nd. ed. Volume 2, no. 2. Chicago: University of Chicago Press, 1979.

Lacan, Jacques. *Écrits: A Selection*. Translated by Alan Sheridan. New York: W. W. Norton, 1977.

———. *The Seminar of Jacques Lacan, Book II: The Ego in Freud's Theory and in the Technique of Psychoanalysis, 1954–1955*. Translated by Sylvan Tomaselli. New York: W. W. Norton, 1988.

Lakoff, George, and Mark Johnson. *Philosophy in the Flesh: The Embodied Mind and Its Challenge to Western Thought*. New York: Basic Books, 1999.

Lambek, Michael, ed. *A Reader in the Anthropology of Religion*. 2d Edition. Malden, MA: Basil Blackwell, 2008.

Larmore, Charles. "Bataille's Heterology." *Semiotexte* 2/2 (1976): 87–104.

Lawson, E. Thomas. "Theory and the Comparativism, Old and New." *Method and Theory in the Study of Religion* 8/1 (1996): 31–35.

Lecog, Dominique, and Jean-Luc Lory. Eds. *Ecrits d' ailleurs: George Bataille et les ethnologues*. Paris: Maison des sciences de l' Home, 1987.

Lévi-Strauss, Claude. *Structural Anthropology*. Translated by Claire Jacobson and Brooke Grundfest Schoefp. New York: Basic Books, 1963.

Lévy-Bruhl, Lucien. *Primitive Mentality*. Translated by Lilian A. Clare. London: George Allen & Unwin, 1923.

Lewis, Bermard. *Islam and the West*. New York: Oxford University Press, 1993.

Lewis, Thomas S. "The Oglala (Teton Dakota) Sun Dance: Vicissitudes of Its Structure and Functions." *Plains Anthropology* 17 (1972): 44–49.

Lincoln, Bruce. *Authority: Construction and Corrosion*. Chicago: University of Chicago Press, 1994.

———. *Theorizing Myth: Narrative, Ideology, and Scholarship*. Chicago: University of Chicago Press, 1999.

Long, Charles H. *Significations: Signs, Symbols, and Images in the Interpretation of Religion*. Philadelphia: Fortress Press, 1986.

Lowe, Lisa. *Critical Terrains: French and British Orientalism*. Ithaca, NY: Cornell University Press, 1991.

Lyotard, Jean-François. *The Inhuman: Reflections on Time*. Translated by Geoffrey Bennington and Rachel Bowlby. Cambridge: Polity Press, 1977.

———. *The Postmodern Condition: A Report on Knowledge*. Translated by Geoff Bennington and Brian Massumi. Theory and History of Literature, volume 10. Minneapolis: University of Minnesota Press, 1984.

———. "Réponse a la question: Qu'est-ce la postmoderne" *Critique* 419 (1982): 356–367.

Lyotard, Jean François, and Jean-Loup Thébaud. *Just Gaming*. Translated by Wlad Goodrich. Theory and History of Literature, volume 20. Minneapolis: University of Minnesota Press, 1985.

MacIntyre, Alistair C. *Three Rival Versions of Moral Enquiry: Encyclopedia, Genealogy, and Tradition*. Notre Dame: University of Notre Dame Press, 1990.

Marino, Adrian. *L'herméneutique de Mircea Eliade*. Translated by Jean Gouillard. Paris: Gallimard, 1981.

Marmande, Francis. *Georges Bataille poltique*. Lyon: Presses universitaires de Lyon, 1985.

Masuzawa, Tomoko. *In Search of Dreamtime: The Quest for the Origin of Religion*. Chicago: University of Chicago Press, 1993.

————. *The Invention of World Religions, or How European Universalism Was Preserved in the Languages of Pluralism.* Chicago: University of Chicago Press, 2005.

Mauss, Marcel. *Essai sur le don: Forms et reason de l' échange dons les sociétés archaiques.* In *Sociologie et anthropology.* 3rd ed. Paris: Presses universitaires de France, 1966.

————. *The Gift: The Form and Reason for Exchange in Archaic Societies.* Trans. W. D. Halls. New York: W. W. Norton, 1990.

————. "Rapports reèls et pratiques de la psychologie et de la sociologie." In *Sociologie et anthropologie.* Paris: Presses universitaries de France, 1966.

McCauley, Thomas. "The Naturalness of Religion and the Unnaturalness of Science." In *Exploration and Cognition.* Eited by Frank Keil and Robert Wilson. Cambridge, MA: Massachusetts Institute of Technology Press, 2000, pp. 61–86.

McCutcheon, Russell T. *Critics Not Caretakers: Redescribing the Public Study of Religion.* Albany: State University of New York Press, 2001.

————. *Manufacturing Religion: The Discourse on Sui Generis Religion and the Politics of Nostalgia.* New York: Oxford University Press, 1997.

McGowan, John. *Postmodernism and Its Critics.* Ithaca, NY: Cornell University Press, 1991.

Megill, Allan. *Prophets of Extremity: Nietzsche, Heidegger, Foucault, Derrida.* Berkeley: University of California Press, 1985.

Mellor, Philip A. "Orientalism, Representation, and Religion: The Reality behind the Myth." *Religion* 14/1 (2004): 99–112.

Melody, Michael E. "The Lakota Sun Dancer: A Composite View and Analysis." *South Dakota History* 6 (1976): 452–454.

Mithen, Steven. "Cognitive Archaeology, Evolutionary Psychology and Cultural Transmission, with Particular References to Religious Ideas." In *Rediscovering Darwin: Evolutionary Theory and Archaeological Explanation.* Edited by Michael Barton and Geoffrey A. Clark. Arlington, VA: American Anthropology Association, 1997, pp. 67–86.

————. "Symbolism and the Supernatural." In *The Evolution of Culture: An Interdisciplinary View.* Edited by Robin Dunbar, Chris Knight, and Camilla Power. New Brunswick, NJ: Rutgers University Press, 1999, pp. 147–172.

Müller, Max. *Chips from a German Workshop.* Volume 1, *Essays on the Science of Religion.* New York: Charles Scribner, 1869; reprint, Chico, CA: Scholars Press, 1985.

————. *Comparative Mythology.* London: Routledge, 1909; reprint, New York: Amo Press, 1977.

————. *Introduction to the Science of Religion.* London: Longmans, Green, 1873.

————. *Natural Religion.* London: Longmans, 1890.

Murphy, Tim. "Eliade, Subjectivity, and Hermeneutics." In *Changing Religious Worlds: The Meaning and End of Mircea Eliade.* Edited by Bryan Rennie. Albany: State University of New York Press, 2001, pp. 35–49.

———. *Representing Religion: Essays in History, Theory and Crisis*. London: Equinox, 2007.

Nandy, Ashis. *Intimate Enemy: Loss and Recovery of Self under Colonialism*. Delhi: Oxford University Press, 1983.

———. *Traditions, Tyranny and Utopias: Essays in the Politics of Awareness*. Delhi: Oxford University Press, 1987.

Nietzsche, Friedrich. *The Birth of Tragedy*. Translated by William A. Haussmann. In Volume 1 of *The Complete Works of Friedrich Nietzsche*. 18 volumes. Edited by Oscar Levy. New York: Russell & Russell, 1964.

———. *The Gay Science*. Translated by Josefine Nauckhoff. Cambridge: Cambridge University Press, 2001.

———. *On the Genealogy of Morals*. Translated by Carol Diethe. Cambridge: Cambridge University Press, 1994.

———. *The Use and Abuse of History*. Translated by Adrian Collins. New York: Macmillan, 1957.

———. *The Will to Power*. Translated by Walter Kaufmann and R. J. Hollingdale. New York: Random House, 1967.

Neville, Robert C. *Reconstruction of Thinking*. Albany: State University of New York Press, 1981.

Nozick, Robert. *The Nature of Rationality*. Princeton, NJ: Princeton University Press, 1993.

Olivelle, Patrick. *The Āśrama System: The History and Hermeneutic of a Religious Institution*. New York: Oxford University Press, 1993.

Olson, Carl. "The Deification of Death in Postmodern Thought: A Critical Examination." *International Journal of Humanistic Ideology* 1/1 (Summer 2008): 25–42.

———. *Indian Philosophers and Postmodern Thinkers: Dialogues on the Margins of Culture*. Delhi: Oxford University Press, 2002.

———. *The Many Colors of Hinduism: A Thematic-Historical Introduction*. New Brunswick, NJ: Rutgers University Press, 2007.

———. "Mircea Eliade, Postmodernism, and the Problematic Nature of Representational Thinking." *Method and Theory in the Study of Religion* 11 (1999): 357–385.

———. *The Theology and Philosophy of Eliade: A Search for the Centre*. London: Macmillan, 1992.

———. *Zen and the Art of Postmodern Philosophy: Two Paths of Liberation from the Representational Mode of Thinking*. Albany: State University of New York Press, 2000.

Parry, Jonathan P. *Death in Benares*. Cambridge: Cambridge University Press, 1994.

———. "The Gift, the Indian Gift, and the 'Indian Gift.'" *Man*, n.s., 24 (1986): 453–473.

Pefanis, Julian. *Heterology and the Postmodern: Bataille, Baudrillard, and Lyotard.* Durham, NC: Duke University Press, 1991.

Perniola, Mario. *L' instant eternal: Bataille et la pensée de la marginalité.* Paris: Medidiens Anthropos, 1982.

Pippin, Robert B. *Modernism as a Philosophical Problem: On the Dissatisfactions of European High Culture.* Cambridge, MA: Basil Blackwell, 1991.

Pocock, John. "Historiography and Enlightenment: A View of Their History." *Modern Intellectual History* 5/1 (2008): 83–96.

Polanyi, Michael. *Personal Knowledge: Towards a Post-Critical Philosophy.* 1958; London: Routledge & Kegan Paul, 1983.

Popper, Karl R. *Conjectures and Refutations: The Growth of Scientific Knowledge.* 4th ed. 1963; London: Routledge & Kegan Paul, 1985.

———. *The Logic of Scientific Discovery.* 1959; London: Hutchinson, 1986.

———. *Objective Knowledge: An Evolutionary Approach.* 1972; Oxford: Clarendon Press, 1986.

Powers, William E. *Oglala Religion.* Lincoln: University of Nebraska Press, 1977.

Preus, J. Samuel. *Explaining Religion: Criticism and Theory from Bodin to Freud.* New Haven, CT: Yale University Press, 1987.

Putnam, Hilary. *Renewing Philosophy.* Cambridge, MA: Harvard University Press, 1992.

Raheja, Gloria. *The Poison in the Gift: Ritual, Possession, and the Dominant Caste in a North Indian Village.* Chicago: University of Chicago Press, 1988.

Rennie, Bryan S. "The Influence of Eastern Orthodox Christian Theology on Mircea Eliade's Understanding of Religion." In *Hermeneutics, Politics and the History of Religions: The Contested Legacies of Joachim Wach and Mircea Eliade.* Edited by Christian K. Wedemeyer and Wendy Doniger. New York: Oxford University Press, 2010, pp. 197–213.

———. *Reconsidering Eliade: Making Sense of Religion.* Albany: State University of New York Press, 1996.

Renou, Louis, and Jean Filliozat. *L'Inde classique: Manuel des etudes indienne.* 2 volumes. 1953; Paris: Imprimerie nationals, 1957.

Rescher, Nicholas. *A System of Pragmatic Idealism.* Volume 1, *Human Knowledge in Idealistic Perspective.* Princeton, NJ: Princeton University Press, 1992.

Richman, Michele. *Reading Georges Bataille: Beyond the Gift.* Baltimore: Johns Hopkins University Press, 1982.

Ries, Julien, "La méthode comparé en histoire des religions selon Georges Dumézil et Mircea Eliade." In *The Notion of "Religion" in Comparative Research: Selected Proceedings of the XVIth Congress of the International Association for the History of Religions.* Rome September, 3–8, 1990. Edited by Ugo Bianchi. Rome: L'Erma di Bretschneder, 1994, pp. 713–719.

Riesebrodt, Martin. *The Promise of Salvation: A Theory of Religion.* Translated by Steven Rendall. Chicago: University of Chicago Press, 2010.

Rocher, Rosane. "British Orientalism in the Eighteenth Century: The Dialectics of Knowledge and Government." In *Orientalism and the Postcolonial Predicament*. Edited by Carol A. Breckenridge and Peter van der Veer. Philadelphia: University of Pennsylvania Press, 1993, pp. 215–249.

Rorty, Richard. "Foucault and Epistemology." In *Foucault: A Critical Reader*. Edited by David Couzens Hoy. London: Basil Blackwell, 1986, pp. 41–49.

———. *Philosophy and the Mirror of Nature*. Princeton, NJ: Princeton University Press, 1979.

Rosen, Stanley. *The Ancients and the Moderns: Rethinking Modernity*. New Haven, CT: Yale University Press, 1989.

———. *The Elusiveness of the Ordinary: Studies in the Possibility of Philosophy*. New Haven, CT: Yale University Press, 2002.

———. *Hermeneutics as Politics*. New York: Oxford University Press, 1987.

Rushdie, Salman. *Midnight's Children*. New York: Alfred A. Knopf, 1980.

Said, Edward W. *Culture and Imperialism*. New York: Vintage Books, 1993.

———. *Orientalism*. New York: Vintage Books, 1979.

———. *The World, the Text, and the Critic*. Cambridge, MA: Harvard University Press, 1983.

Saler, Benson. "Towards a Realistic and Relevant 'Science of Religion.'" *Method and Theory in the Study of Religion* 16/3 (2004): 205–233.

Saliba, John A. *Homo Religiosus in Mircea Eliade: Anthropological Evaluation*. Leiden: E. J. Brill, 1976.

Sardar, Siauddin. *Orientalism*. Buckingham: Open University Press, 1999.

Schillbrack, Kevin. "Religions: Are There Any?" *Journal of the American Academy of Religion* 78/4 (2010): 1112–1138.

Schopen, Gregory. *Bones, Stones, and Buddhist Monks: Collected Papers on the Archaeology, Epigraphy, and Texts in India*. Honolulu: University of Hawaii Press, 1997.

———. *Buddhist Monks and Business Matters: Still More Papers on Monastic Buddhism in India*. Honolulu: University of Hawaii Press, 2004.

———. *Figments and Fragments of Mahāyāna Buddhism in India: More Collected Papers*. Honolulu: University of Hawaii Press, 2005.

Schrag, Calvin O. *The Resources of Reason: A Response to the Postmodern Challenge*. Bloomington: Indian University Press, 1992.

Searle, John R. *The Construction of Social Reality*. New York: Free Press, 1995.

Segal, Robert. "Classification and Comparison in the Study of Religion: The Work of Jonathan Z. Smith." *Journal of the American Academy of Religion* 73/4 (2005): 1175–1188.

Smart, Ninian. "Beyond Eliade: The Future of Theory in Religion." *Numen* 25/2 (1978): 171–183.

Smith, David. "Orientalism and Hinduism." In *The Blackwell Companion to Hinduism*. Edited by Gavin Flood. Oxford: Basil Blackwell, 2003, pp. 45–63.

Bibliography

Smith, Jonathan Z. "Acknowledgments: Morphology and History in Mircea Eliade's *Patterns in Comparative Religion* (1949–1999), Part 1: The Work and Its Contexts; Part 2: The Texture of the Work." *History of Religions* 39/4 (2000): 315–351.

———. *Drudgery Divine: On the Comparison of Early Christianities and the Religions of Late Antiquity*. Chicago: University of Chicago Press, 1990.

———. *Imagining Religion: From Babylon to Jonestown*. Chicago: University of Chicago Press, 1982.

———. *Map Is Not Territory: Studies in the History of Religions*. Leiden: E. J. Brill, 1978.

———. "Prologue: In Comparison a Magic Dwells." In *A Magic Still Dwells: Comparative Religion in the Postmodern Age*, ed. Kimberley C. Patton and Benjamin C. Ray. Berkeley: University of California Press, 2000, pp. 23–44.

———. *Relating Religion: Essays in the Study of Religion*. Chicago: University of Chicago Press, 2004.

———. *To Take Place: Toward Theory in Ritual*. Chicago: University of Chicago Press, 1987.

Soloman, Robert. "Nietzsche's *ad hominem*: Perspectives, Personality, and *Ressentiment* Revisited." In *The Cambridge Companion to Nietzsche*. Edited by Bernd Magnus and Kathleen M. Higgins. Cambridge: Cambridge University Press, 1996, pp. 180–222.

Spencer, Herbert. *The Principles of Sociology*. 3 volumes. New York: Appleton, 1898.

Spivak, Gayatri Chakravorty. *A Critique of Postcolonial Reason: Toward a History of the Vanishing Present*. Cambridge, MA: Harvard University Press, 1999.

———. "Can the Subaltern Speak? Speculations on Widow Sacrifice." *Wedge* 7/8 (1985): 120–130.

———. "The Rani of Sirmur." In *Europe and Its Others*. 2 volumes. Edited by Francis Barker et al. Colchester: University of Essex, 1985, 1: 128–151.

Stark, Rodney. "Micro-Foundation of Religion: A Revised Theory." *Sociological Theory* 17/3 (1999): 264–289.

Starobinski, Jean. *Largesse*. Translated by Jane Marie Todd. Chicago: University of Chicago Press, 1997.

Stoekl, Alan. Ed. "On Bataille." *Yale French Studies* 78 (1990).

———. "Truman's Apotheosis: Bataille, 'Planisme,' and Headless." *Yale French Studies* 78 (1990): 181–205.

Strenski, Ivan. "Ad Hominem Reviews and Rejoinders: Their Uses and Abuses." *Method and Theory in the Study of Religion* 16/4 (2004): 367–385.

———. *Four Theories of Myth in Twentieth-Century History: Cassirer, Eliade, Lévi-Strauss and Malinowski*. London: Macmillan; Iowa City: University of Iowa Press, 1987.

———. "Ideological Critique in the Study of Religion: Real Thinkers, Real Contexts, and a Little Humility." In *New Approaches to the Study of Religion*. Volume 1, *Regional, Critical, and Historical Approaches*. Edited by Peter Antes, Armin W. Geertz, and Randi R. Warne. Berlin: Walter de Gruyter, 2008, pp. 271–293.

———. *Religion in Relation: Method, Application, and Moral Location.* Columbia, SC: University of South Carolina Press, 1993.

Surya, Michel. *Georges Bataille: La Mort à l' oeuvre.* Paris: Séguier, 1987. Translated by Krzysztof Fijalkowski and Michael Richardson as *Georges Bataille: An Intellectual Biography.* London: Verso, 2002.

Svendsen, Lars. *Fashion: A Philosophy.* Translated by John Irons. London: Reaktion Books, 2006.

Tambiah, Stanley. "The Magical Power of Words." *Man,* n.s., 3/2 (1968): 175–208.

———. "A Performative Approach to Ritual." *Proceedings of the British Academy* 65 (1979): 113–169.

Taves, Ann. "No Field Is an Island: Fostering Collaboration between the Academic Study of Religion and the Sciences." *Method and Theory in the Study of Religion* 22 (2010): 170–188.

———. *Religious Experience Reconsidered: A Building-Block Approach to the Study of Religion and Other Special Things.* Princeton, NJ: Princeton University Press, 2009.

Taylor, Charles. *Philosophical Arguments.* Cambridge, MA: Harvard University Press, 1985.

———. *Philosophical Papers I: Human Agency and Language.* Cambridge: Cambridge University Press, 1985.

———. *A Secular Age.* Cambridge, MA: Belknap Press of Harvard University Press, 2007.

———. *Sources of the Self: The Making of Modern Identity.* Cambridge: Cambridge University Press, 1989.

Taylor, James. *Buddhism and Postmodern Imaginings in Thailand: The Religiosity of Urban Space.* Farnham, England: Ashgate, 2008.

Taylor, Mark C. *After God.* Chicago: University of Chicago Press, 2007.

———. *Altarity.* Chicago: University of Chicago Press, 1987.

———. *Erring: A Postmodern A/theology.* Chicago: University of Chicago Press, 1984.

———. *Nots.* Chicago: University of Chicago Press, 1993.

———. *Tears.* Albany: State University of New York Press, 1990.

Tetlock, Philip E. "Thinking the Unthinkable: Sacred Values and Taboos Cognitions." *Trends in Cognitive Science* 7/17 (2003): 320–324.

Thapar, Romila. "Sacrifice, Surplus, and the Soul." *History of Religions* 33 (1994): 305–324.

Tiele, Cornelis P., *Elements of the Science of Religion.* 2 volumes. 1897; London: William Blackwood & Sons, 1899.

Tilly, Charles. *Big Structures, Large Processes, Huge Comparisons* New York: Russell Sage Foundation, 1984.

Toynbee, Arnold. *A Study of History.* 3 volumes. London: Oxford University Press, 1939–1961.

Turner, Victor. *Dramas, Fields and Metaphors: Symbolic Action in Human Society.* Ithaca, NY: Cornell University Press, 1975.

———. *The Drums of Affliction: A Study of Religious Processes among the Ndembu of Zambia.* Oxford: Clarendon Press, 1968.

———. *The Forest of Symbols: Aspects of Ndembu Ritual.* Ithaca, New York: Cornell University Press, 1967.

———. *Image and Pilgrimage in Christian Culture.* New York: Columbia University Press, 1978.

———. *The Ritual Process: Structure and Anti-Structure.* Chicago: Aldine, 1969.

Tylor, Edward B. *Primitive Culture: Researches into the Development of Mythology, Philosophy, Religion, Language, Art and Customs.* 2 volumes. 3rd ed. New York: H. Holt, 1983.

Urban, Hugh B. *The Power of Tantra: Religion, Sexuality and the Politics of South Asian Studies.* London: I. B. Tauris, 2010.

———. "The Remnants of Desire: Sacrificial Violence and Sexual Transgression in the Cult of the Kāpālikas and in the Writings of Georges Bataille." *Religion* 25 (1995): 67–90.

———. *Tantra, Sex, Secrecy, Politics, and Power in the Study of Religion.* Berkeley: University of California Press, 2003.

Varisco, Daniel Martin. *Reading Orientalism: Said and the Unsaid.* Seattle: University of Washington Press, 2007.

Vial, Theodore. "How Does the Cognitive Science of Religion Stack Up as a Big Theory, A La Hume." *Method and Theory in the Study of Religion* 18/4 (2006): 351–371.

Viswanathan, Gauri, ed. *Power, Politics, and Culture: Interviews with Edward W. Said.* New York: Pantheon Books, 2001.

Vries, Hent de. "Introduction: Why Still 'Religion'?" In *Religion: Beyond a Concept.* Edited by Hent de Vries. New York: Fordham University Press, 2008, pp. 1–98.

Waardenburg, Jacques. *Reflections on the Study of Religion.* The Hague: Mouton, 1978.

———. "Religion between Reality and Idea." *Numen* 19/2–3 (1972): 128–203.

———. "*Religionswissenschaft* New Style: Some Thoughts and Afterthoughts." *Annual Review of the Science of Religion* 2 (1978): 116–125.

Walker, James R. *Lakota Belief and Ritual.* Edited by Rayond J. de Maillie and Elaine A. Jahner. Lincoln: University of Nebraska Press, 1980.

Wasserstrom, Steven M. *Religion after Religion: Gershom Scholem, Mircea Eliade and Henry Corbin at Eranos.* Princeton, NJ: Princeton University Press, 1999.

Weber, Max. *The Sociology of Religion.* Translated by Ephram Fishoff. Boston: Beacon Press, 1964.

———. *The Theory of Social and Economic Organization.* Translated by A. M. Henderson and T. Parsons. New York: Free Press, 1947.

Wedemeyer, Christian K. "Introduction I: Two Scholars, a 'School,' and a Conference." In *Hermeneutics, Politics, and the History of Religions: The Contested Legacies of Joachim Wach and Mircea Eliade.* Edited by Christian K. Wedemeyer and Wendy Doniger. Oxford: Oxford University Press, 2010, pp. xv–xxxiv.

———. *The Politics of Religious Studies: The Continuing Conflict with Theology in the Academy.* New York: St. Martin's Press, 1991.

Weiss, Allen S. *The Aesthetics of Excess.* Albany: State University of New York Press, 1989.

White, Hayden V. *Topics of Discourse: Essays in Cultural Criticism.* Baltimore: Johns Hopkins University Press, 1978.

Whitehouse, Harvey. *Modes of Religiosity: A Cognitive Theory of Religious Transmission.* Walnut Creek, CA: AltaMira Press, 2004.

Widengren, Geo. "La Methode Comparative: Entre Philologie et Phenomenologie." *Numen* 15/3 (December 1971): 161–172.

———. *Religionsphanomenologie.* Berlin: Walter de Gruyter, 1969.

Wiebe, Donald. "Is a Science of Religion Possible?" *Studies in Religion* 7/1 (Winter 1978): 5–17.

———. "Is the New Comparativism Really New?" *Method and Theory in the Study of Religion* 8/1 (1996): 21–29.

———. *The Politics of Religious Studies: The Continuing Conflict with Theology in the Academy.* New York: St. Martin's Press, 1991.

———. "A Positive Episteme for the Study of Religion." *Scottish Journal of Religious Studies* 6/2 (Autumn 1985): 78–95.

Yao, Xinzhong, and Yanxia Zhao. *Chinese Religion: A Contextual Approach.* London: Continuum, 2010.

Young, Robert J. C. *Postcolonialism: An Historical Introduction.* Oxford: Basil Blackwell, 2001.

———. *White Mythologies: Writing History and the West.* London: Routledge, 1990.

Index

Abraham 53
Acéphale 18, 45
agency 165n.14
Aion 105
alterity 118–119
Amée sociologique, L' 35
American Academy of Religion 148
animism 4, 85
anthropology 4, 14
Apollonian 22
aporia 35
arborescent thinking 115, 122
archaeology 110–111
Archaeology of Knowledge 110
Artaud, Antonin 114
ascetic 51
*Asceticism and Eroticism in the
    Mythology of Śiva* 102
Aufklärung 8
Augustine, Saint 3
auspicious 50–51

Bakhtin, Mikhail 138
Banaras 51
Barthes, Roland 100, 138
Bataille, Georges 11, 15, 17–345, 40, 49,
    80, 129–130, 150, 157n.20, 159n.59
  gift 41–44, 47, 129
  hermeneutics of 34
  and human situation 20–21
  theory of eroticism 23–25, 37,
    150, 156n.7, 159n.39

theory of religion 21–23, 34–35,
    80–81
  violence and sacrifice 25–27
Baudrillard, Jean 10, 124–125, 133,
    157n.34, 159n.42–43
Bedrick, The 97
Beidelman, T. O. 161n.82
Bell, Catherine 52
Bhabha, Homi K. 59–60, 65, 70–71
  cosmopolitanism 70
  secularism 70
Biardeau, Madeleine 49
Black Elk 28
Black Skin, White Masks 69
Blanchot, Maurice 151
Bloch, Maurice 153n.6
Blue of Noon, The 33
body 21, 74, 135–136, 160n.93,
    162n.20
Boehme, Jacob 135
Bourdieu, Pierre 52, 141–142
Brahmins 50–51
Breton, André 17
bricoleur 71
Buddhism 4, 136–137

capitalism 7
Capps, Walter H. 119
carnivalesque 149–150
Carrette, Jeremy 6, 13
caste 49
castration 46

Cavell, Stanley 13
Chantepie de la Saussaye, P. D. 87
Clarke, J. J. 66–67
cognitive science 4, 141, 144–145, 151, 179n.38
coincidentia oppositorum (conjunction of opposites) 13, 25, 44
colonialism 59–60, 68, 70, 101
Combs-Schilling, M. E. 43
common sense 137–141, 149
comparison 83–84, 86–88, 91–92, 99–100, 104, 113, 119, 126, 128, 130, 133, 135, 148, 169n.27, 170n.50
Comte, Auguste 85
consciousness 93
Contre-Allaque 18
corroboration 142
Courtright, Paul 60
Critique 19
Critique Sociale, La 18
culture 64, 69–70, 75, 77, 100, 179n.38
Culture and Imperialism 67

Daksha 98
daksilā (gift) 47–48
    and *śraddhā* (faith) 48
Dali, Salvador 20
dan (gift) 41, 47–48, 50–51
Darwin, Charles 3
death 19, 22, 26, 31, 51, 146, 151
    and eroticism 23–25, 33–34
decadence 11, 33–334, 148–151
deconstruction 13, 35, 47, 56–57, 71–72, 76–77, 95, 116, 118–119, 123, 130–132
Deleuze, Gilles 10, 81–82, 84, 90–93, 96, 98–99, 104–105, 107, 114–116, 118, 120, 123, 131–133, 136, 147, 150
    and body without organs 114
    desire 96, 114
    difference 82, 105, 107, 122, 125
democracy 7
dépense 41, 43

Derrida, Jacques 13, 15, 17, 35, 44–57, 71–73, 76, 78, 108, 113, 116–118, 122–124, 129, 133, 149, 151, 157 n.18, n.25
    deconstruction 118–119
    gift in time 44–47, 129
    meaning 113
    play 149–150
    and pure gift 52–54
    and reason 122
De Sade, Marquis 18, 33
desire 24, 96, 114, 121, 132, 150, 158n.92
De Vries, Hent 13–14, 152
dharma 5
différance 113, 116, 157n.18, n.25
difference 9–12, 20–21, 26–27, 30, 32, 34–35, 46, 62, 76, 81–82, 89–91, 93–96, 101, 103–107, 109–110, 112, 115, 117, 122, 124, 129, 132–131–134, 138, 147, 170n.50
Dionysian 22, 57, 126, 150
discourse 59, 62–65, 74, 80, 92, 104–105, 110, 137, 147
Doniger, Wendy 15, 60, 81, 132
    comparison 94–100
    and methodological problems 99–104
    myths and dreams 98
    toolbox approach 97–98
Douglas, Mary 160n.93
dream 98
Dupré, Louis 7
Durcharbeitung (working through) 11
Durkheim, Emile 22, 38, 55, 84–85, 87

Eastern Orthodox Christianity 109
Edelstein, Dan 8
Eliade, Mircea 15–16, 22, 81, 104–105, 107–108, 110, 112, 116–127, 131–132, 151, 157n.25, 169n.27, 173n.111, 176n.62

hermeneutics 81–84
  history 112–114
  morphology 114–115, 119–121
  predecessors 84–88
Encyclopédie 8
Enlightenment 6–9, 11, 15, 57, 108–109,
    119, 121–122, 126–128, 130, 141,
    144, 150–151, 173n.115
epistemology 65–66, 97, 118–120,
    176n.62
eroticism 12, 17–19, 23, 31, 33, 37, 41, 43,
    52–53, 99, 1218–129, 135, 150,
    159n.39
  and death 23–27
essentialism 101, 145
ethnocentrism 106–107
Eurocentrism 137, 147
event 45–46
evolution 3–4, 84–85, 132, 141
excess 19, 21–22, 26–27, 29, 32–34,
    41–43, 46, 130, 133, 139, 150
  of gift 46–47, 49, 52–53, 129
exergue (inscription) 76
explanation 144

faith 7, 53
falsification 96–94, 141
Fanon, Frantz 69–70
Fascism 18
Fasolt, Constantin 167n.53
feminism 71–72
Filliozat, Jean 48
flesh 25–26, 29–32, 34
Flood, Gavin 146–147, 179n.38
Foucault, Michel 11, 15, 17, 60, 62, 64–65,
    68–69, 73, 76, 108, 111–113, 121–122,
    131, 150, 158n.39, 167n.53, n.59
  discourse 63–64
  genealogy 74–75, 110–111, 122, 130
  on religion 12–13
Frazer, James G. 4, 84–87, 151
Freud, Sigmund 4, 151

Gallagher, Catherine 66
Gay, Peter 8
Gay Science, The 74, 111
Geisteswissenschaft 86, 145
genealogy 59–60, 73–73, 110–111,
    130–132, 138
gift 35–57, 128–129, 162n.20
  Hindu notion of 37
  irrational 42
  and obligation 37–40
  pure gift 35, 52–54
Gill, Sam 93, 170n.50
Girard, René 25
Glas 46
Gnaski 28
God 8, 13, 19, 153
  death of 10, 151
Goethe, Wolfgang von 84, 109
Gonda, Jan 48–50, 52–53
grammatology 123–124
Grimes, Ronald L. 160n.93
Guattari, Félix 10, 114–116, 122, 131–132,
    136, 147, 150

Habermas, Jürgen 19
habitus 140–141
Haida 41
Halbfass, Wilhelm 65–66
Hassrick, R. B. 27
Hatcher, Brian 97
Heesterman, J. C. 49–50, 52
Hegel, G. W. F. 9, 19, 21, 44, 47,
    157n.18
Heidegger, Martin 12, 35, 55, 76, 117, 131
Helmont, Jean 157n.18
hermeneutics 21, 34, 66, 75, 78,
    80–107, 115, 128, 132
heterology 19, 21–22, 30, 34, 49, 52–54,
    75, 122, 130, 134, 146, 148, 151,
    157n.18, n.20
hierophany 81, 116, 118, 160n93
Hiltebeitel, Alf 93–94

Hiroshima 12
history 8, 54, 71, 74–75, 81, 84, 100,
        109–116, 122, 124, 128, 130–132,
        137, 141, 149, 167n.53
holocaust 47, 53
Holzwege 117
homo ludens 93
homo religiosus 115–116
Hubert, Henri 23, 43
Hultkrantz, Ake 27
Husserl, Edmund 120

Indra 48
imagination 142–143
immanence 10, 20, 22, 82, 90, 114,
        115, 131
inauspicious 50–51
initiation 33, 126–127
intuition 120, 142–143
Islam 65
Iya 28

Jabés, Edmond 151
Jameson, Fredric 11, 34
Jesus 98
Johnson, Mark 145
Jorgensen, Joseph 27
Joyce, James 18
Jung, Carl 4

Kālī 67
Kane, P. V. 48–50, 52–53
Kant, I. 9–10, 55, 121, 125–126, 176n.62
khora 46, 129
King, Richard 167n.59
Kippenberg, Hans G. 9, 75
knowledge 109, 111–112, 118–121, 130,
        132, 134–136, 141, 143–144, 146,
        149, 170n.50
    three modes of 141
Kojève, Alexandre 19
Kristeva, Julia 18, 108, 112, 121–122, 150

Kripal, Jeff 61, 133, 135–136
Kuhn, Thomas S. 142–143
Kwakiutl 41

Lacan, Jacques 117
Laine, James 60
Lakoff, George 145
Lambek, Michael 14
language 19, 35, 89, 92–93, 96, 100,
        116, 123, 137–138, 141
Larmore, Charles 157n.18
Levinas, Emmanuel 35, 44
Lévi-Strauss, Claude 46, 99–100,
        102–104
Lévy-Bruhl, Claude 4, 84–85
Lewis, Bernard 65
Lincoln, Bruce 172n.86
Location of Culture 70
logocentrism 11, 57, 118, 123, 131
Long, Charles 88
Lowe, Lisa 64
Lyotard, Jean-François 11–12. 109,
        121–122, 132

McCutcheon, Russell 96, 133–135
McGowan, John 64
madness 46, 53, 150
magic 4, 85
Mahābhārata 48
Malamoud, Charles 49
Malhotra, Ashok 72–73
Manusmrti 48–49
Mao Tse-tung 150
Masuzawa, Tomoko 147–148
Marion, Jean Luc 44, 152
Marx, Karl 18, 63
Marxism 71–72, 77, 91
masochism 29
Masuzawa, Tomoko 4
Mauss, Marcel 15, 17, 23, 35–36
    on gift 37–43, 46–50, 52,
        54–57, 129

meaning 87, 89, 92–93, 100, 102, 113,
  119, 124, 132, 134, 138, 144, 147
Mephistopheles 34
metaphysics 57, 112, 115, 119, 122–123,
  131, 133, 142, 150
méthode de meditation 34
Metraux, Alfred 17
Midnight's Children 59
modernity 11–12, 136
moon 33
Müller, Max 87
Murphy, Tim 133, 137–138
My Mother 25, 33
myth 89, 98–103, 116, 158n.42,
  172n.86

narrative 8, 11–12, 71, 73, 89, 94, 98,
  110102, 109–110, 131–132, 135, 145,
  147, 149, 151–152, 172n.86
nature 20
Naturwissenschaft 86, 145
Neville, Robert 56
Nietzsche, Friedrich 11–12, 18–19, 22,
  57, 60, 62–63, 68, 80, 111, 122,
  125, 151
  on genealogy 73–75
nihilism 11, 149
Nozick, Robert 150

Occidentalism 40
ontology 115–118
ordinary experience 138–139
Orientalism 15, 40, 60–62, 66, 68–69,
  73–76, 79, 130, 166n.25
*Origins of Evil in Hindu Mythology,
  The* 102
other 19, 35, 60, 92–95, 106, 148
  wholly other 118
Otto, Rudolf 121

pain 31
Parry, J. P. 37, 48, 51–53

Patterns in Comparative Religion 88
Pefanis, Julian 34
Peirce, Charles Sanders 96
Pentheus 98
pharmakon 133, 136
pietism 8
Plato 99
play 23–24, 76, 113, 119, 135,
  149–150, 152
Polanyi, Michael 143
Popper, Karl R. 142–144
postcolonialism 59–60, 69–72
postmodernism 6–7, 9–12, 34, 77,
  108–109, 120, 133–134, 139, 149–151,
  173n.111
  challenge of 15–16, 128–151
  promise of 133–141
poststructuralism 6, 62
potlatch 37, 40–43, 49, 54, 57, 129
power 4, 12–14, 27, 30–31, 34, 41–42,
  52, 59, 68, 74, 78, 89, 110–111, 115,
  130–131, 147, 158n.39
  of gift 39, 41
  of reason 7
  texts and discourse 62–64
  will to 125
pragmatic test 128, 138–139, 147–148
pragmatism 97
presence 19, 37, 44, 57, 76,
  116–117, 132
profane 4, 20, 21–22, 34, 43, 91, 118,
  121–122, 157n.25
Psyché: Inventions de l'autre 44
Putnam, Hilary 150

Raheja, Gloria 48, 50–53
rationality 37, 55, 75, 84–85, 87, 120,
  123, 150–151
reason 7, 9, 11, 22, 45–46, 55–56, 85,
  96, 105, 121–124, 129–130, 132,
  135, 150
reflexivity 102, 139, 141

religion 3, 9, 15–16, 33, 43, 86, 89, 93,
    104, 132, 134, 141, 152
  in China 4–5
  in India 5
  limitations of 4–6
  origin of 3–4
  and postmodernists 12–14,
    133–134, 137
  science of 141–146, 147
  semiotic theory of 137
  sui generis 9, 137, 173n.115
religious studies 3–6, 9, 60, 81, 108,
    128, 137, 141, 145–146, 151
  postmodern challenge to 15–16,
    133–134
  religare 3
  religere 3
  religio 3
Rennie, Bryan S. 173n.111, 176n.62
Renou, Louis 48
repetition 64, 89–91, 93, 102
representational thinking 7, 15–16,
    56–57, 60, 62, 71–77, 82, 84, 90,
    93, 104, 108–127, 132, 141, 146,
    167n.59, 176n.62
Rescher, Nicolas 144, 149–151
rewriting 11–12
rhizome 90, 96, 115, 122, 13, 147
Riesebrodt, Martin 15
ritual 159n.59, n.60, n.62, 160n.93
Rocher, Rosane 65
Roman Catholic Church 7
Romanticism 6–9, 109
Rorty, Richard 112, 123
Rosen, Stanley 139–140, 150
Rushdie, Salman 59, 79

sacred 4, 20–23, 27, 29–30, 33–343, 43,
    81, 83, 89, 91, 115, 118, 120–122,
    127, 132, 157n.25
  pipe 32
sacrifice 17, 19, 23, 25–26, 33–34, 40,

    43, 47, 50, 53, 128–129
Sacrifice: Its Nature and Function 43
sadism 29
Said, Edward W. 15, 60, 70, 76–78, 138,
    166n.38, 167n.59
  critics of 64–68
  his children 69–72
  and Orientalism 61–62, 130–131,
    166n.25
  political agenda 68–69
  texts, power and discourse 62–63
Saler, Benson 144–145
Sardar, Siauddhin 165n.22
Satre, Jean-Paul 19
Satz vom Grund, Der 55
scatology 21
schizoanalysis 132
Schopen, Gregory 93–94
Schrag, Calvin 56
science 4, 7, 21, 85, 141–146
  of religion 141–146
secularization 7, 136
self 10, 20, 22, 24, 29, 43, 117, 148
semiotics 137–138
sexuality 24, 26–34, 43–45, 158n.39
shaman 29, 33
simulacrum 10–11, 93, 99, 114, 116,
    123–127, 133, 135–136, 149–150,
    156n.7
silence 12, 42
Sioux 19, 27, 33–34
Śiva 99
skepticism 11, 58, 77, 119, 123, 136, 143,
    146, 149
Smith, David 64
Smith, Jonathan Z. 15, 81, 96, 104–105,
    107, 115, 121, 132, 137, 147, 169n.27
  comparison 88–93
  map and territory 87–90
Soloman, Robert 73
Sorel, Georges 18
Souvarine, Boris 18

Spencer, Herbert 3, 84–85, 87
Spivak, Gayatri Chakravarty 60, 70–73, 76–77, 79
Stark, Rodney 162n.21
Starobinski, Jean 162n.20
Stoekl, Alan 18
Story of the Eye 33
Strenski, Ivan 96
structuralism 99, 102–104
Sun Dance 19, 27–34, 80
Surrealism 17–18

Tambiah, Stanley 159
Taves, Ann 153n.6
Taylor, Charles 106, 150–151, 165n.14
Taylor, James 133, 136–137
Taylor, Mark C. 12, 14, 108, 113–114, 117–118, 124, 133, 157n.20
Tedlock, Philip E. 162n.21
Temps Modernes, Les 19
text 62, 78
Thapar, Romila 49
Thus Spoke Zarathustra 80
Tiele, Cornelius 87
time 7, 11, 37, 44–53, 86, 129
    gift in 44–47, 53
    in Hinduism 47–52
Tlingit 41
Toynbee, Arnold 11
trace 45, 55, 116, 136
transcendence 10, 13
truth 7, 9, 12, 17, 25, 112–113, 120, 1126–127, 132, 135, 137, 141, 144, 146, 156n.7

Tsimshiao 41
Turner, Victor 159n.62
Tylor, Edward B. 4, 43, 84–87

universalism 101–102
Urban, Hugh 67

Van der Leeuw, Gerardus 49
Varisco, Daniel Martin 67
verification 142
victim 25–26, 33–35, 50, 98
violence 17–24, 29–32, 34, 40, 69, 71, 98, 130
    and death 25–27, 53
    and discourse 63–64
    and gift 46–47
Viswanathan, Gauri 167n.59

Wach, Joachim 86–87
Wakan-tanka 28–29, 32
Walker, J. R. 27, 29, 33
Weber, Max 85, 87
wen (culture) 5
Wesenschau 120
White, Hayden 130
Wittgenstein, Ludwig 91
world religions 141, 146–148
Wretched of the Earth, The 69
xiao (filial piety) 5

Young, Robert 60, 65

Zarathustra 80
zongjiao 4–5